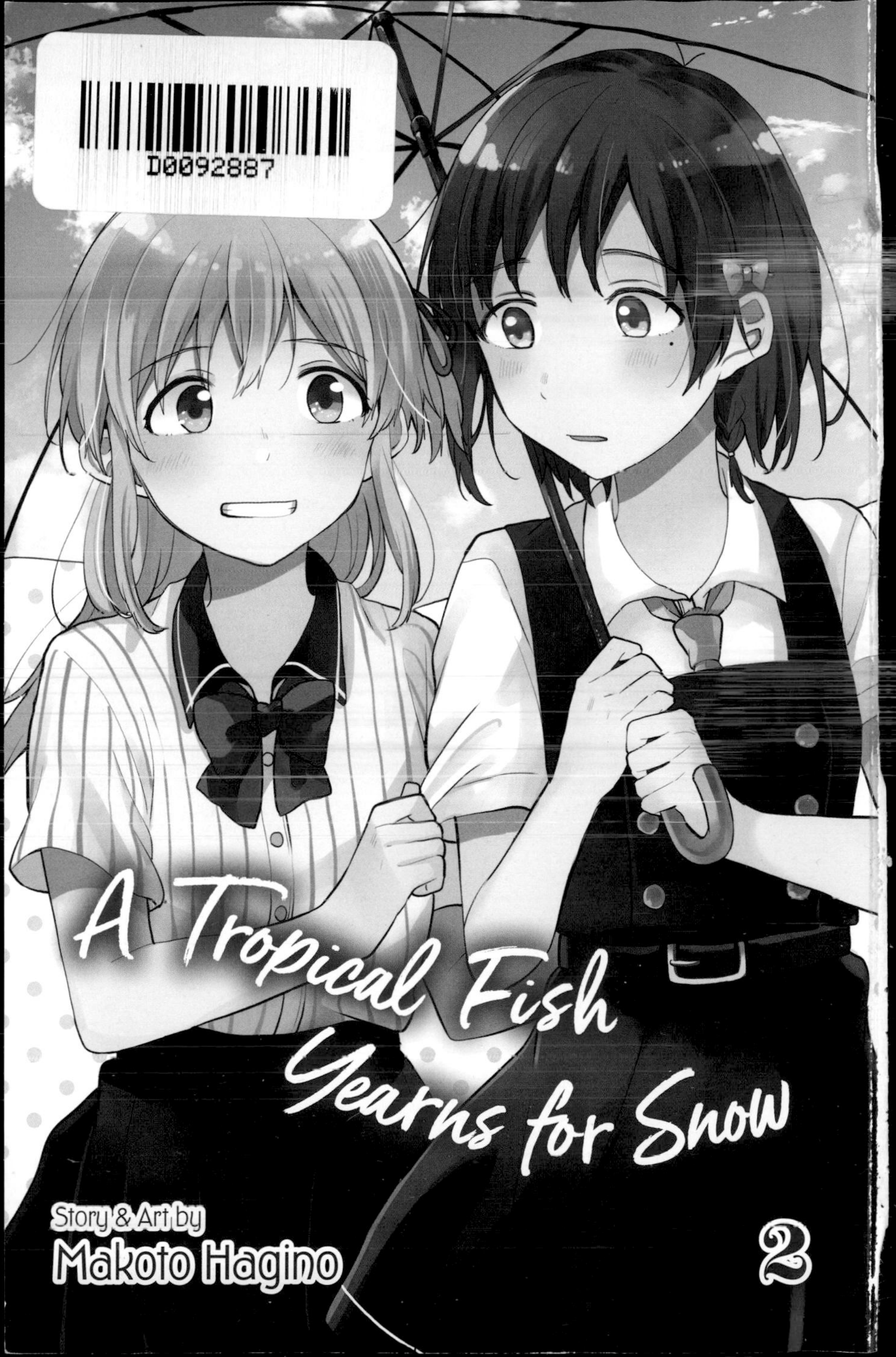
A Tropical Fish Yearns for Snow
Story & Art by
Makoto Hagino
2

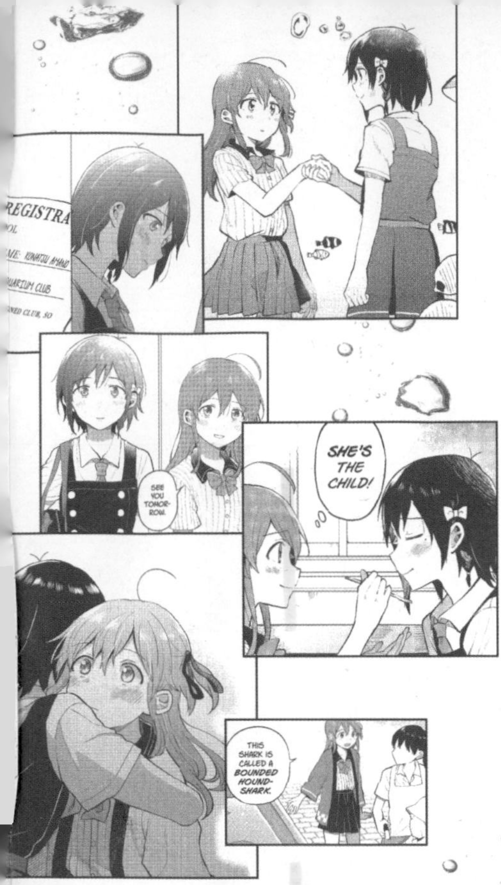
SHE'S THE CHILD!
SEE YOU TOMORROW.
THIS SHARK IS CALLED A BOUNDED HOUND-SHARK.

The Story So Far

Konatsu has trouble adapting to her new surroundings after she moves from Tokyo to a rural seaside town and starts attending school there.

When she meets Koyuki, the sole member of the Aquarium Club, Konatsu decides to join the club too. The two girls are drawn to each other because they're both lonely.

The first time Konatsu participates in an open house for the school aquarium, Koyuki is overcome by inexpressible feelings and she suddenly pulls Konatsu close!

Characters

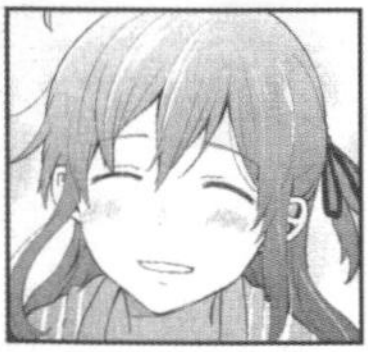

Konatsu Amano

A first-year transfer student. She has trouble adapting to her new surroundings until she decides to join her new friend Koyuki in the Aquarium Club.

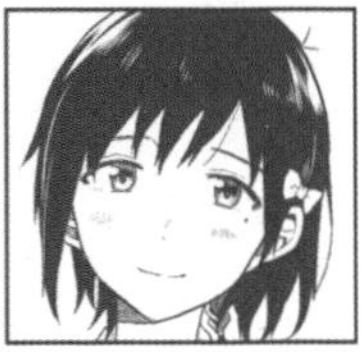

Koyuki Honami

Head of the Aquarium Club. Everyone puts her on a pedestal, and she tries to satisfy their expectations even though she finds them suffocating and feels lonely.

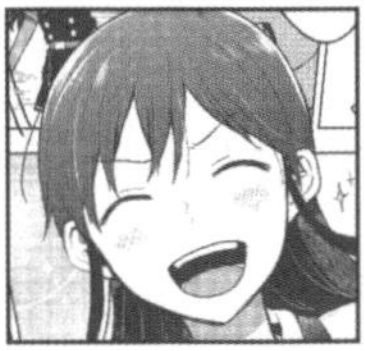

Kaede Hirose

Konatsu's classmate. Due to her perky personality, she has many friends and doesn't hesitate to extend a hearty welcome to Konatsu.

A Tropical Fish Yearns for Snow

A Tropical Fish
Yearns for Snow

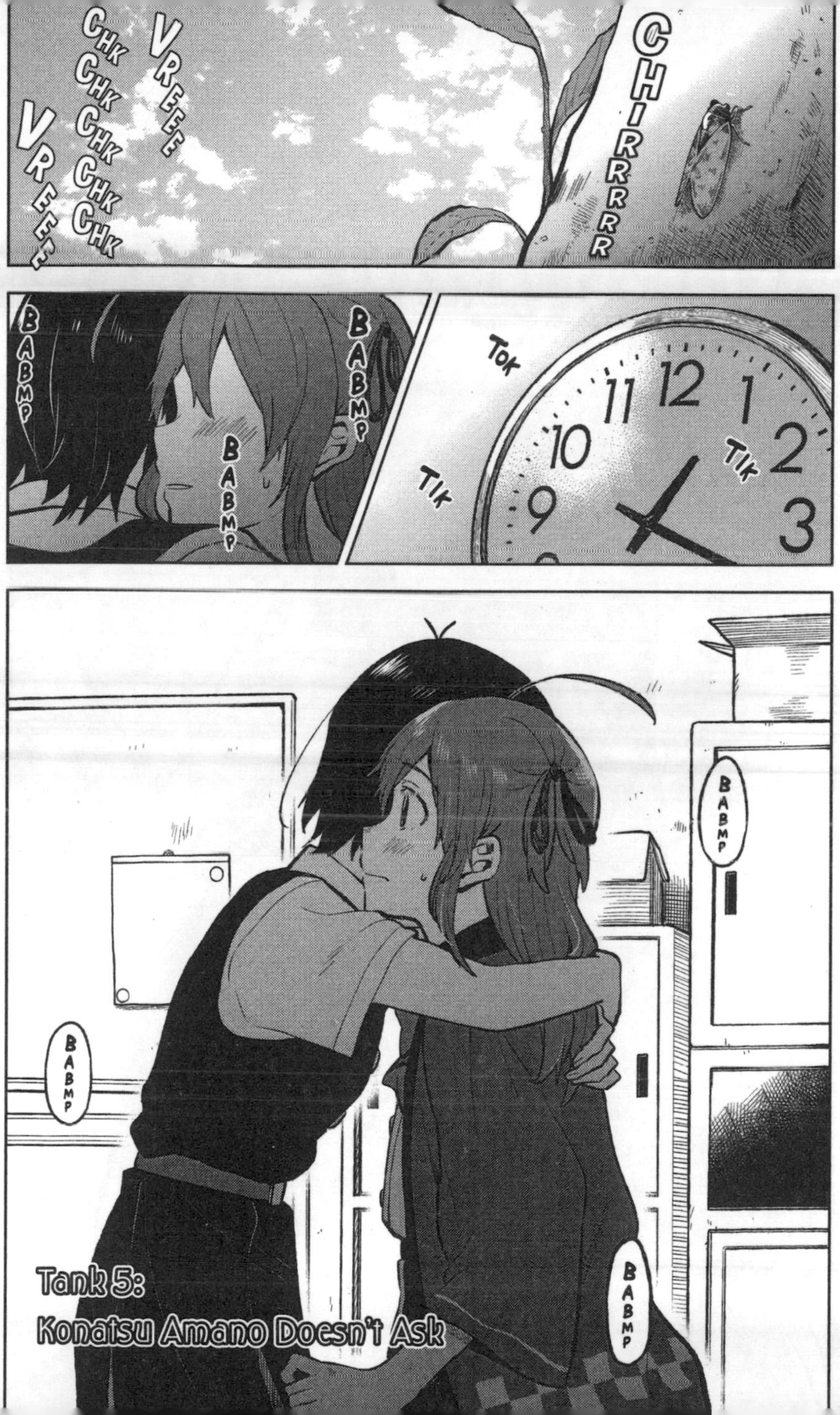
CHIRRRRRR
VREEEE
CHK CHK CHK CHK CHK
VREEEE
TOK
TIK
TIK
BABMP
BABMP
BABMP
BABMP
BABMP
BABMP

Tank 5: Konatsu Amano Doesn't Ask

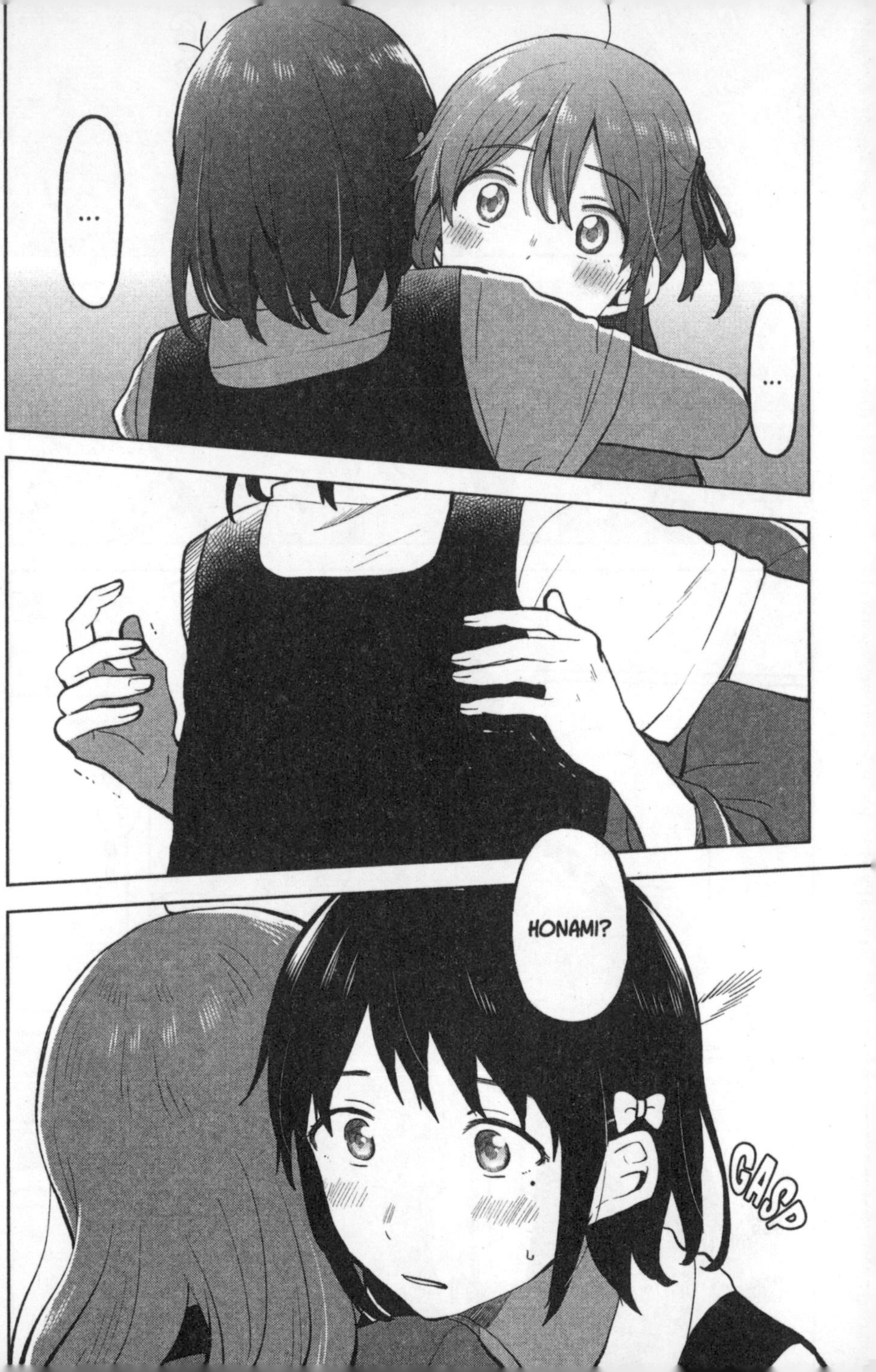
...
...
HONAMI?
GASP

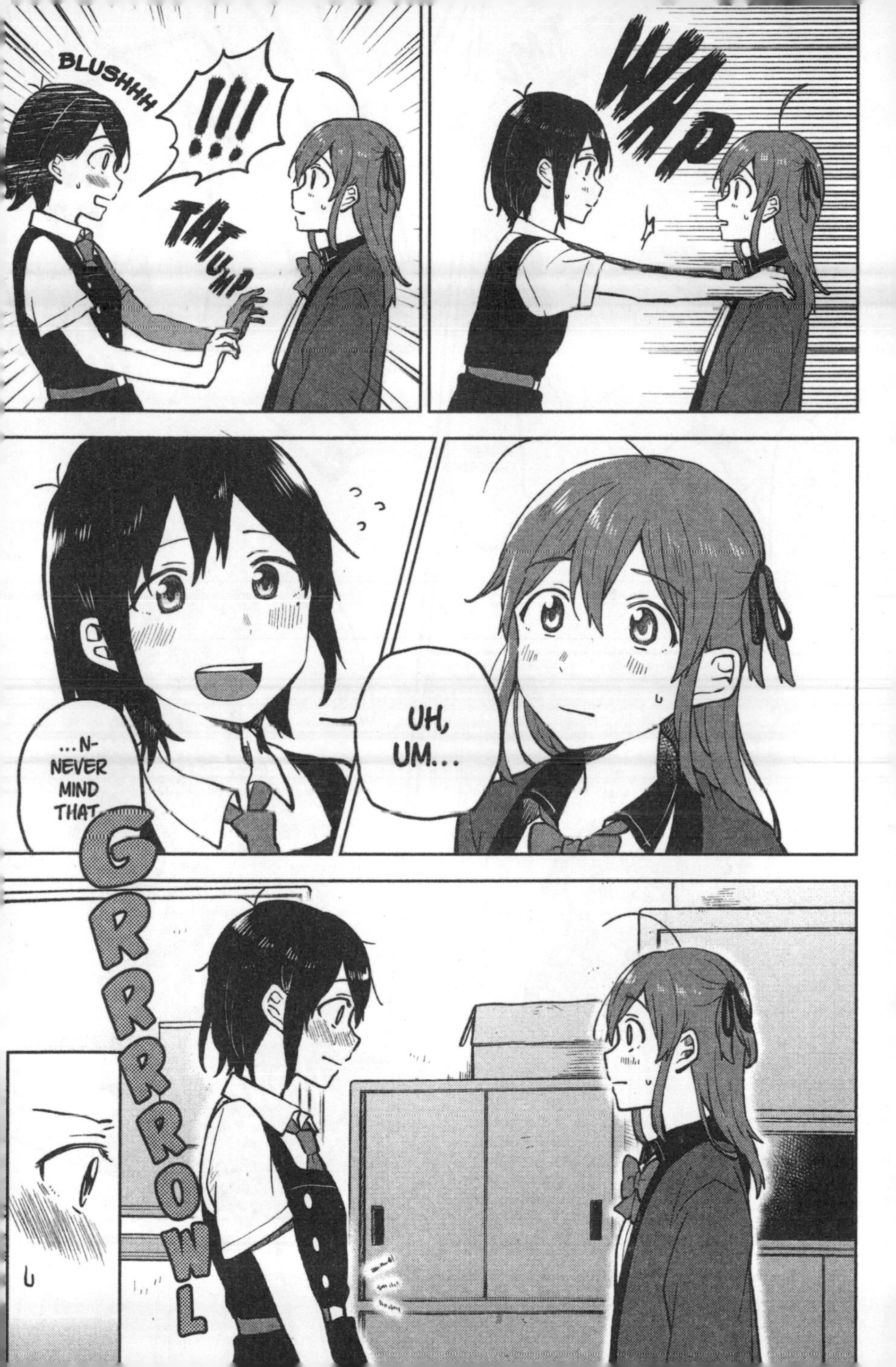
WAP
BLUSHHH
!!!
TATUMP
UH, UM...
...N-NEVER MIND THAT.
GRRROWL

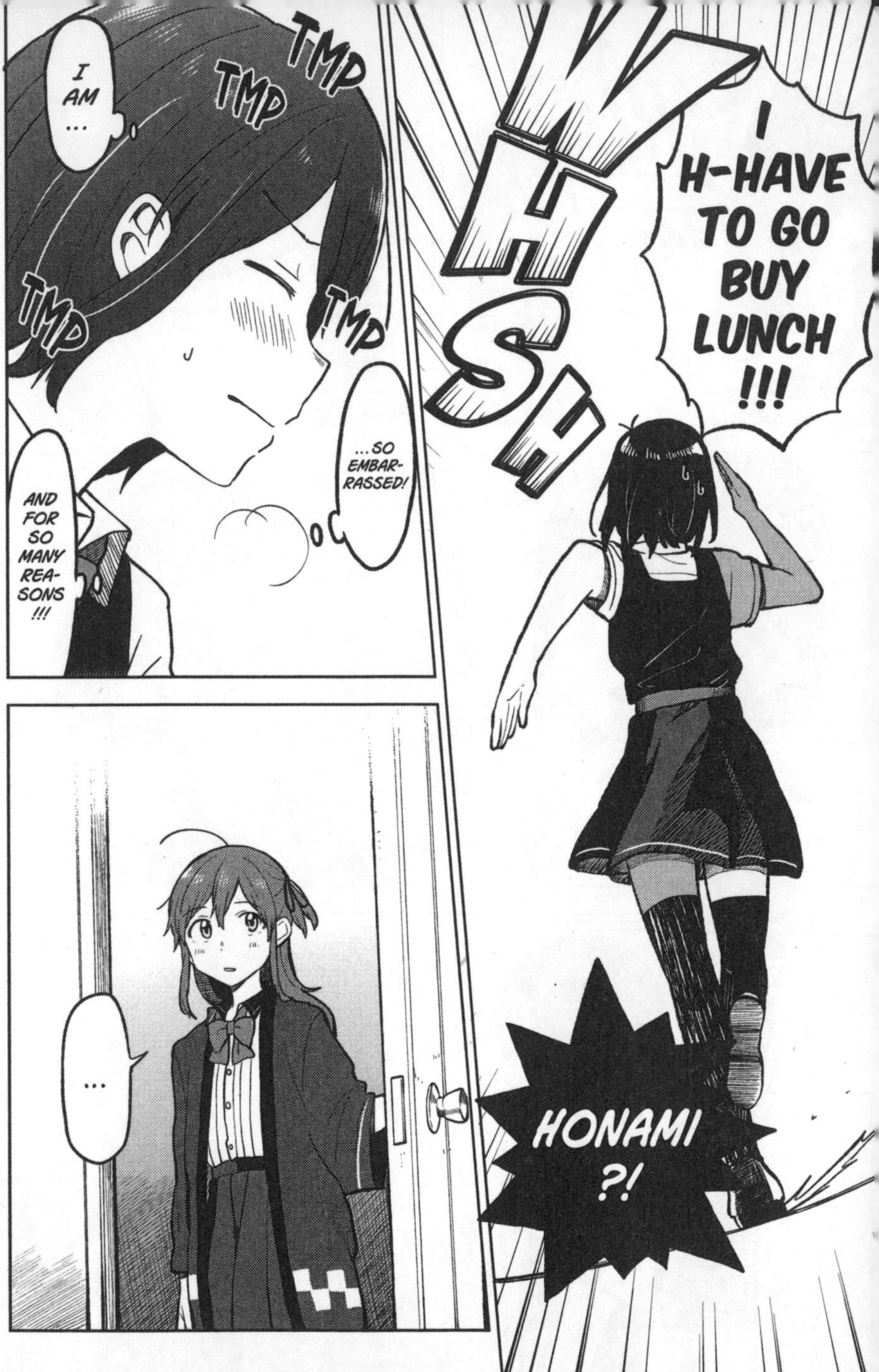
WHSH
I H-HAVE TO GO BUY LUNCH!!!
HONAMI?!
I AM...
TMP
TMP
TMP
TMP
...SO EMBARRASSED!
AND FOR SO MANY REA-SONS!!!
...

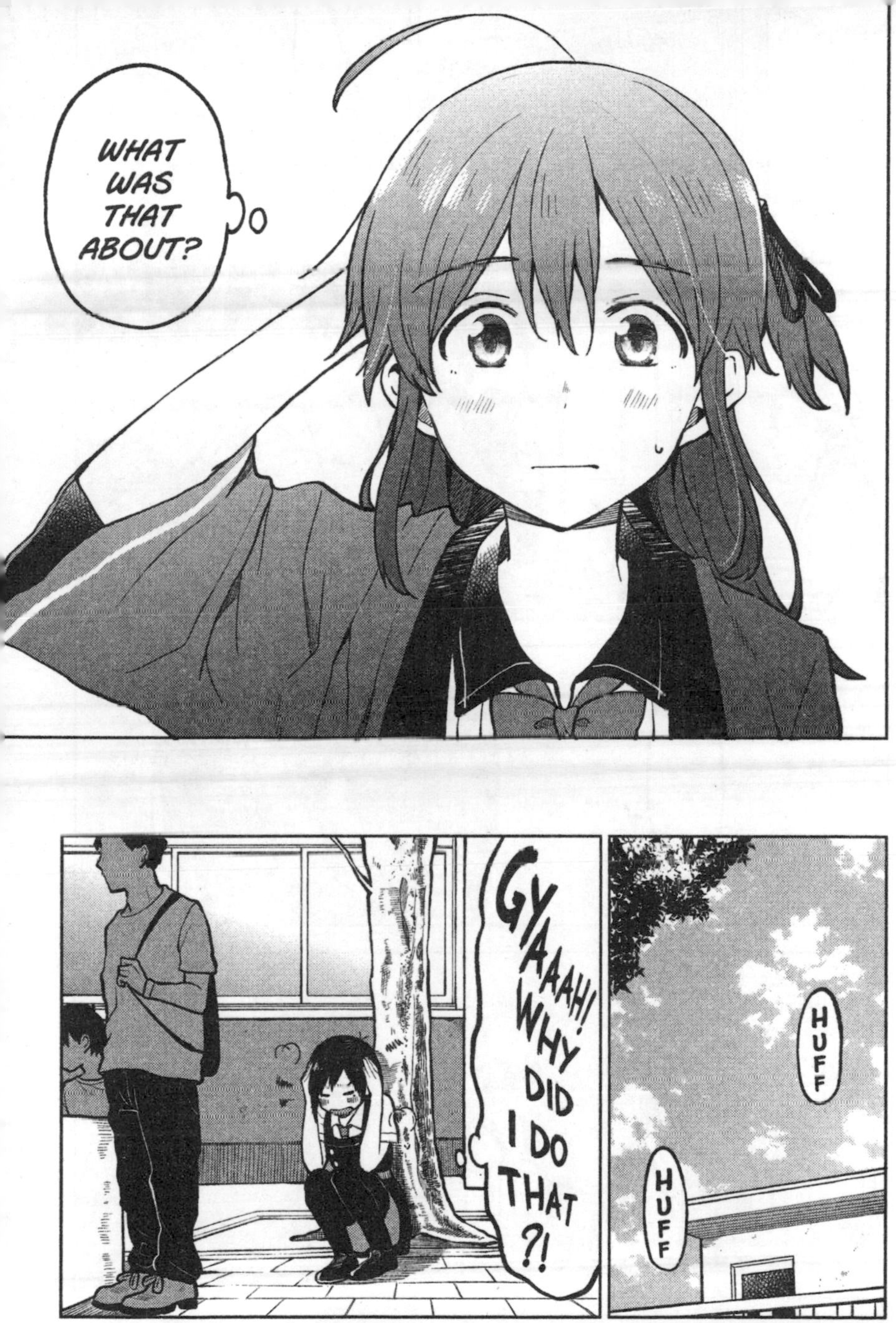
WHAT WAS THAT ABOUT?
HUFF
HUFF
GYAAAH! WHY DID I DO THAT?!

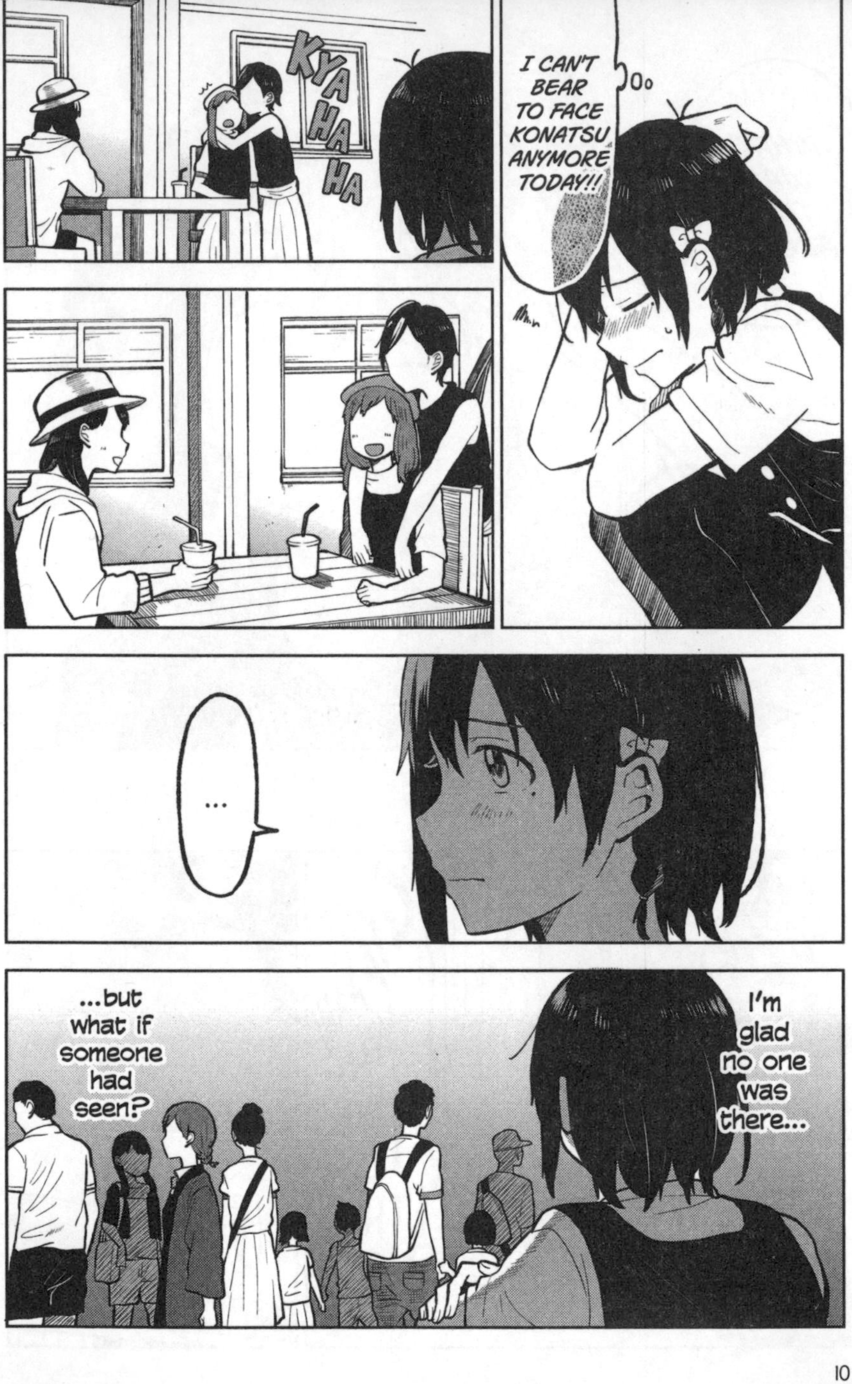
I CAN'T BEAR TO FACE KONATSU ANYMORE TODAY!!
KYAHAHAHA
...
I'm glad no one was there...
...but what if someone had seen?

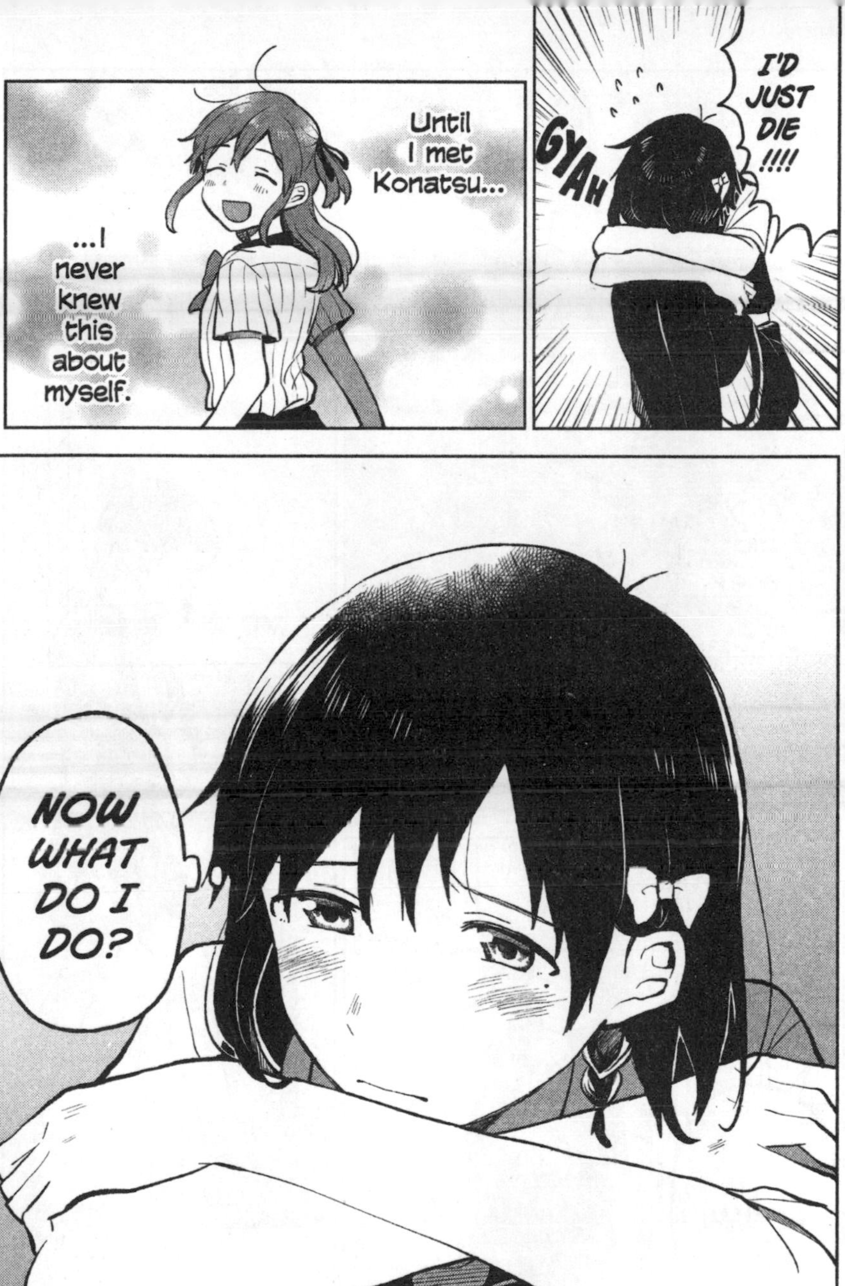
I'D JUST DIE !!!!
GYAH
Until I met Konatsu...
...I never knew this about myself.
NOW WHAT DO I DO?

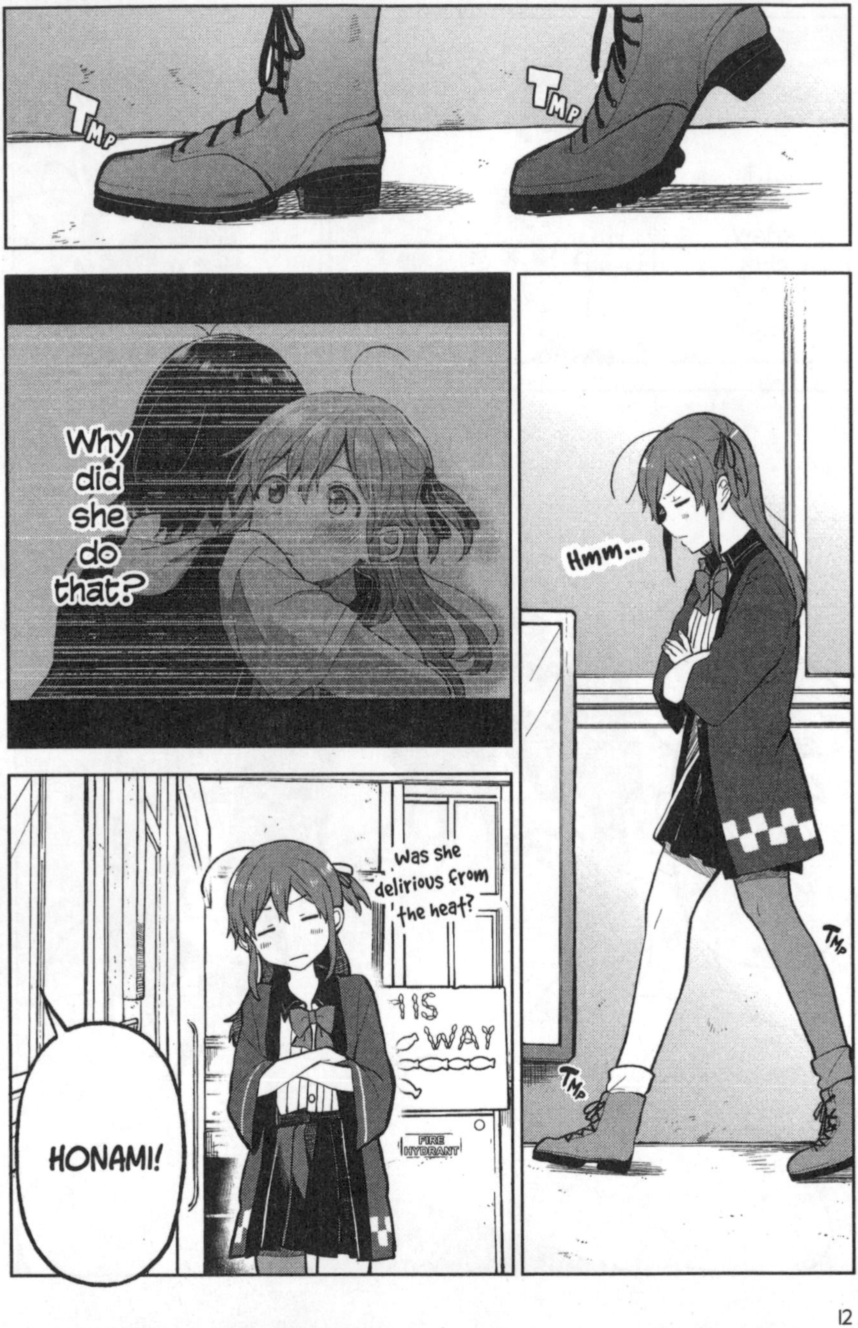
TMP
TMP
Hmm...
TMP
TMP
Why did she do that?
Was she delirious from the heat?
FIRE HYDRANT
HONAMI!

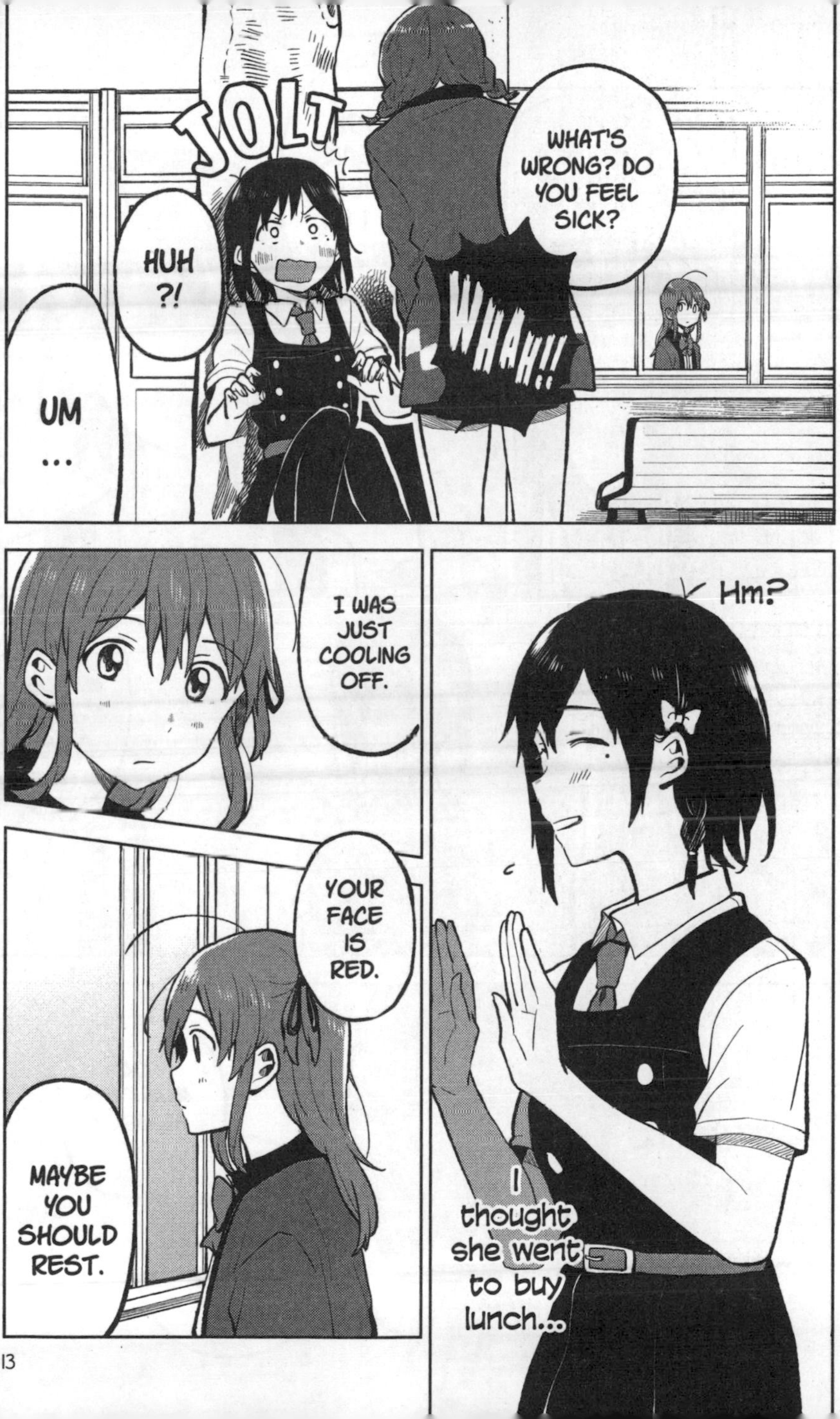
WHAT'S WRONG? DO YOU FEEL SICK?
WHAH!!
JOLT
HUH ?!
UM ...
Hm?
I thought she went to buy lunch...
I WAS JUST COOLING OFF.
YOUR FACE IS RED.
MAYBE YOU SHOULD REST.

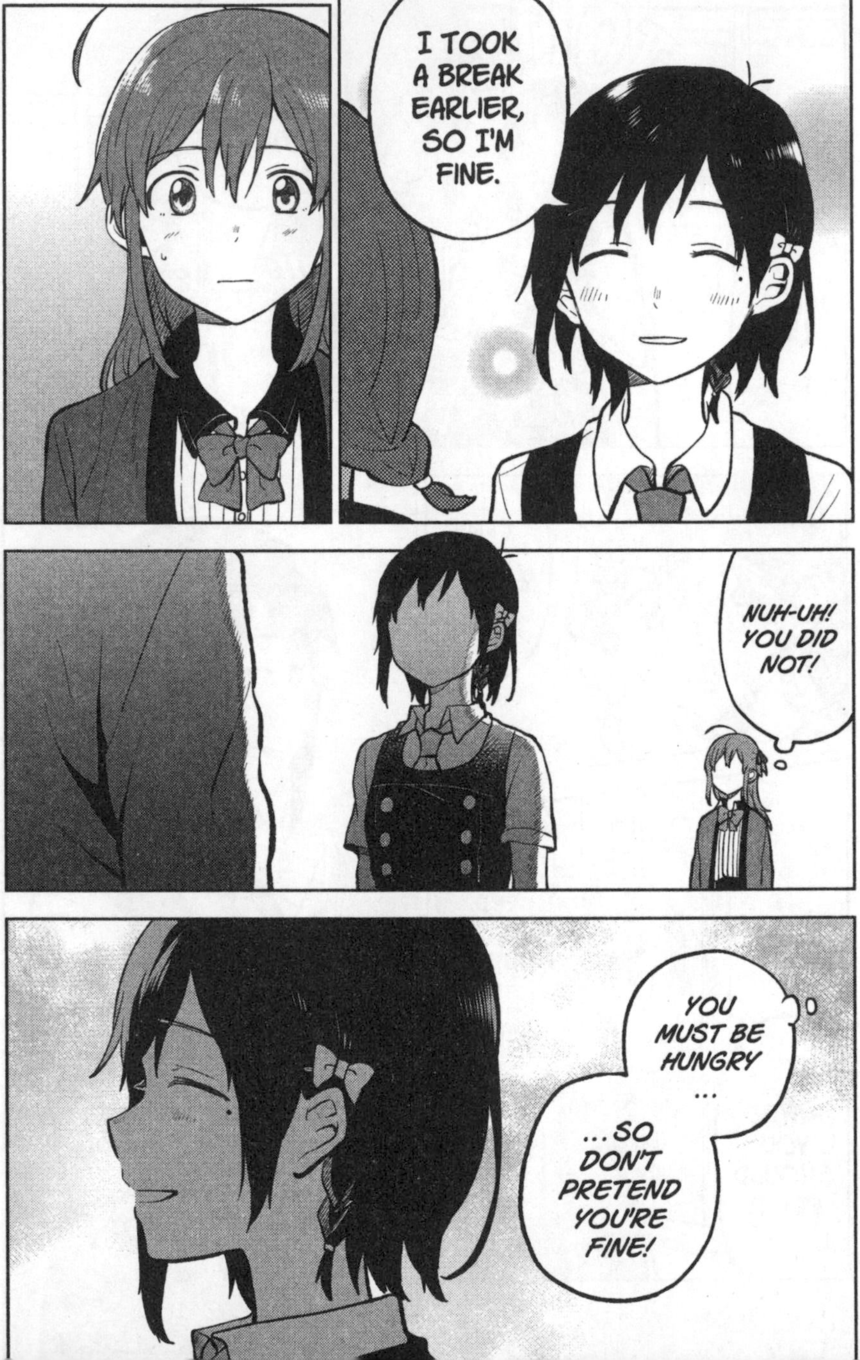
I TOOK A BREAK EARLIER, SO I'M FINE.
NUH-UH! YOU DID NOT!
YOU MUST BE HUNGRY ...
...SO DON'T PRETEND YOU'RE FINE!

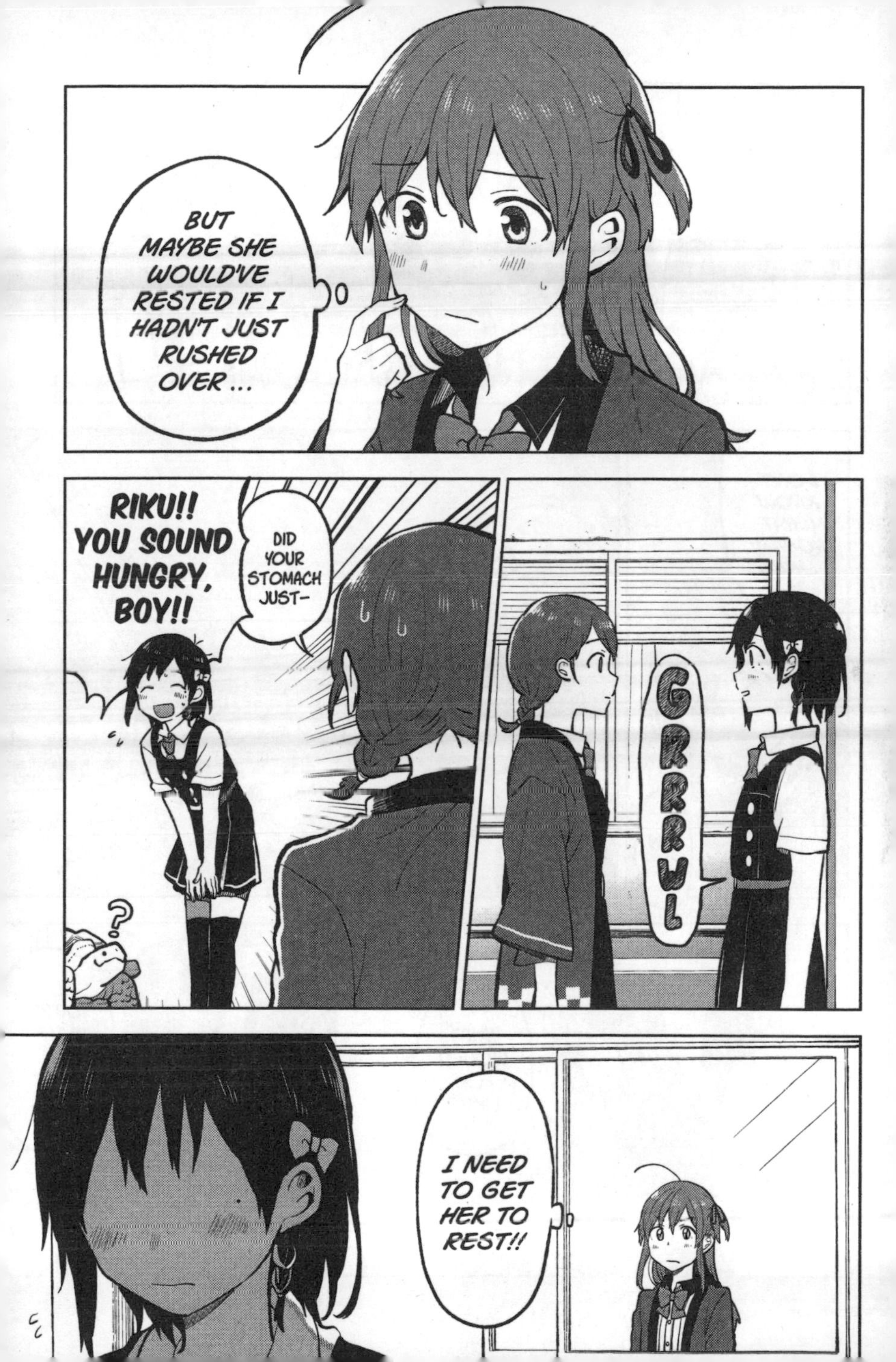
BUT MAYBE SHE WOULD'VE RESTED IF I HADN'T JUST RUSHED OVER ...
GRRRUL
DID YOUR STOMACH JUST-
RIKU!! YOU SOUND HUNGRY, BOY!!
I NEED TO GET HER TO REST!!

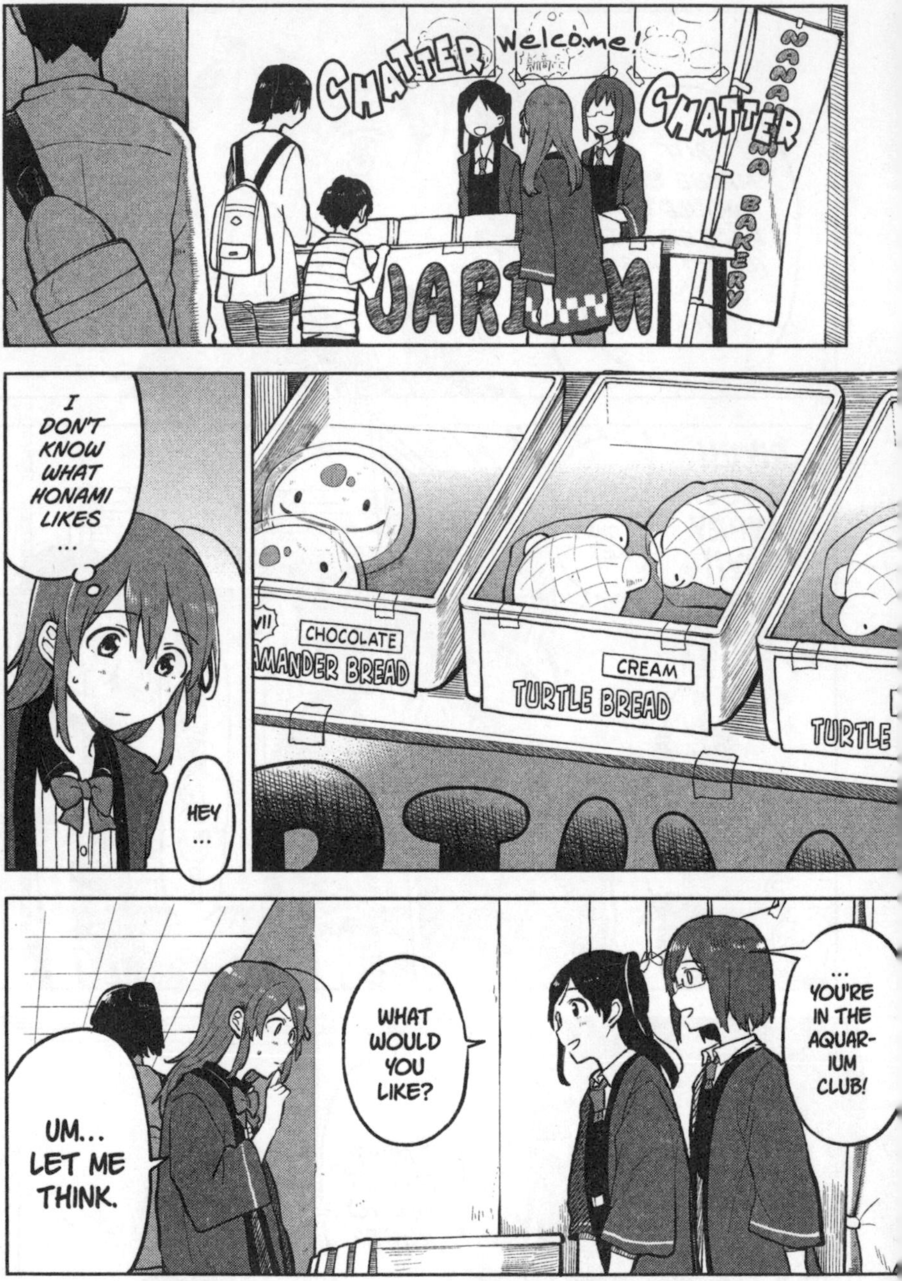
CHATTER
Welcome!
新商品
CHATTER
BAKERY
UARIUM
CHOCOLATE
AMANDER BREAD
CREAM
TURTLE BREAD
TURTLE
I DON'T KNOW WHAT HONAMI LIKES...
HEY...
...YOU'RE IN THE AQUARIUM CLUB!
WHAT WOULD YOU LIKE?
UM... LET ME THINK.

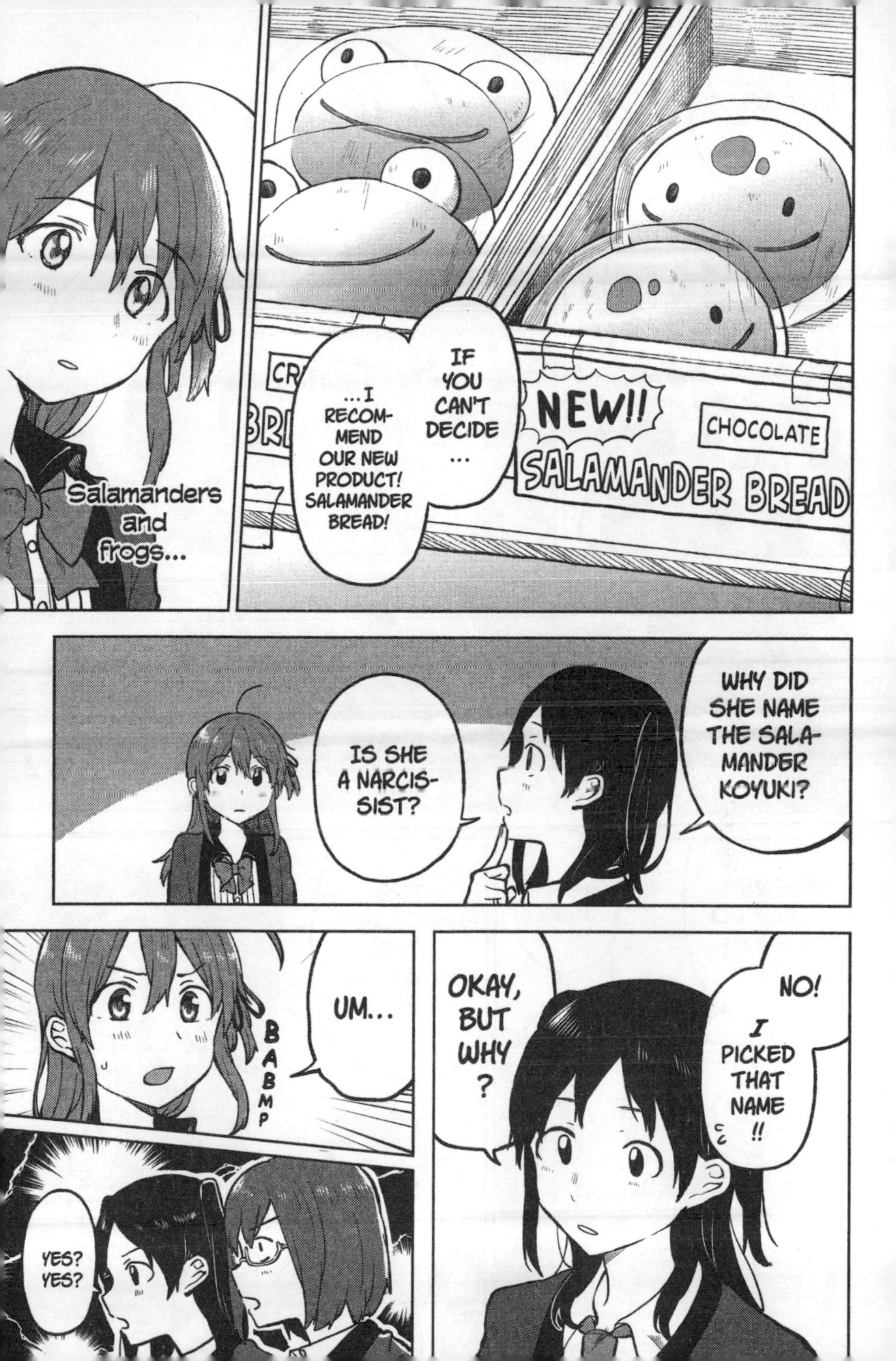
IF YOU CAN'T DECIDE ...
...I RECOMMEND OUR NEW PRODUCT! SALAMANDER BREAD!
NEW!!
CHOCOLATE
SALAMANDER BREAD
Salamanders and frogs...
WHY DID SHE NAME THE SALAMANDER KOYUKI?
IS SHE A NARCISSIST?
NO!
I PICKED THAT NAME!!
OKAY, BUT WHY?
UM...
BABMP
YES? YES?

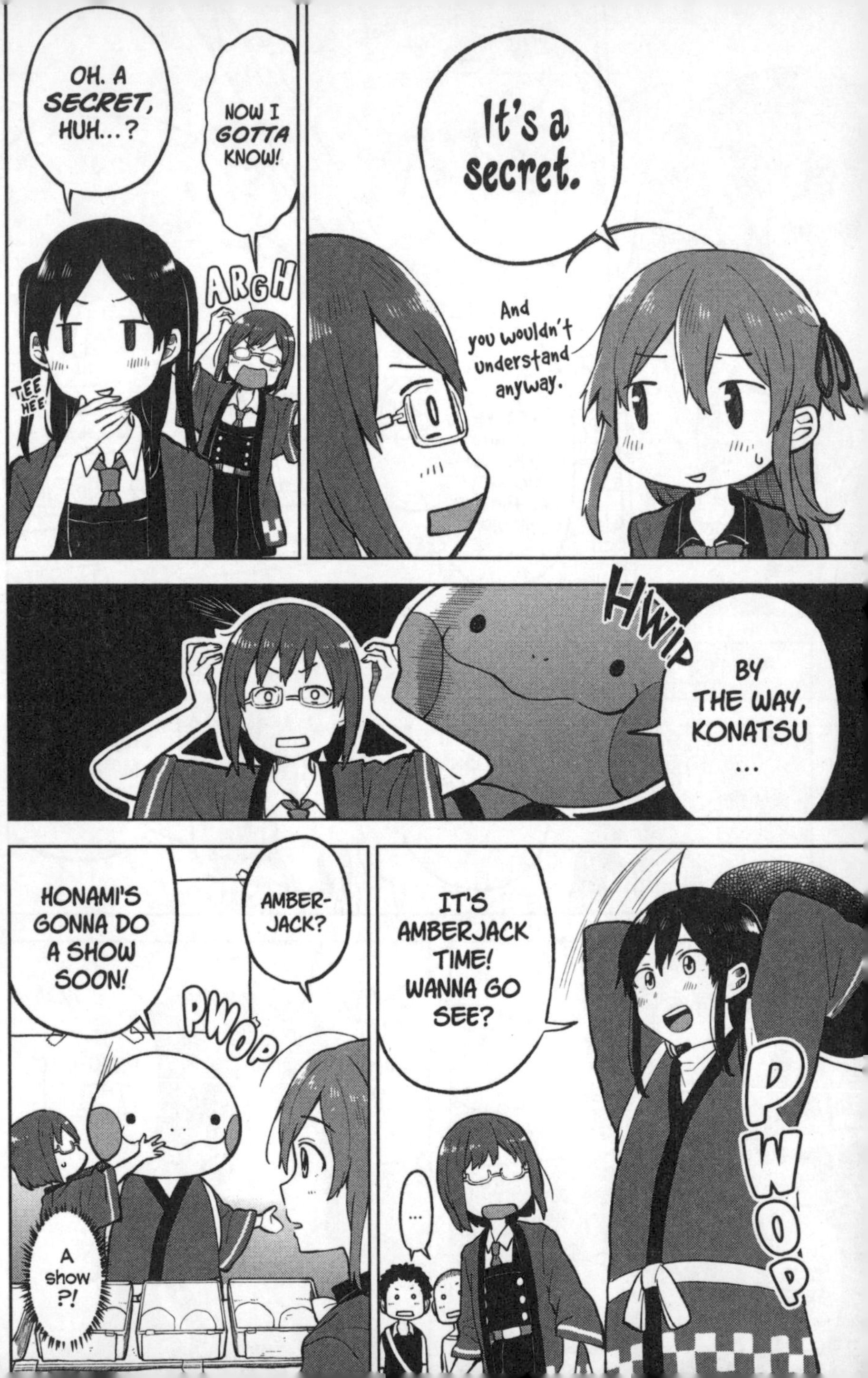
It's a secret.
And you wouldn't understand anyway.
NOW I GOTTA KNOW!
OH. A SECRET, HUH...?
ARGH
TEE HEE
HWIP
BY THE WAY, KONATSU ...
IT'S AMBERJACK TIME! WANNA GO SEE?
PWOP
...
AMBER-JACK?
HONAMI'S GONNA DO A SHOW SOON!
PWOP
A show?!

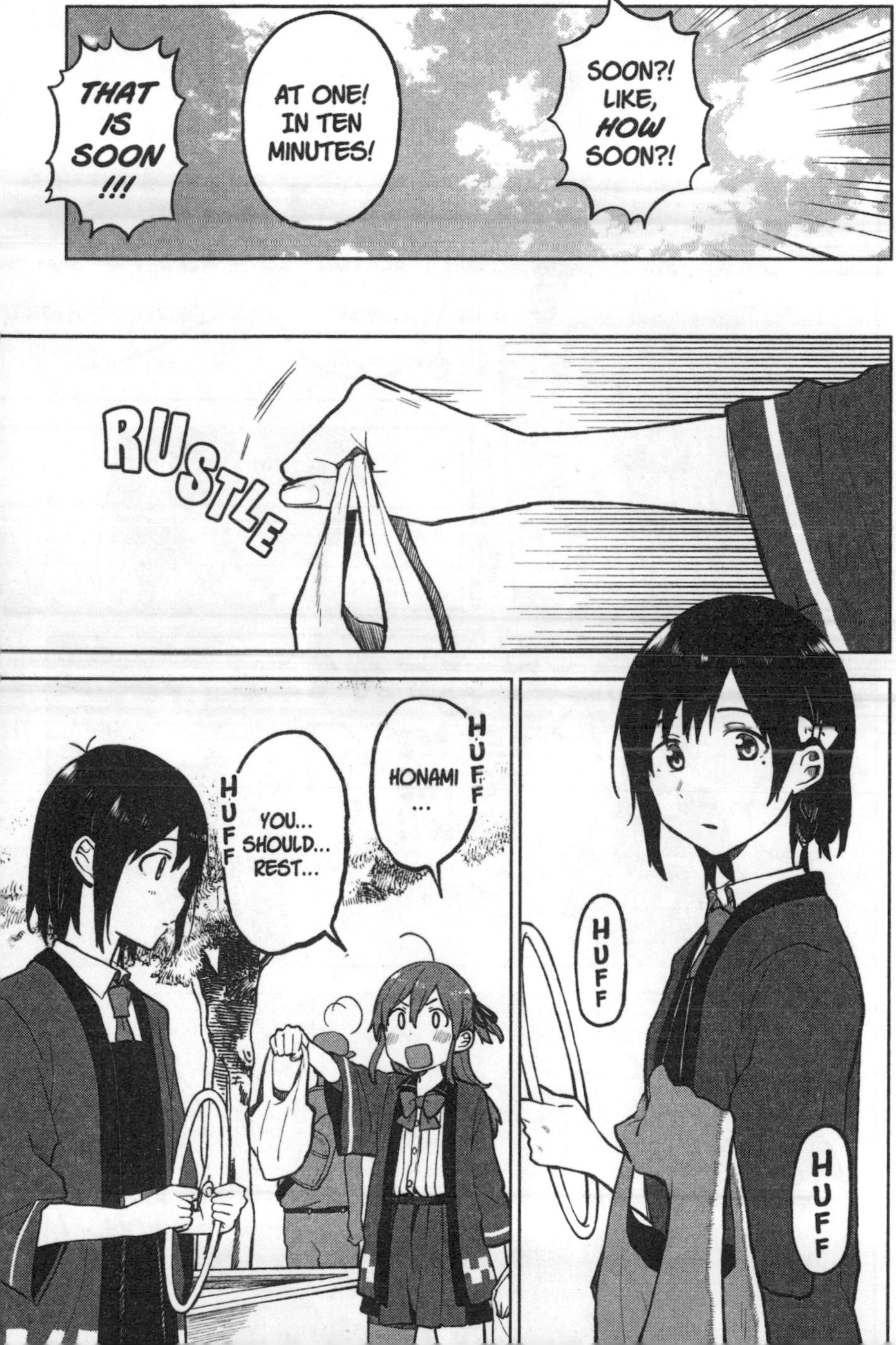
SOON?! LIKE, *HOW* SOON?!
AT ONE! IN TEN MINUTES!
THAT IS SOON!!!
RUSTLE
HUFF
HUFF
HUFF HUFF
HONAMI ...
HUFF HUFF
YOU... SHOULD... REST...

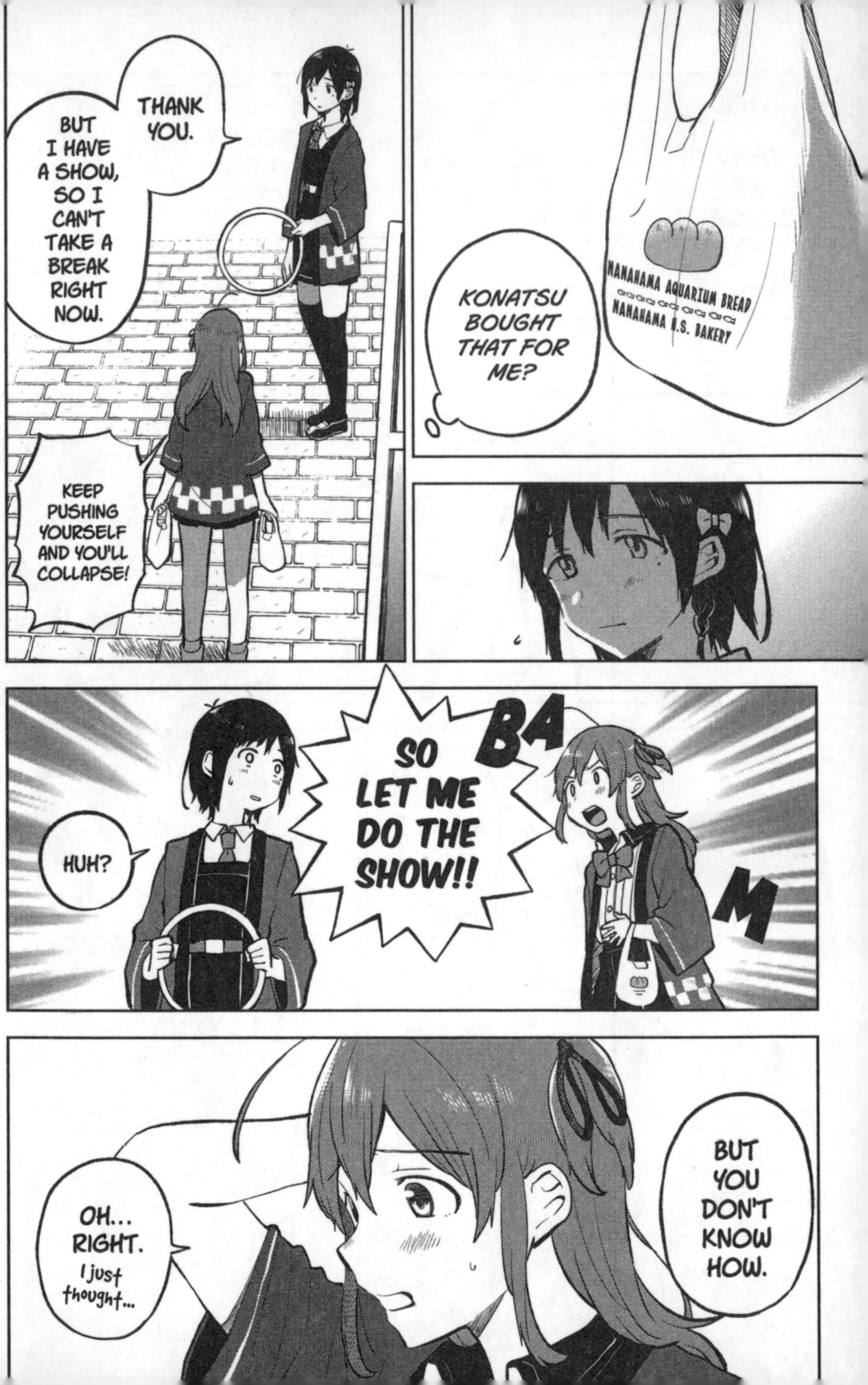
NANAHAMA AQUARIUM BREAD
NANAHAMA H.S. BAKERY
KONATSU BOUGHT THAT FOR ME?
THANK YOU.
BUT I HAVE A SHOW, SO I CAN'T TAKE A BREAK RIGHT NOW.
KEEP PUSHING YOURSELF AND YOU'LL COLLAPSE!
BAM
SO LET ME DO THE SHOW!!
HUH?
BUT YOU DON'T KNOW HOW.
OH... RIGHT. I just thought...

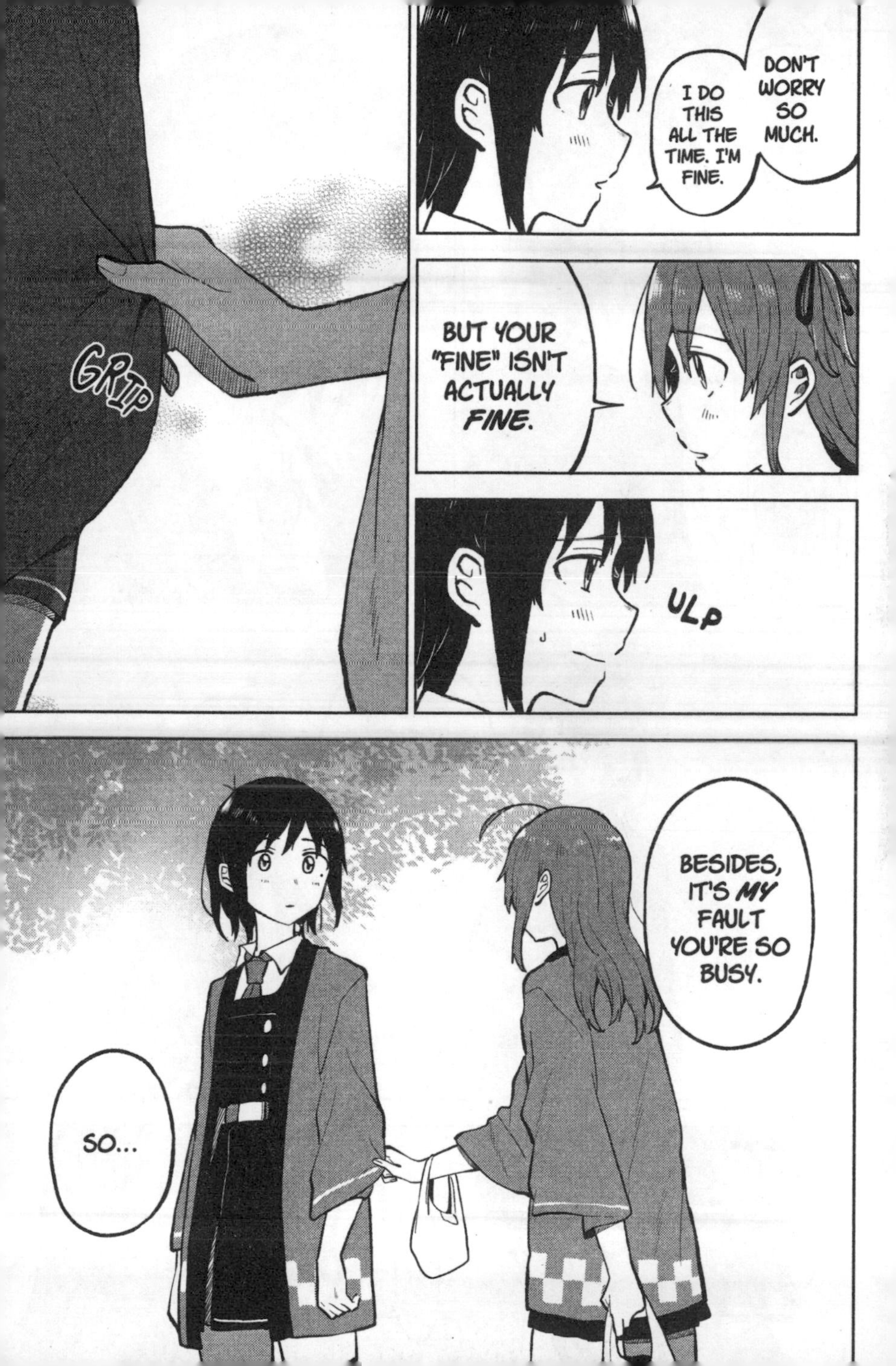
DON'T WORRY SO MUCH.
I DO THIS ALL THE TIME. I'M FINE.
BUT YOUR "FINE" ISN'T ACTUALLY FINE.
ULP
GRIP
BESIDES, IT'S MY FAULT YOU'RE SO BUSY.
SO...

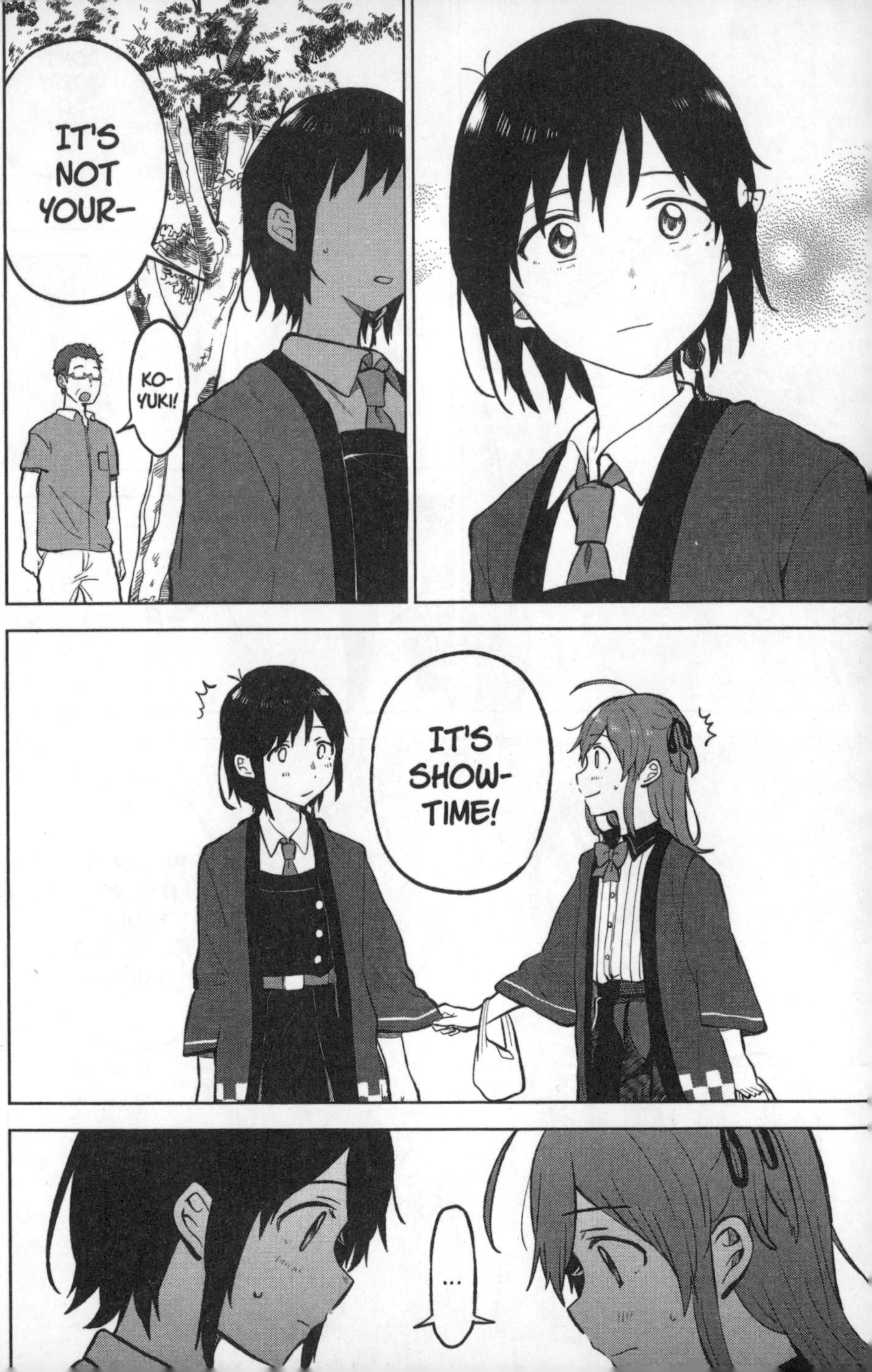
IT'S NOT YOUR–
KO-YUKI!
IT'S SHOW-TIME!
...

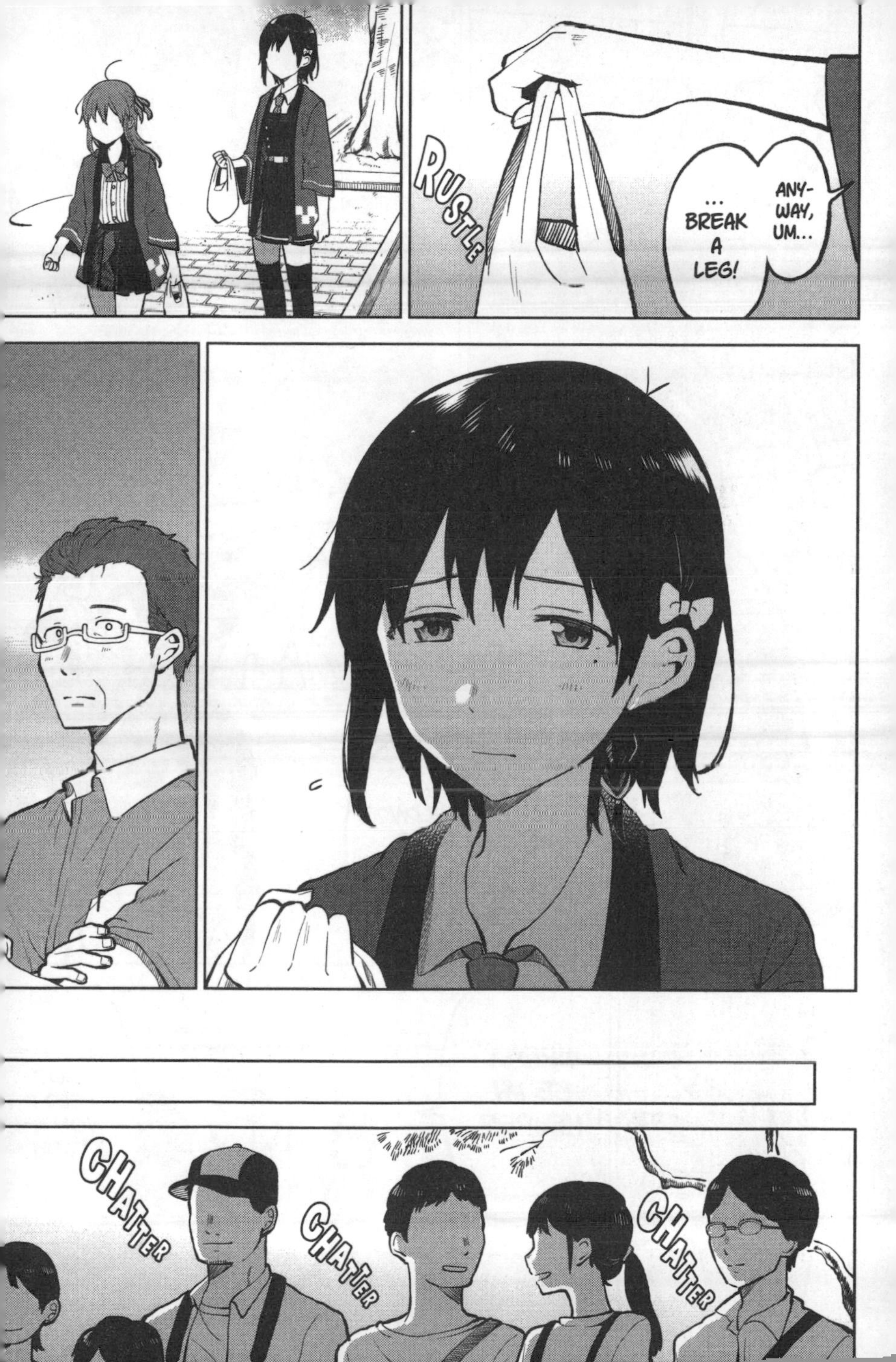
RUSTLE
ANYWAY, UM...
... BREAK A LEG!
CHATTER
CHATTER
CHATTER

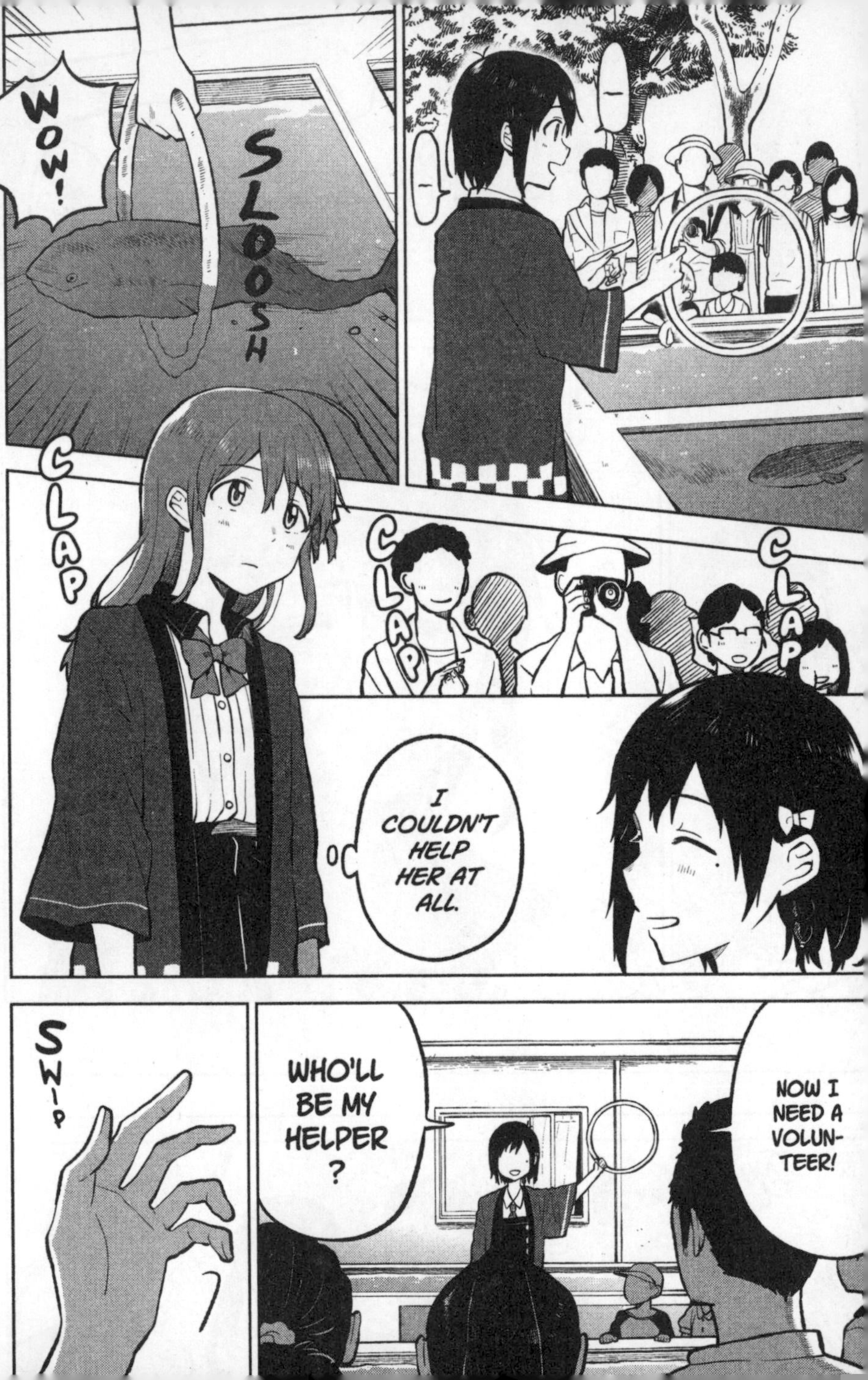
WOW!
SLOOSH
CLAP
CLAP
I COULDN'T HELP HER AT ALL.
CLAP
NOW I NEED A VOLUNTEER!
WHO'LL BE MY HELPER?
SWIP

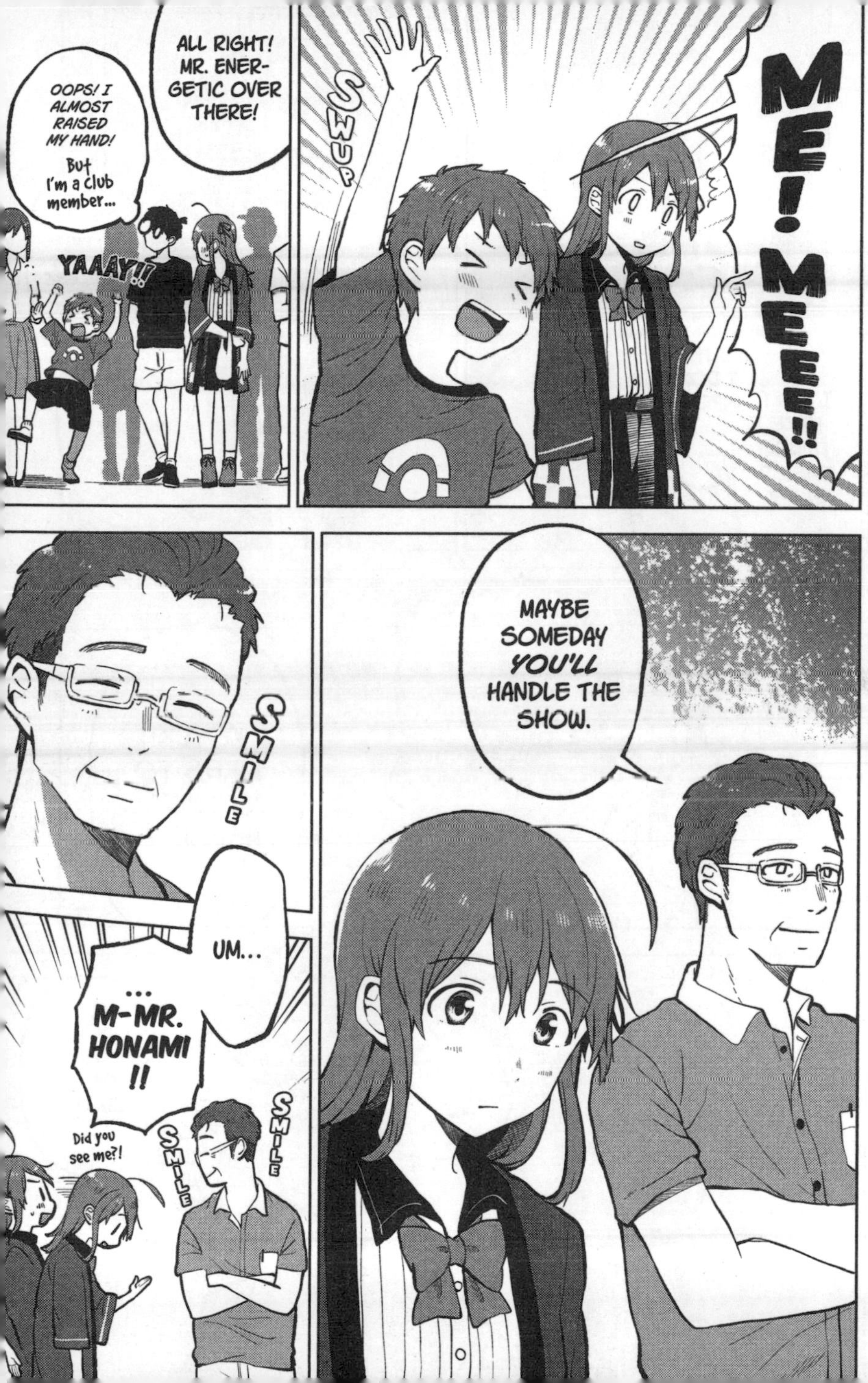
ME! MEEE!!
SWUP
ALL RIGHT! MR. ENER-GETIC OVER THERE!
OOPS! I ALMOST RAISED MY HAND!
But I'm a club member...
YAAAY!!
MAYBE SOMEDAY YOU'LL HANDLE THE SHOW.
SMILE
UM...
... M-MR. HONAMI!!
SMILE
SMILE
Did you see me?!

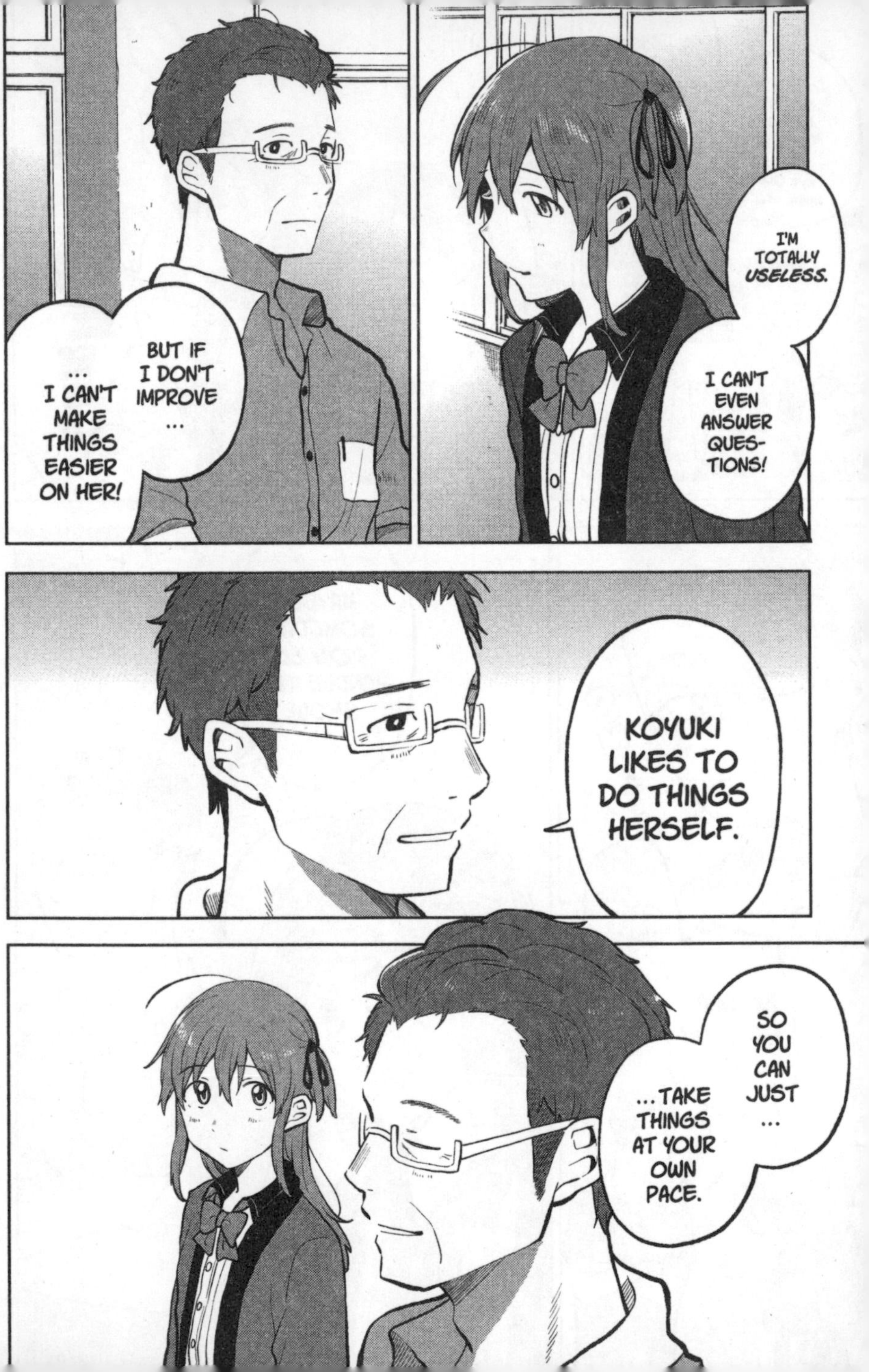
I'M TOTALLY USELESS.
I CAN'T EVEN ANSWER QUES-TIONS!
BUT IF I DON'T IMPROVE ...
... I CAN'T MAKE THINGS EASIER ON HER!
KOYUKI LIKES TO DO THINGS HERSELF.
SO YOU CAN JUST ...
...TAKE THINGS AT YOUR OWN PACE.

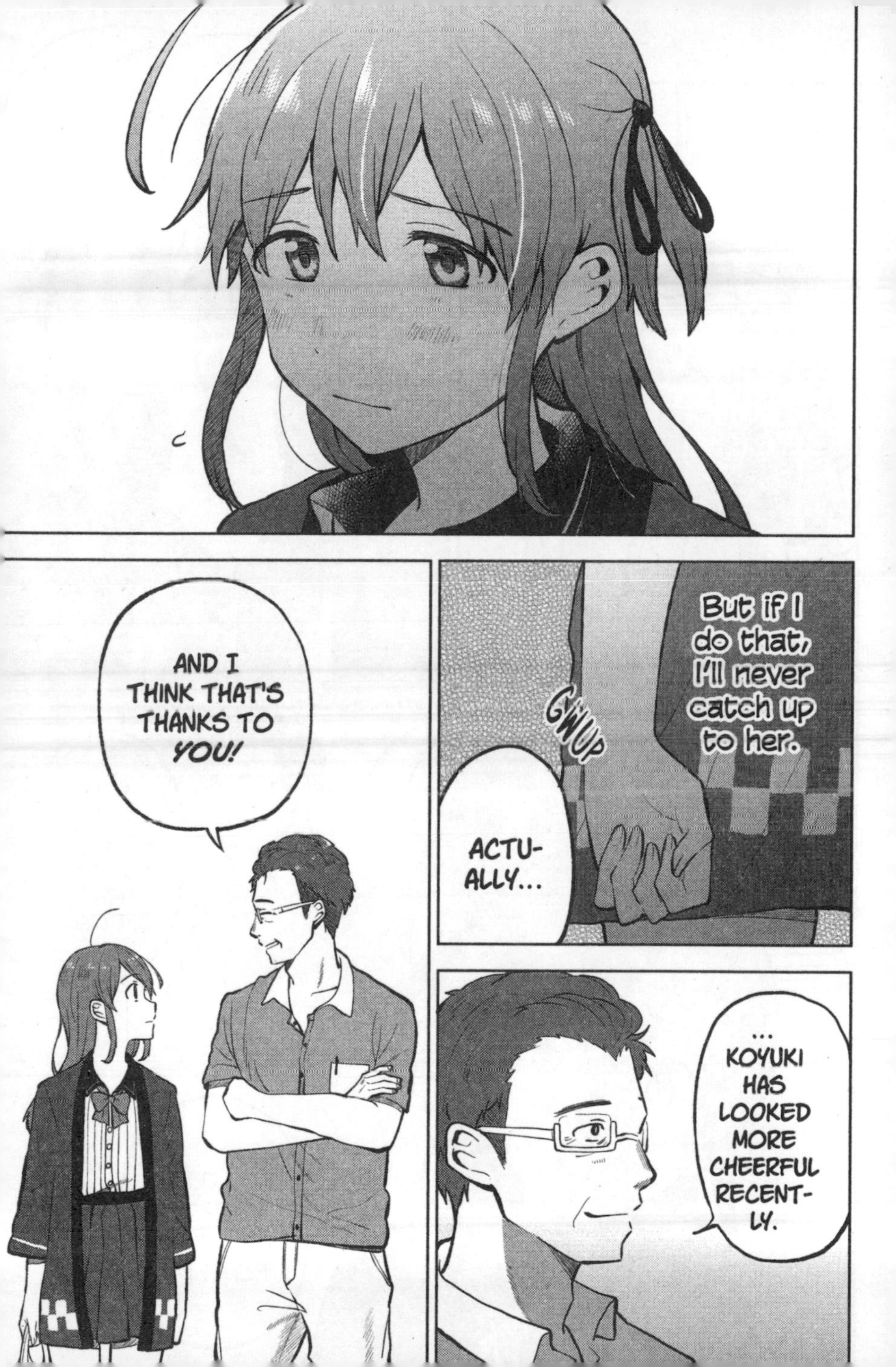
But if I do that, I'll never catch up to her.
GWUP
ACTU-ALLY...
... KOYUKI HAS LOOKED MORE CHEERFUL RECENT-LY.
AND I THINK THAT'S THANKS TO YOU!

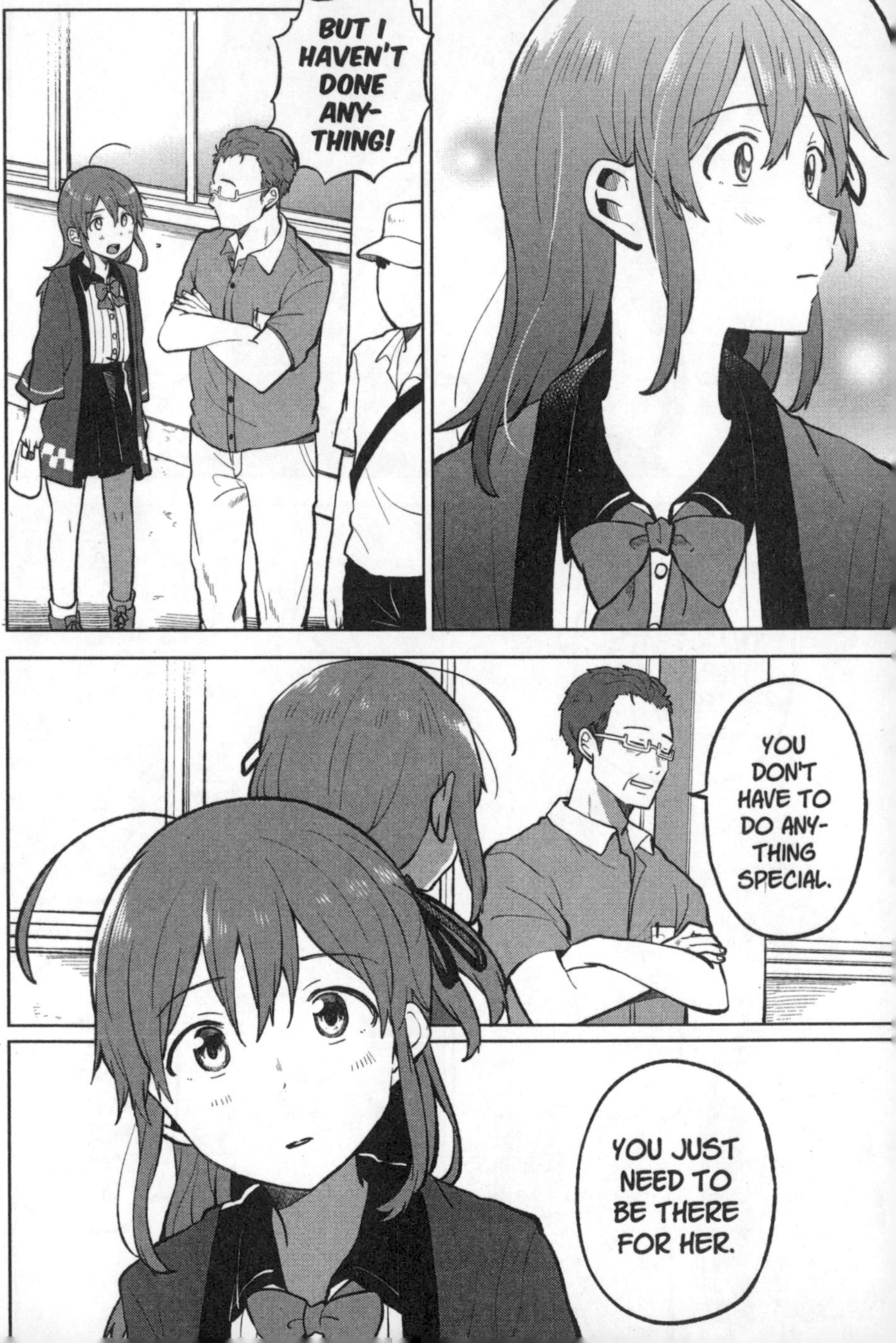
BUT I HAVEN'T DONE ANY-THING!
YOU DON'T HAVE TO DO ANY-THING SPECIAL.
YOU JUST NEED TO BE THERE FOR HER.

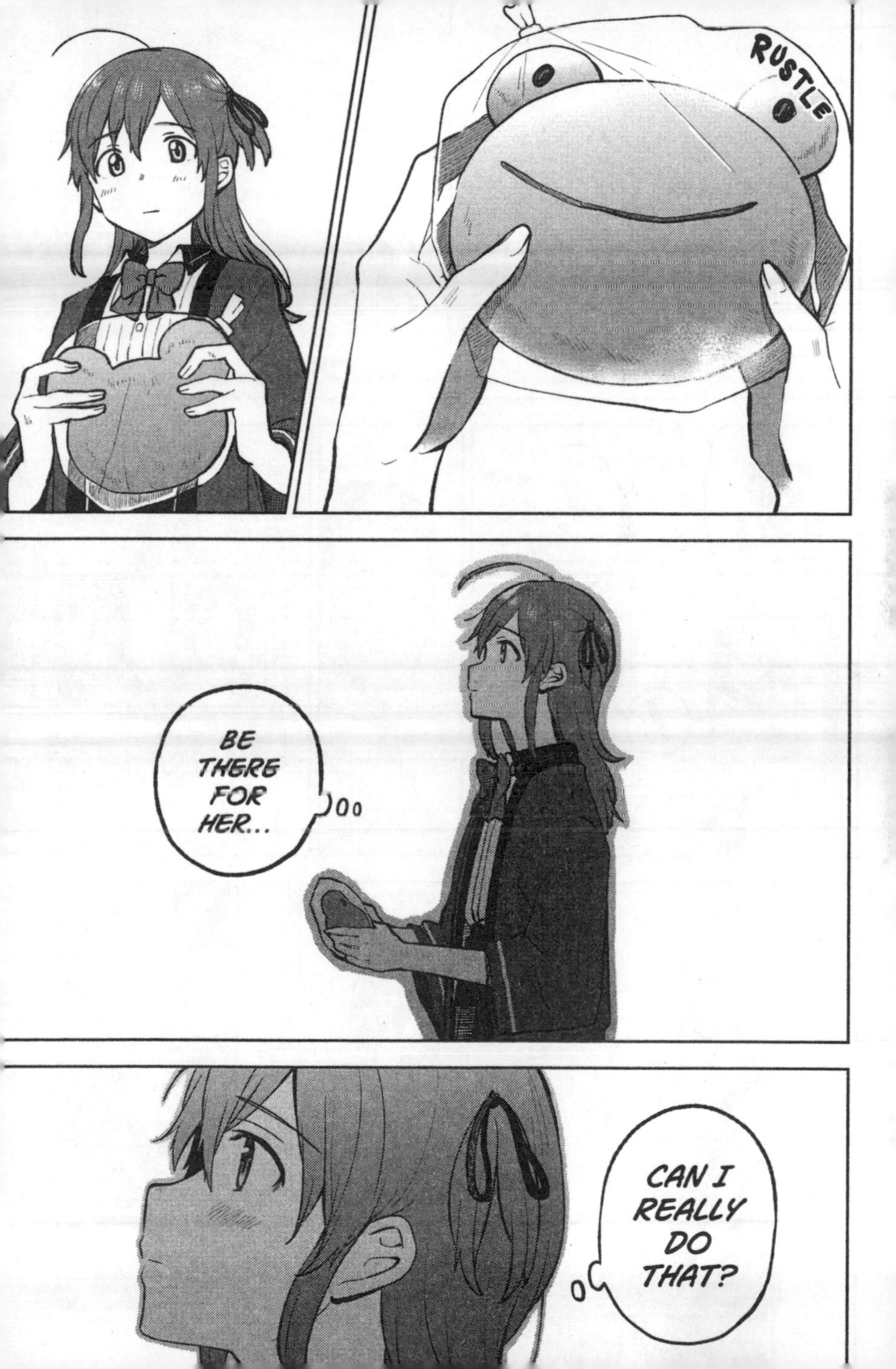
RUSTLE
BE THERE FOR HER...
CAN I REALLY DO THAT?

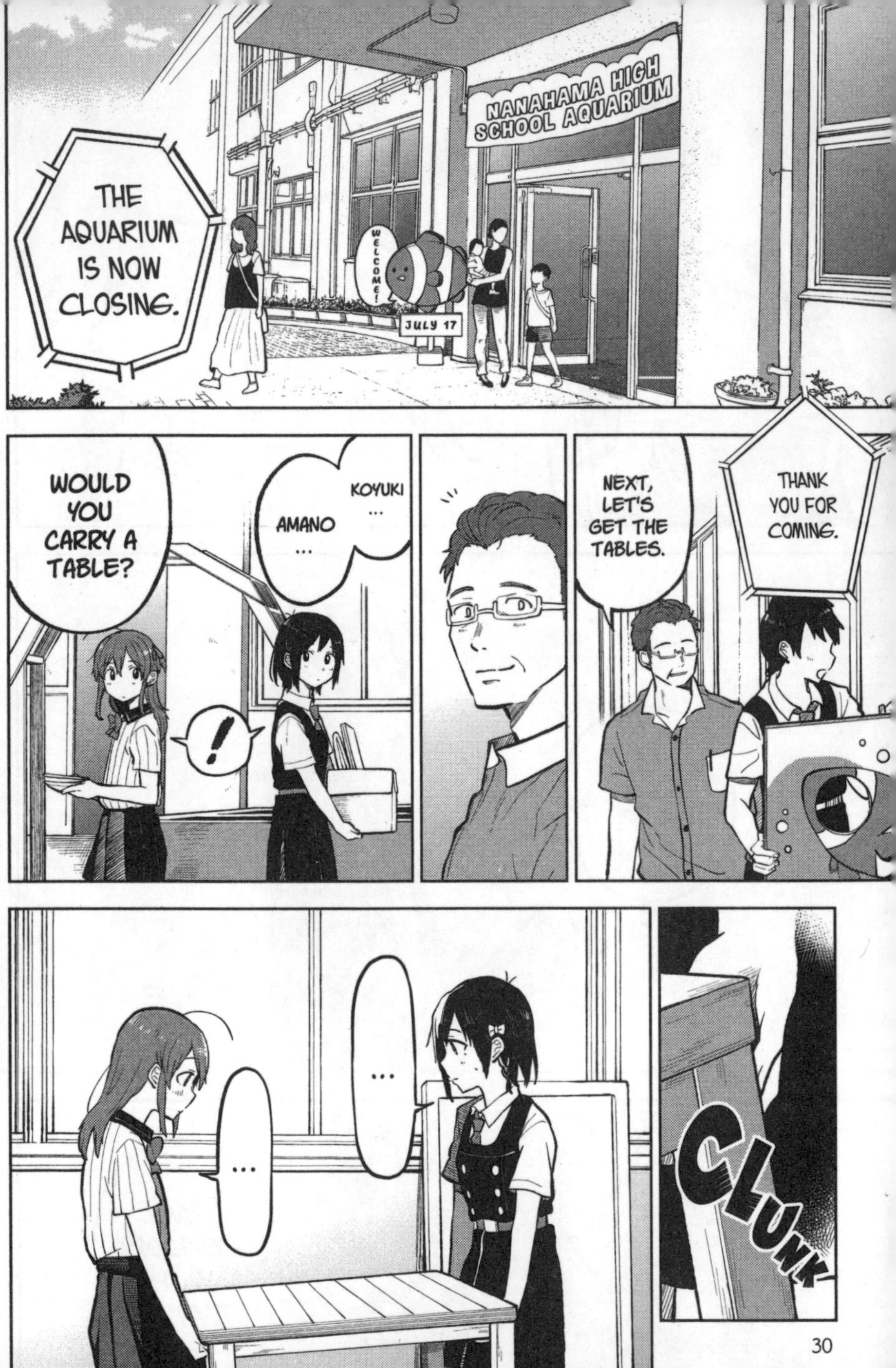
NANAHAMA HIGH SCHOOL AQUARIUM
THE AQUARIUM IS NOW CLOSING.
WELCOME!
JULY 17
THANK YOU FOR COMING.
NEXT, LET'S GET THE TABLES.
KOYUKI ...
AMANO ...
WOULD YOU CARRY A TABLE?
!
CLUNK
...
...

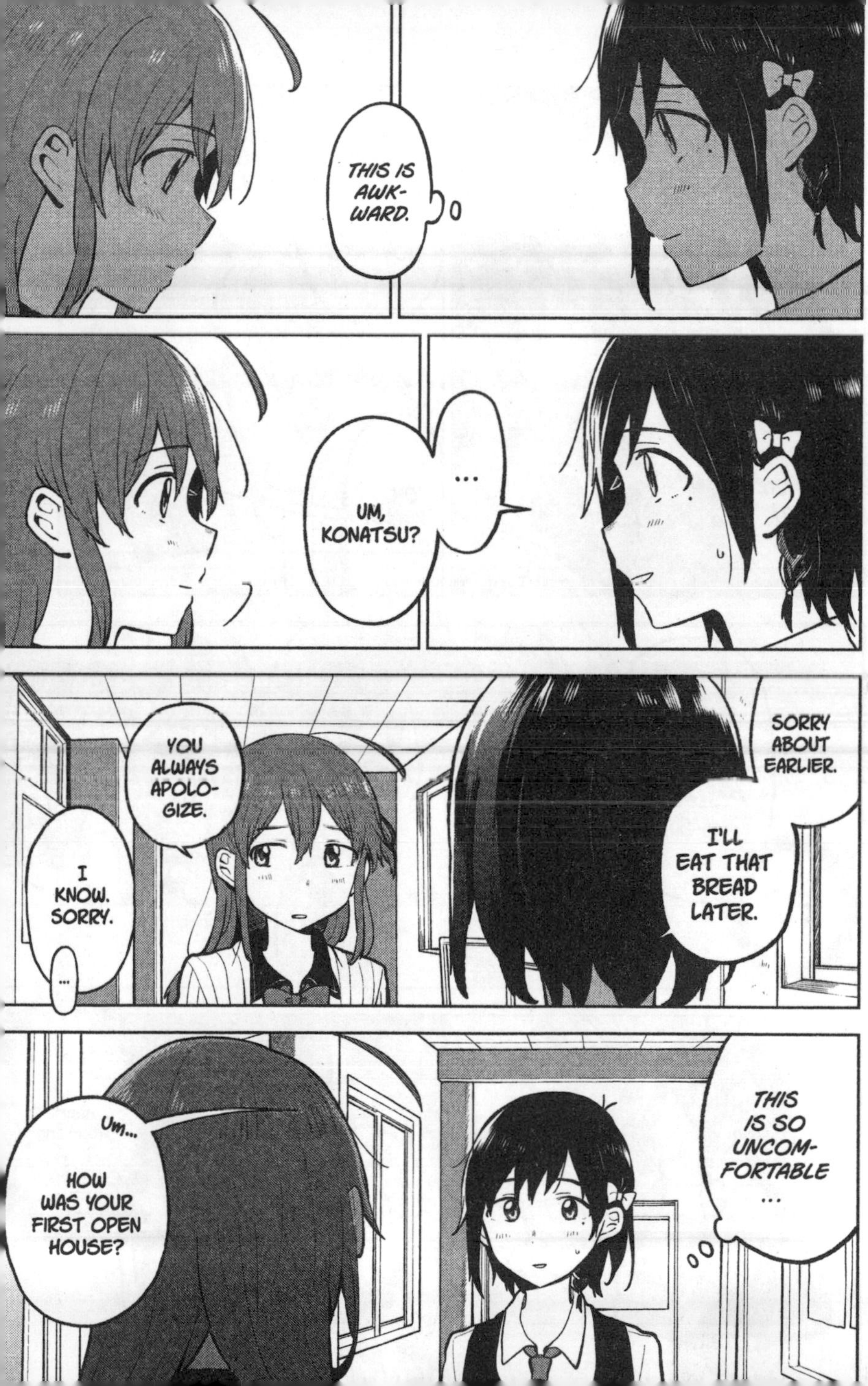
THIS IS AWK-WARD.
...
UM, KONATSU?
SORRY ABOUT EARLIER.
I'LL EAT THAT BREAD LATER.
YOU ALWAYS APOLO-GIZE.
I KNOW. SORRY.
...
THIS IS SO UNCOM-FORTABLE ...
Um...
HOW WAS YOUR FIRST OPEN HOUSE?

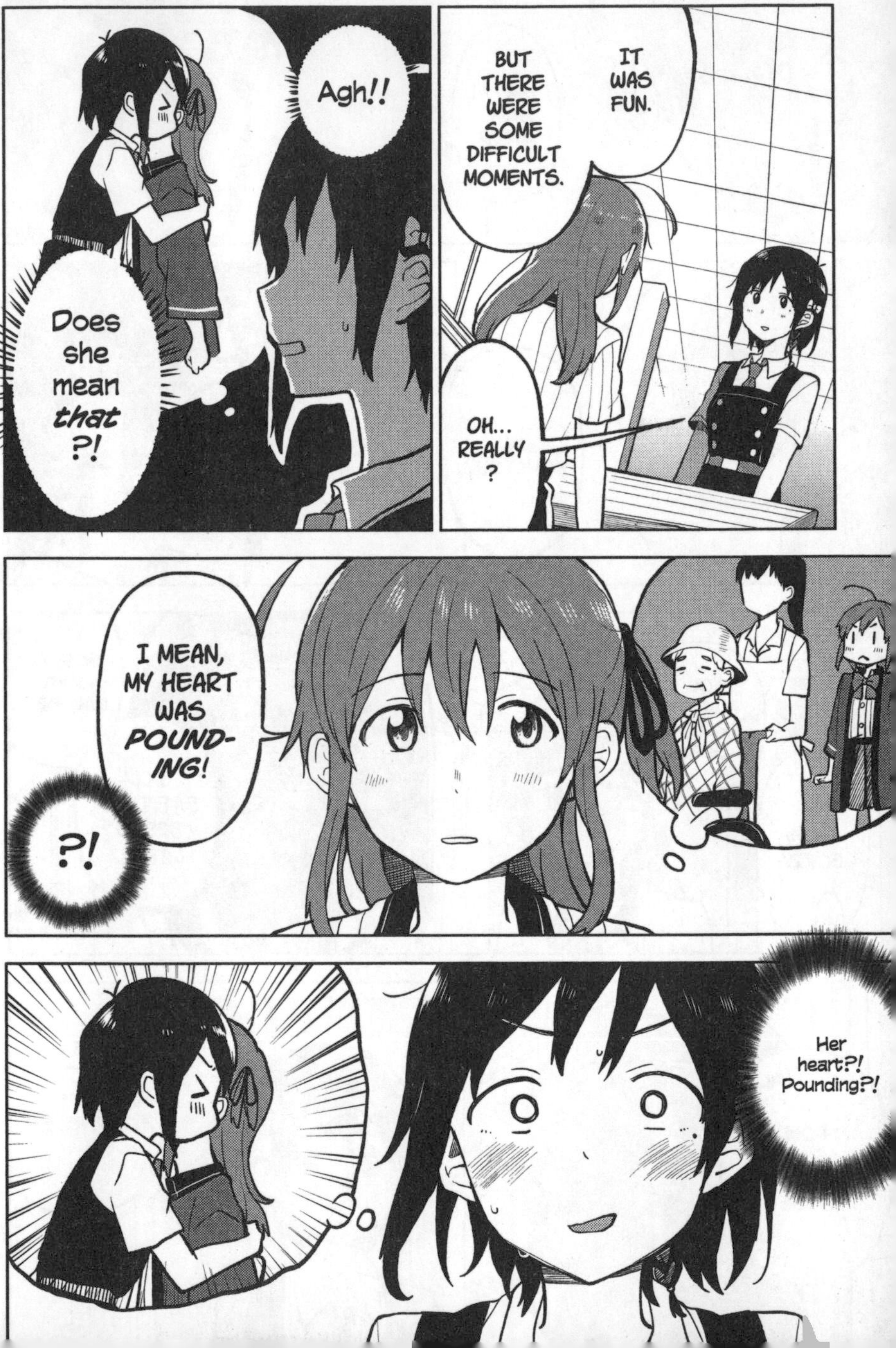
IT WAS FUN.
BUT THERE WERE SOME DIFFICULT MOMENTS.
OH... REALLY?
Agh!!
Does she mean *that*?!
I MEAN, MY HEART WAS *POUNDING*!
?!
Her heart?! Pounding?!

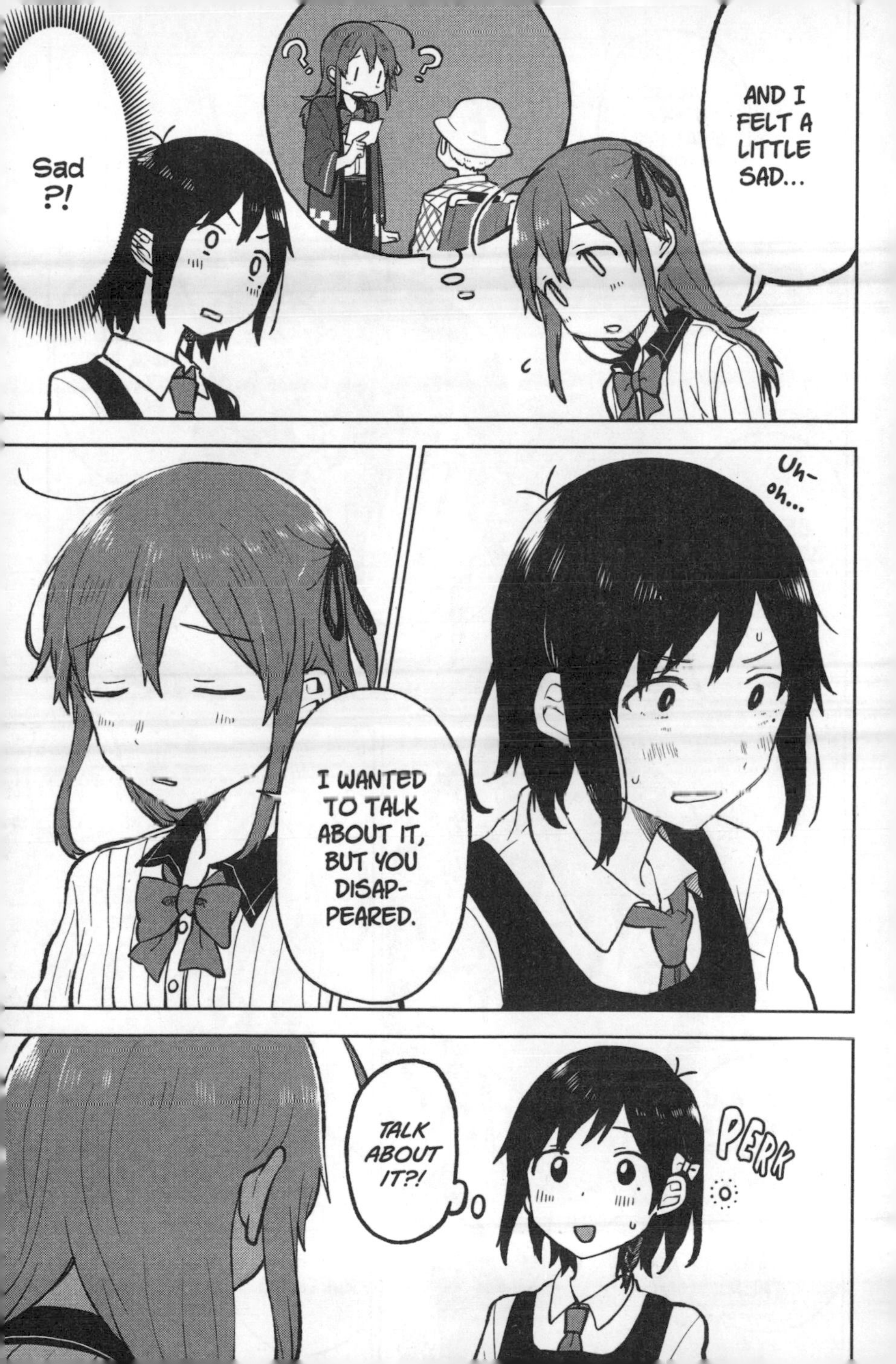
AND I FELT A LITTLE SAD...
Sad ?!
Uh-oh...
I WANTED TO TALK ABOUT IT, BUT YOU DISAPPEARED.
PERK
TALK ABOUT IT?!

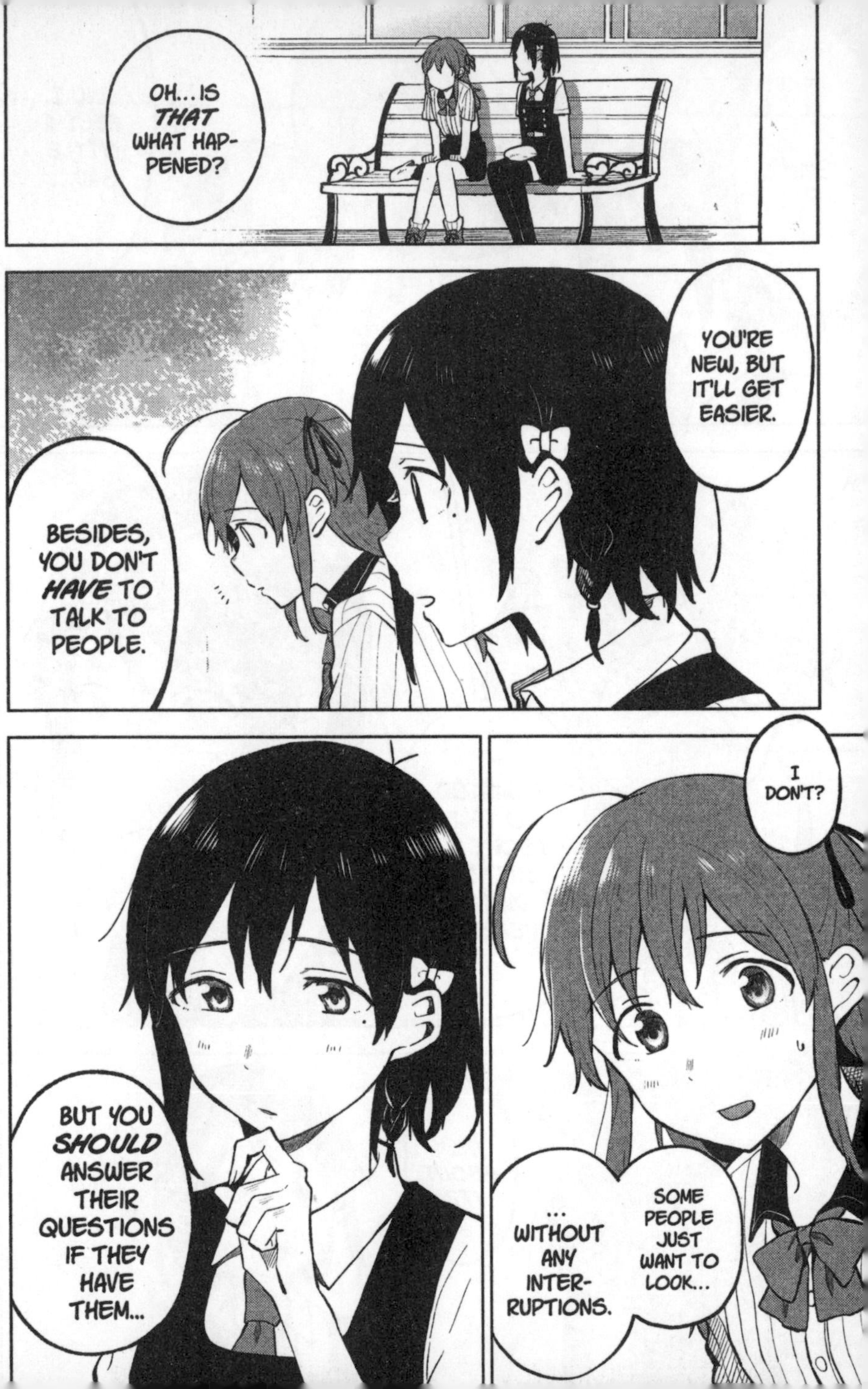
OH... IS THAT WHAT HAP-PENED?
YOU'RE NEW, BUT IT'LL GET EASIER.
BESIDES, YOU DON'T HAVE TO TALK TO PEOPLE.
I DON'T?
SOME PEOPLE JUST WANT TO LOOK...
...WITHOUT ANY INTER-RUPTIONS.
BUT YOU SHOULD ANSWER THEIR QUESTIONS IF THEY HAVE THEM...

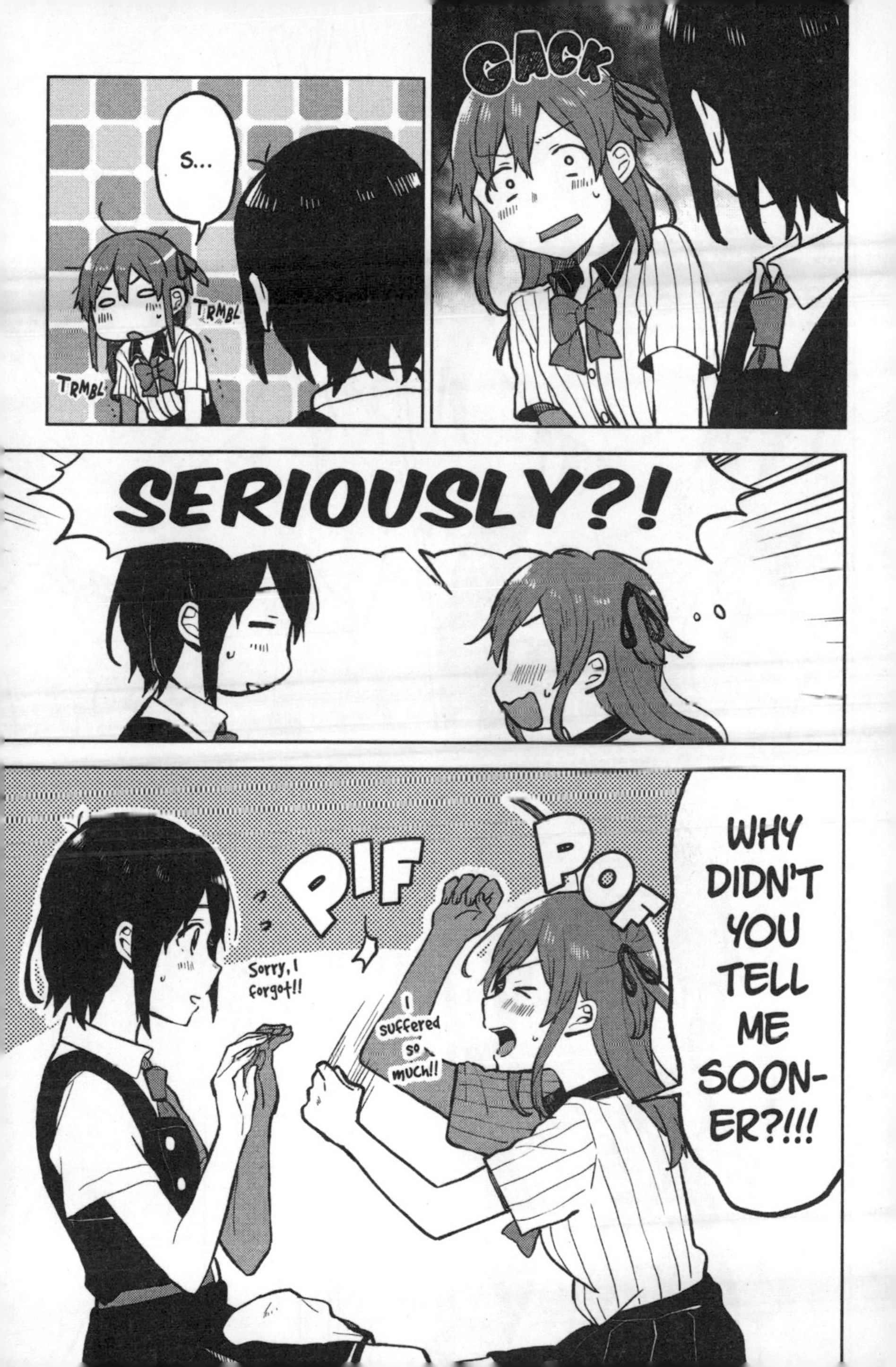
GACK
S...
TRMBL
TRMBL
SERIOUSLY?!
WHY DIDN'T YOU TELL ME SOON-ER?!!!
POF
PIF
I suffered so much!!
Sorry, I forgot!!

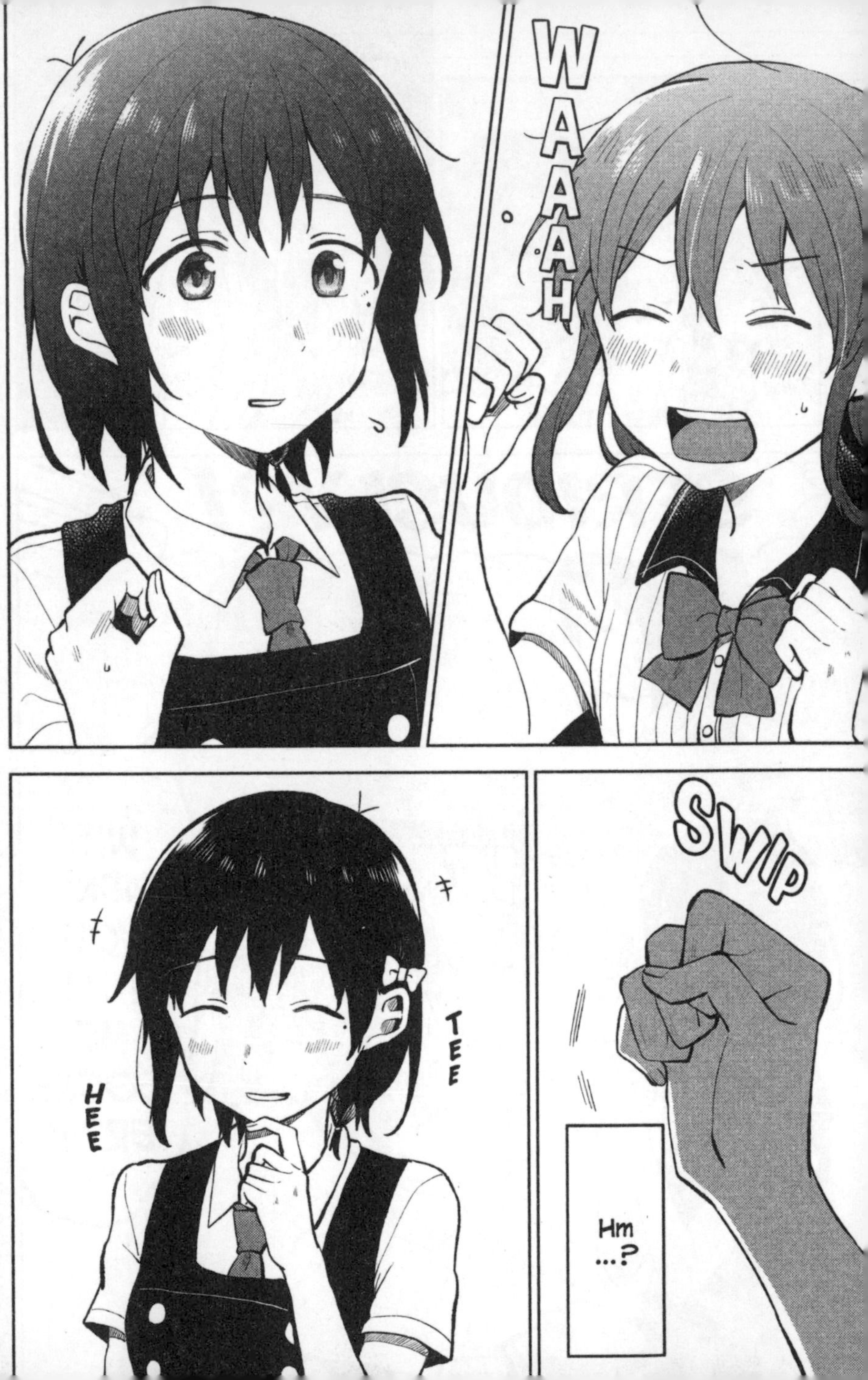
WAAAAH
SWIP
Hm ...?
TEE HEE

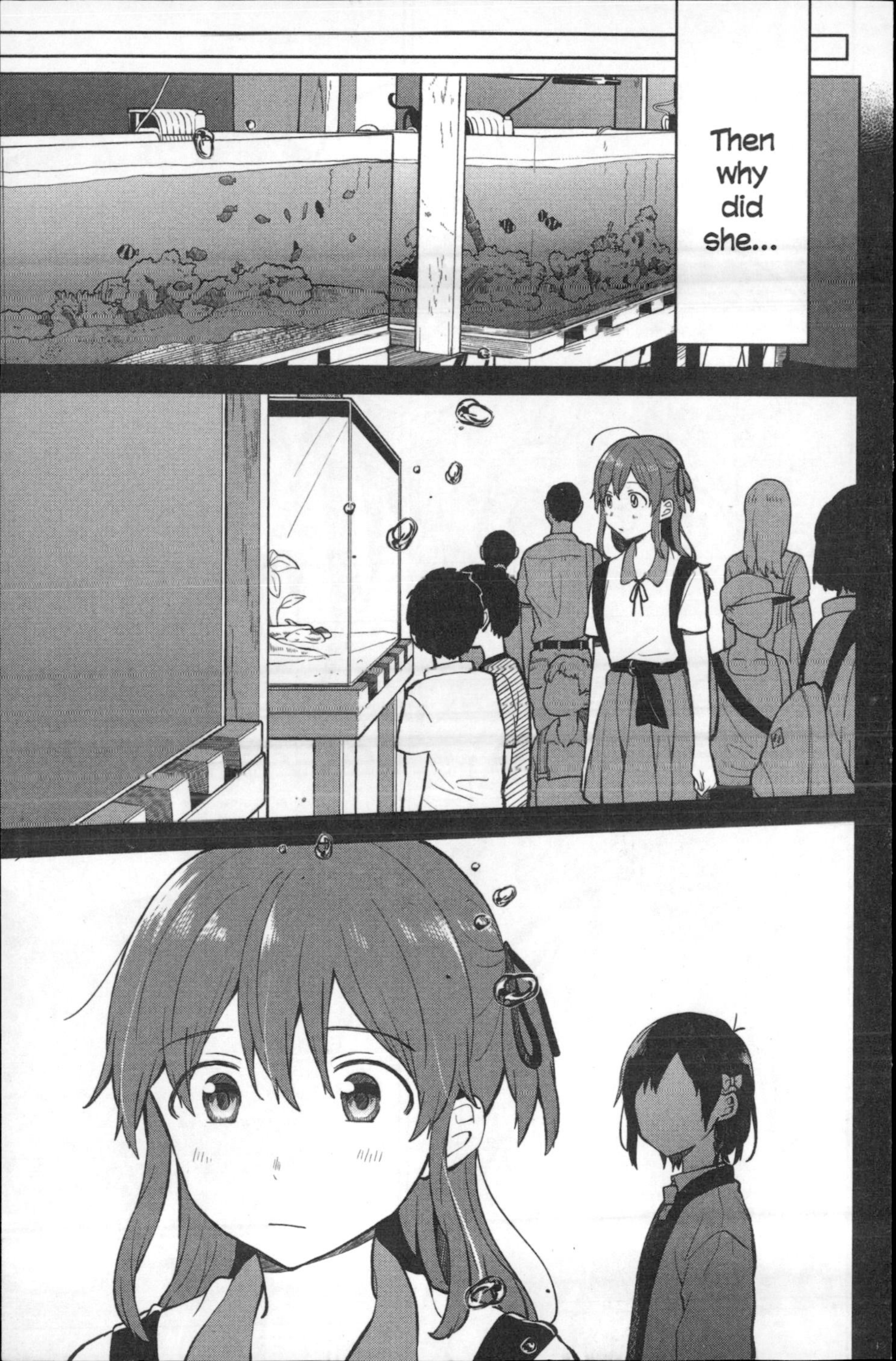
Then why did she...

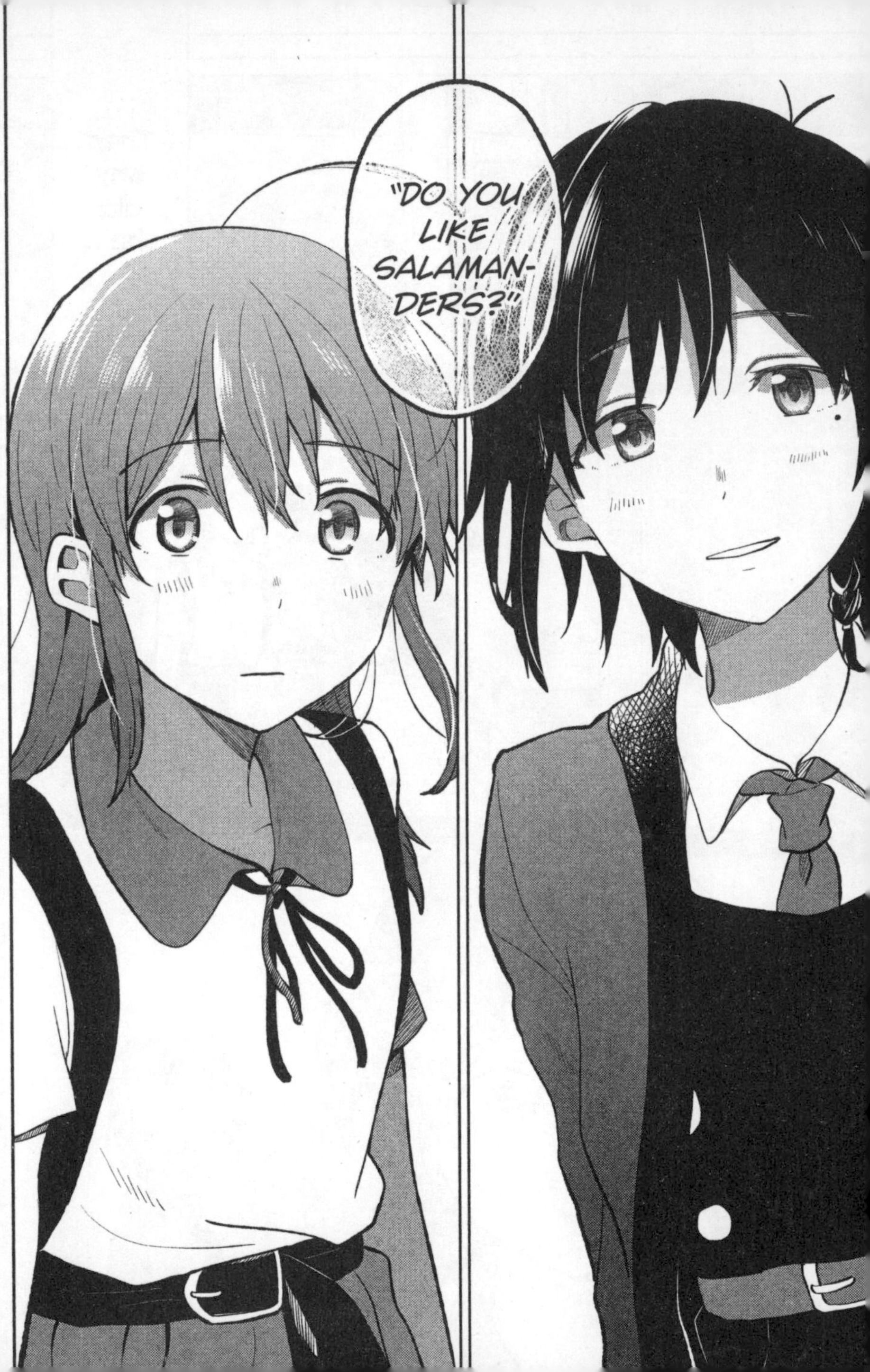
"DO YOU LIKE SALAMANDERS?"

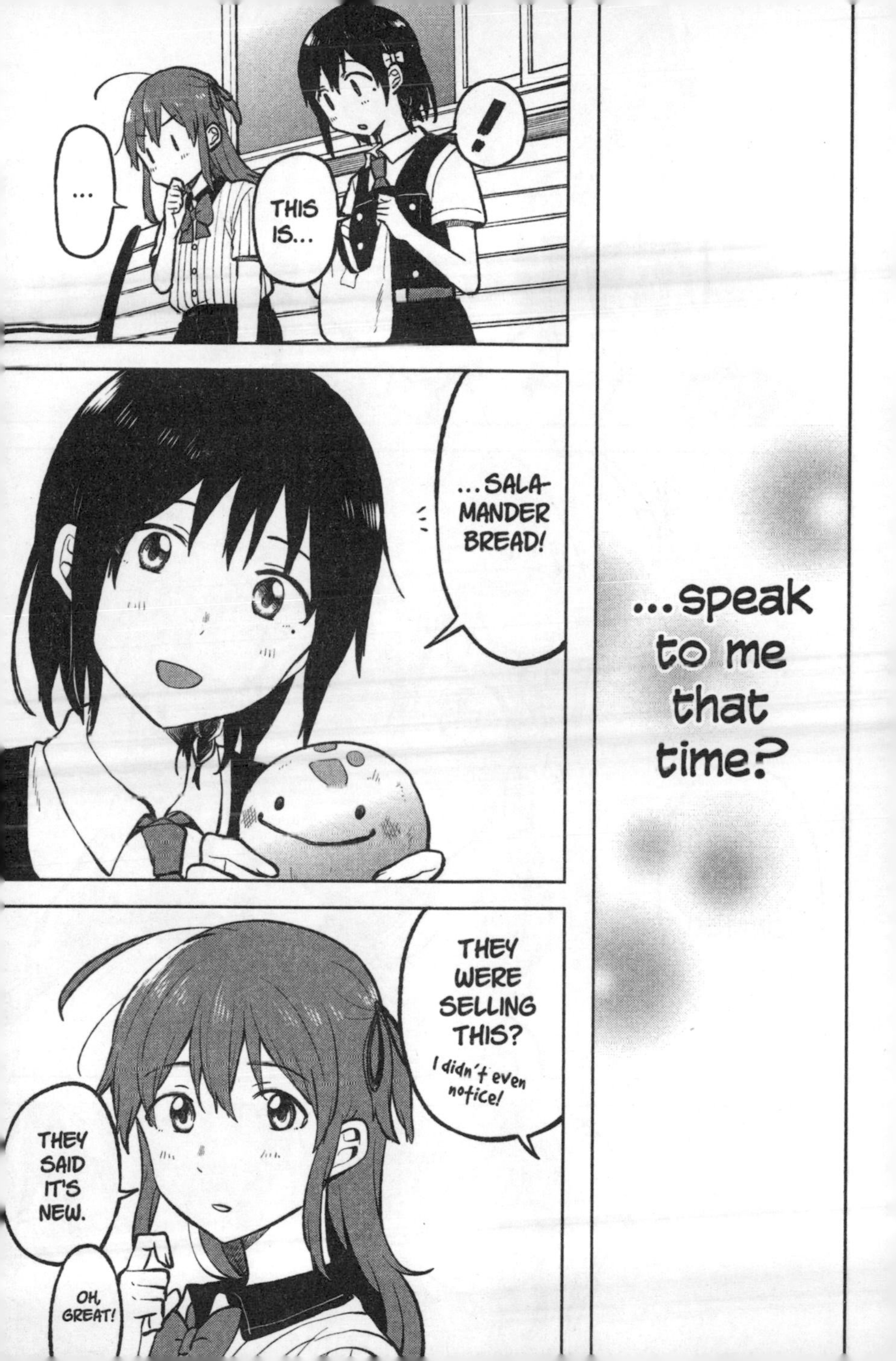
...speak to me that time?
!
THIS IS...
...
...SALAMANDER BREAD!
THEY WERE SELLING THIS?
I didn't even notice!
THEY SAID IT'S NEW.
OH, GREAT!

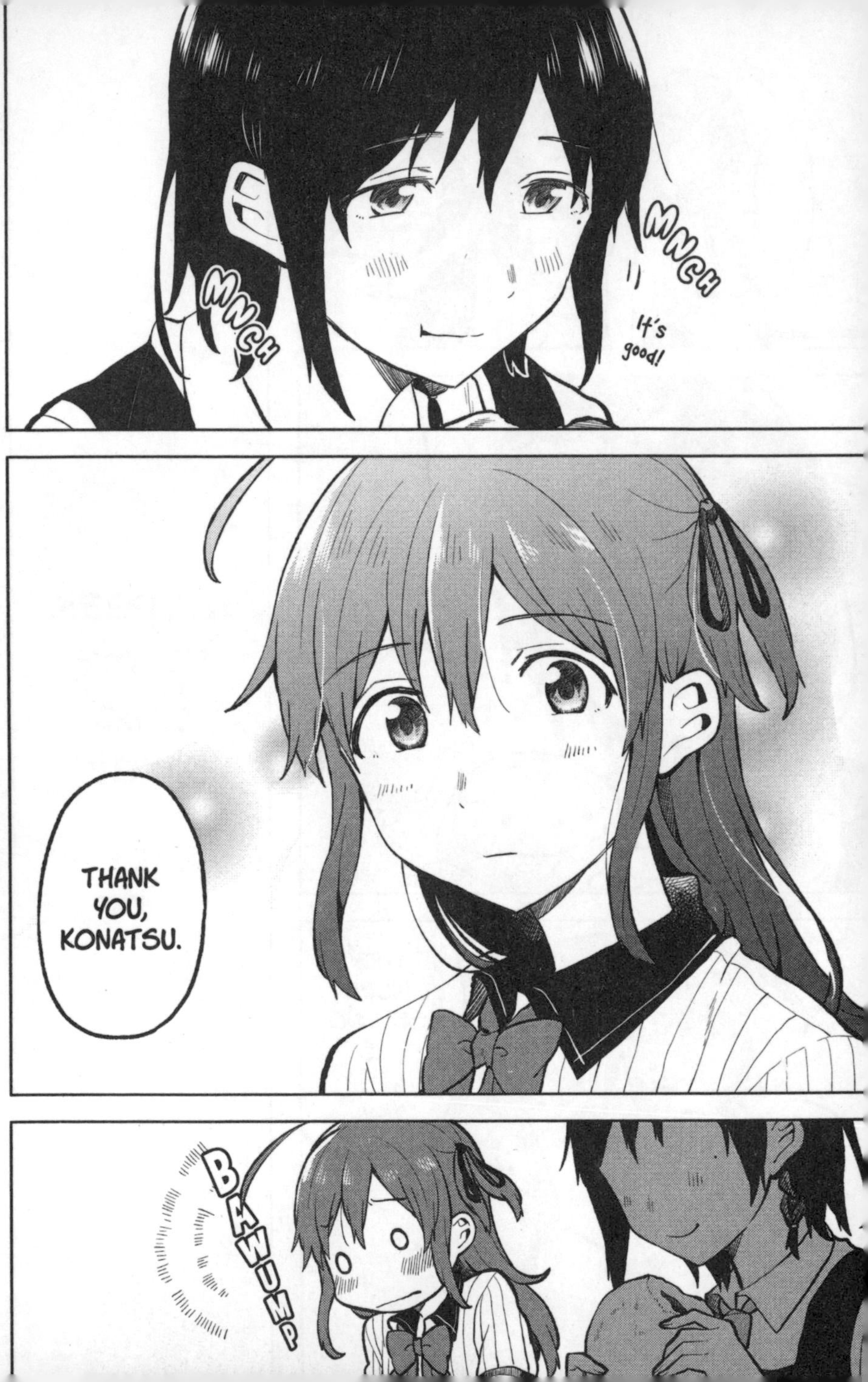
MNCH
MNCH
It's good!
THANK YOU, KONATSU.
BAWUMP

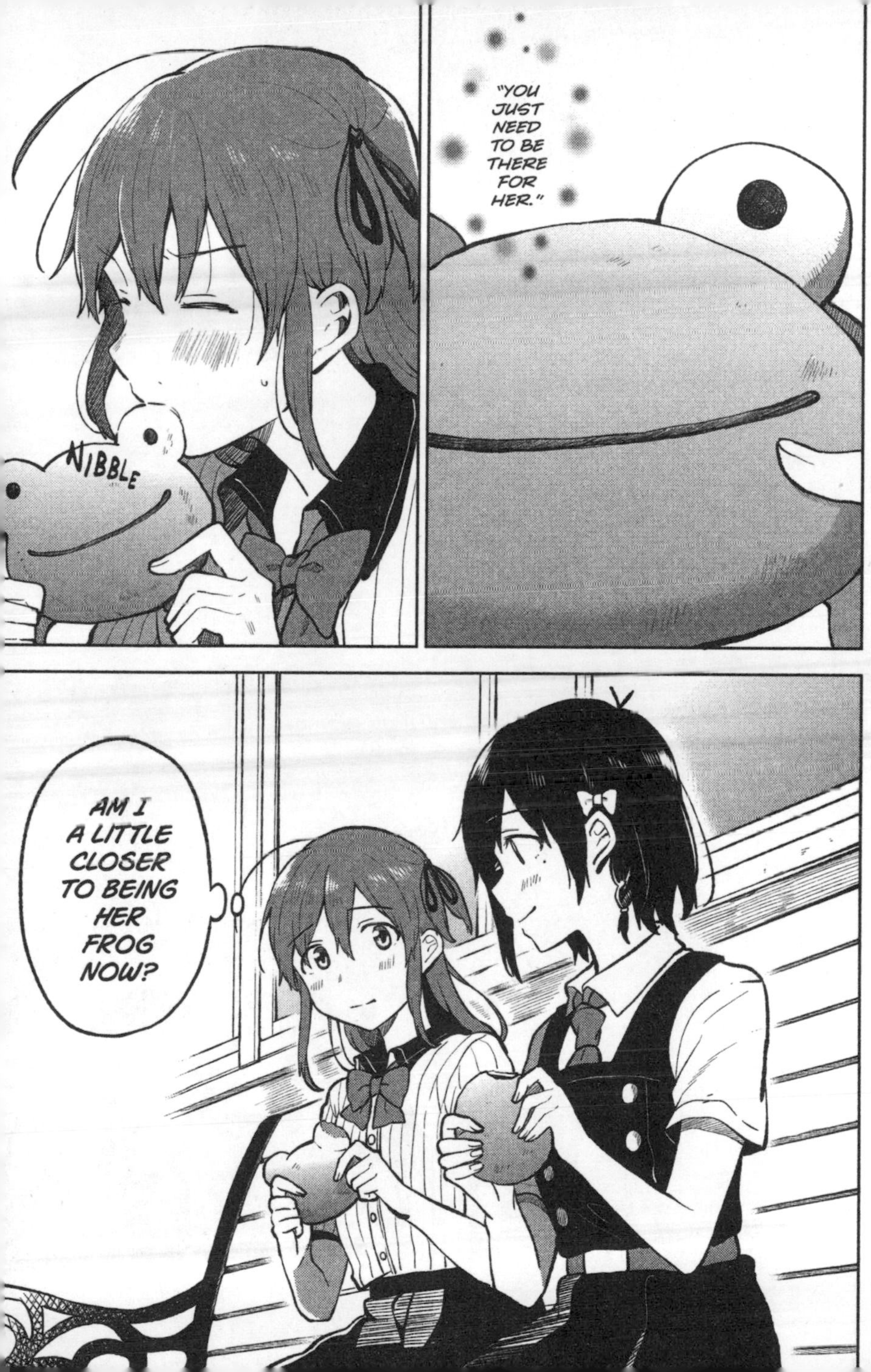
"YOU JUST NEED TO BE THERE FOR HER."
NIBBLE
AM I A LITTLE CLOSER TO BEING HER FROG NOW?

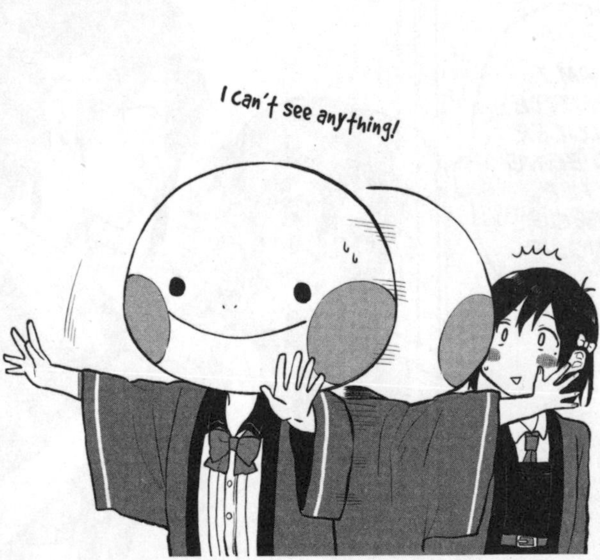
I can't see anything!

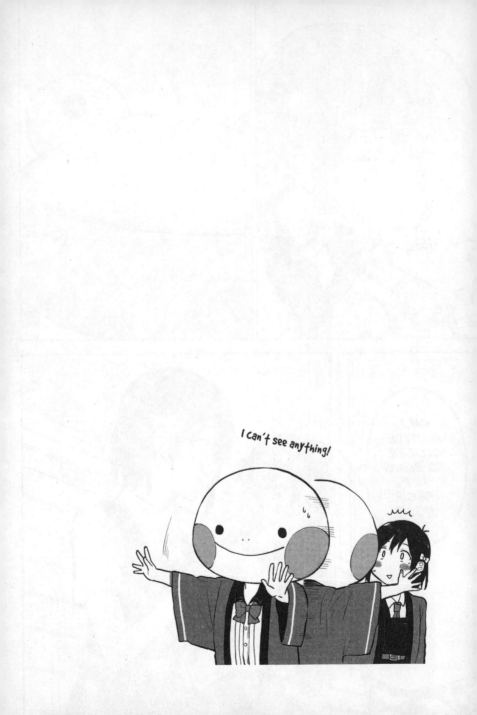

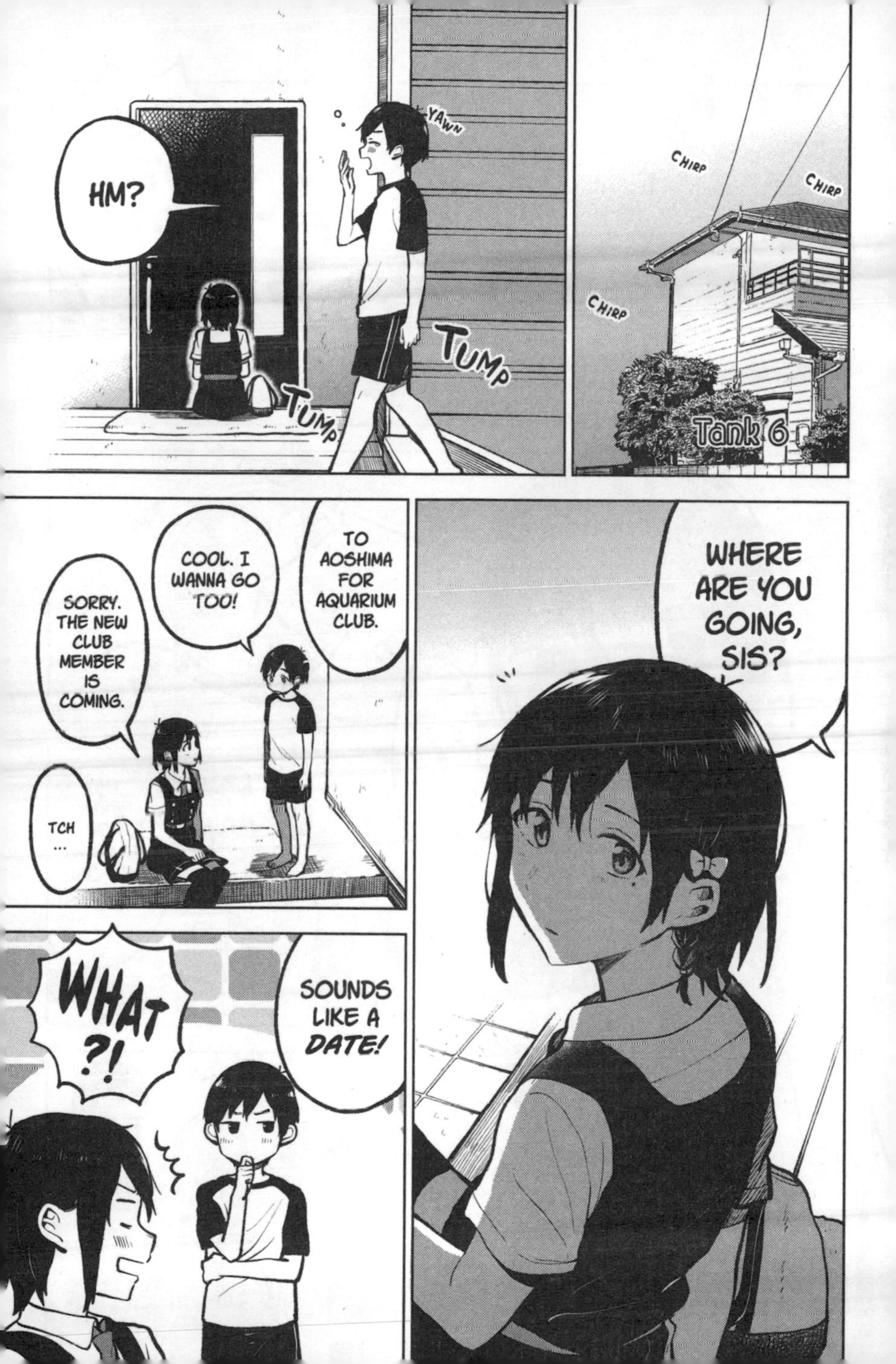

Tank 6
CHIRP
CHIRP
CHIRP
YAWN
TUMP
TUMP
HM?
WHERE ARE YOU GOING, SIS?
TO AOSHIMA FOR AQUARIUM CLUB.
COOL. I WANNA GO TOO!
SORRY. THE NEW CLUB MEMBER IS COMING.
TCH ...
SOUNDS LIKE A *DATE!*
WHAT ?!

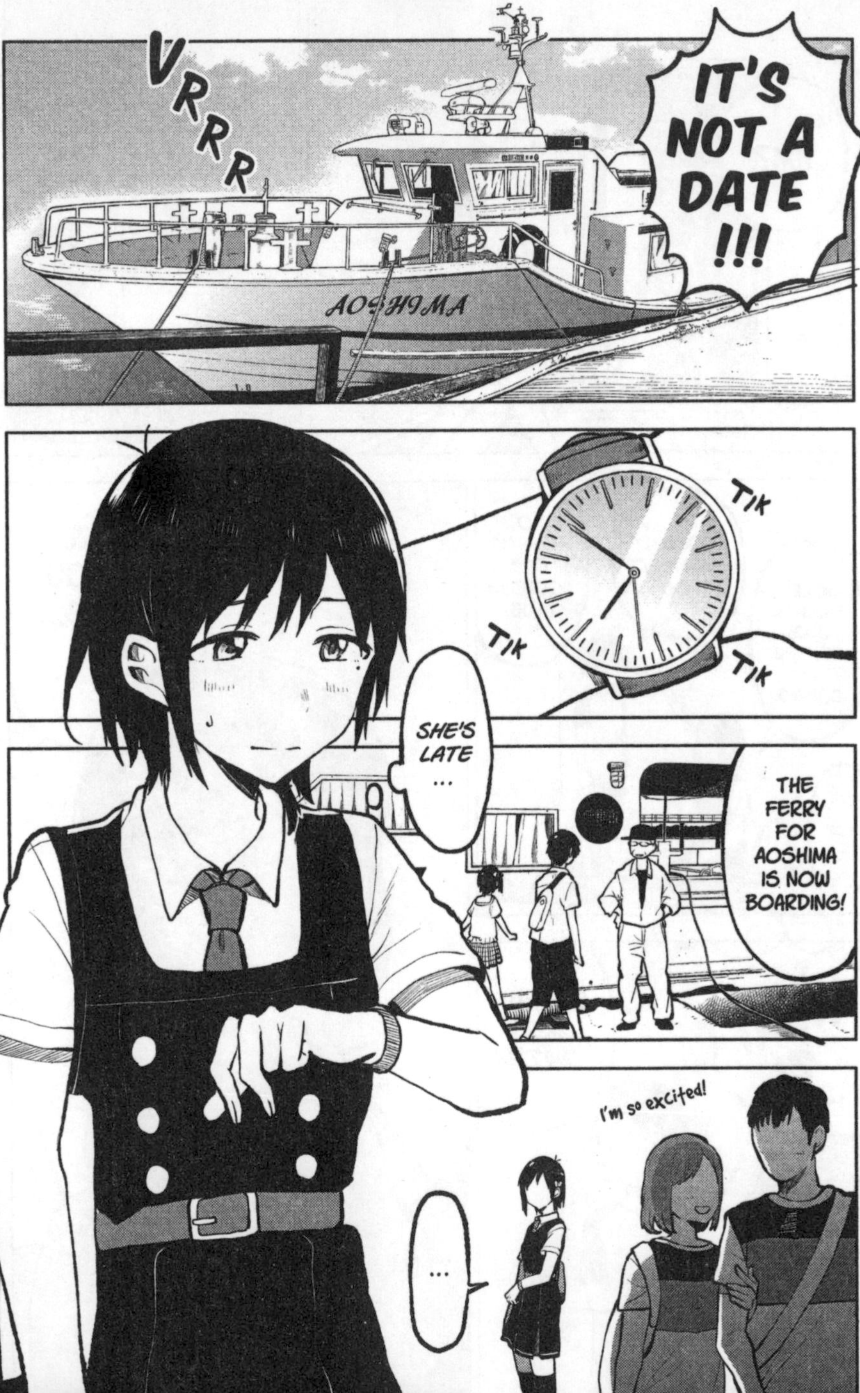
IT'S NOT A DATE !!!
VRRR
TIK
TIK
TIK
THE FERRY FOR AOSHIMA IS NOW BOARDING!
SHE'S LATE ...
I'm so excited!
...

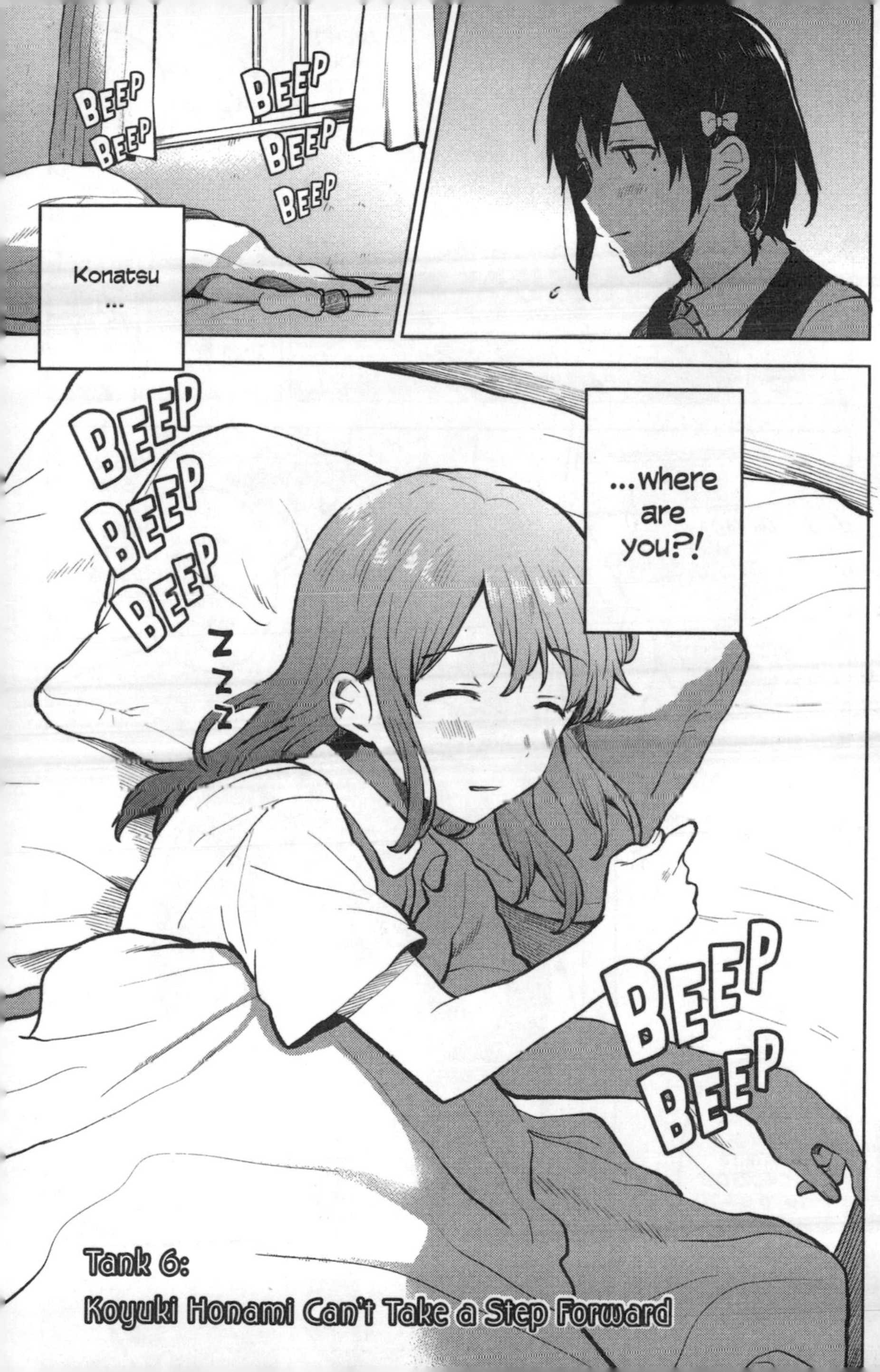
BEEP
BEEP
BEEP
BEEP
BEEP
Konatsu
...
...where are you?!
BEEP
BEEP
BEEP
ZZZ
BEEP
BEEP
Tank 6:
Koyuki Honami Can't Take a Step Forward

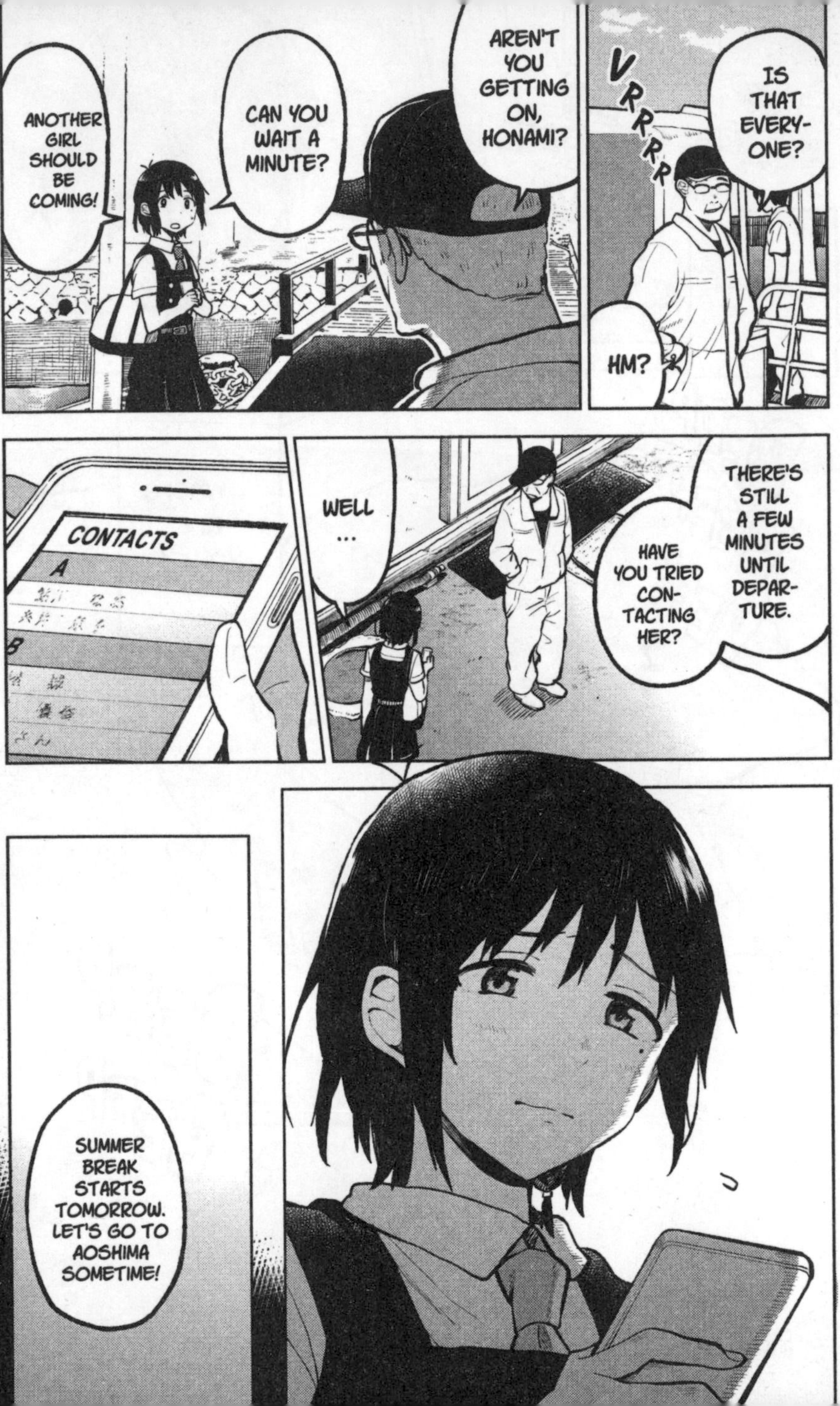
VRRRR
IS THAT EVERY-ONE?
HM?
AREN'T YOU GETTING ON, HONAMI?
CAN YOU WAIT A MINUTE?
ANOTHER GIRL SHOULD BE COMING!
THERE'S STILL A FEW MINUTES UNTIL DEPAR-TURE.
HAVE YOU TRIED CON-TACTING HER?
WELL ...
CONTACTS
A
B
SUMMER BREAK STARTS TOMORROW. LET'S GO TO AOSHIMA SOMETIME!

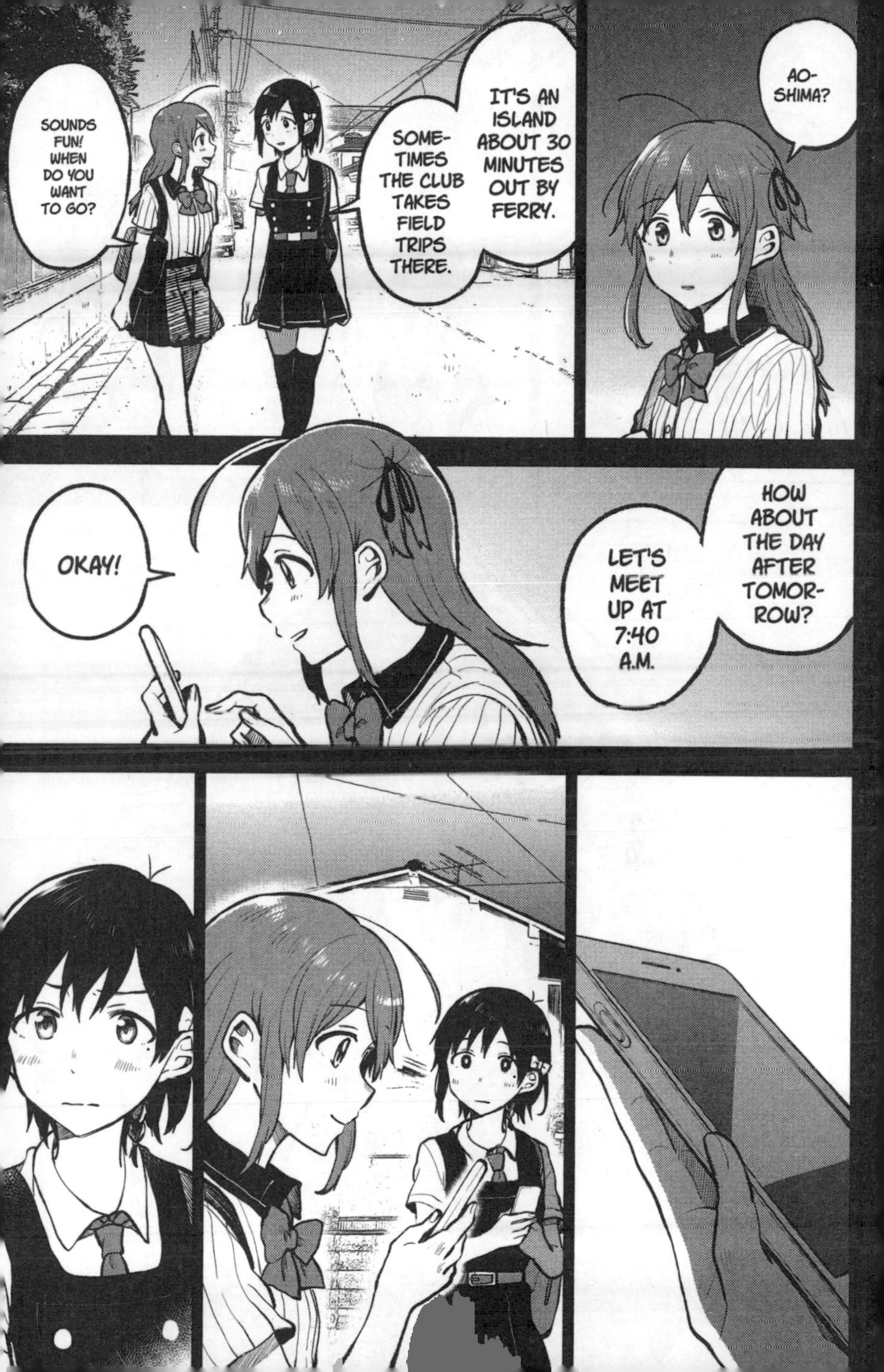
AO-SHIMA?
IT'S AN ISLAND ABOUT 30 MINUTES OUT BY FERRY.
SOME-TIMES THE CLUB TAKES FIELD TRIPS THERE.
SOUNDS FUN! WHEN DO YOU WANT TO GO?
HOW ABOUT THE DAY AFTER TOMOR-ROW?
LET'S MEET UP AT 7:40 A.M.
OKAY!

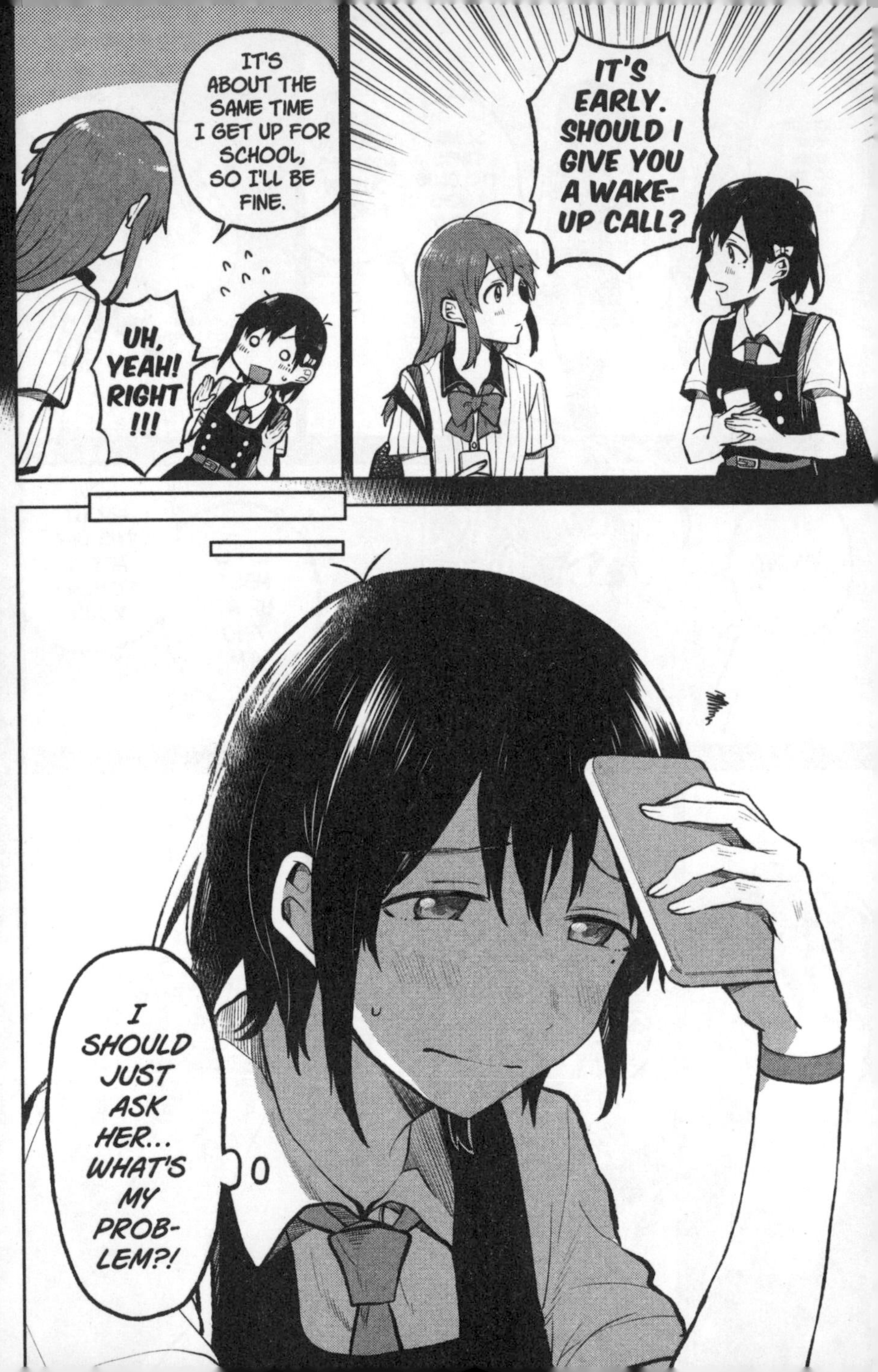
IT'S EARLY. SHOULD I GIVE YOU A WAKE-UP CALL?
IT'S ABOUT THE SAME TIME I GET UP FOR SCHOOL, SO I'LL BE FINE.
UH, YEAH! RIGHT!!!
I SHOULD JUST ASK HER... WHAT'S MY PROB-LEM?!

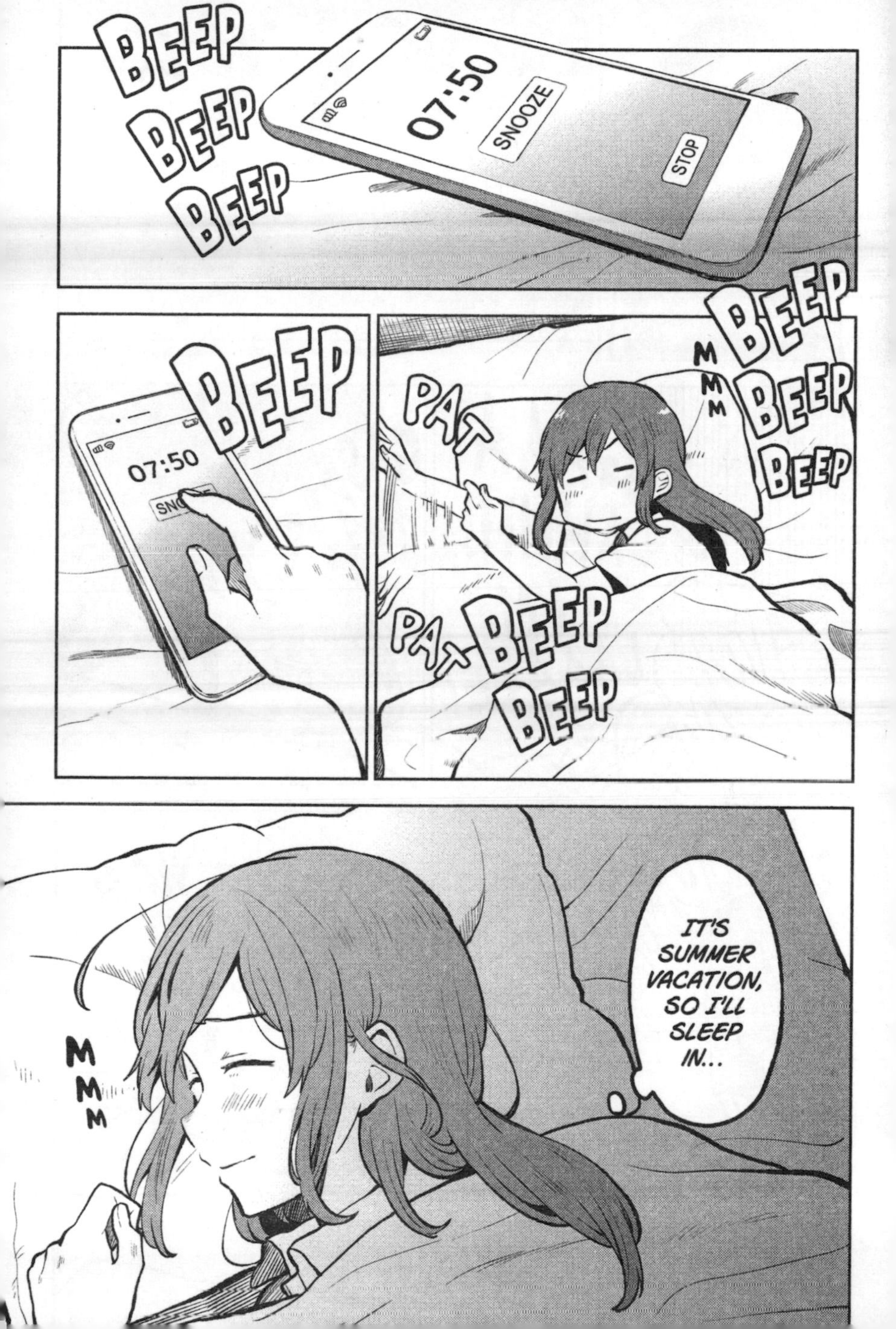
BEEP
BEEP
BEEP
07:50
SNOOZE
STOP
BEEP
BEEP
BEEP
MMM
PAT
PAT
BEEP
BEEP
BEEP
07:50
IT'S SUMMER VACATION, SO I'LL SLEEP IN...
MMM

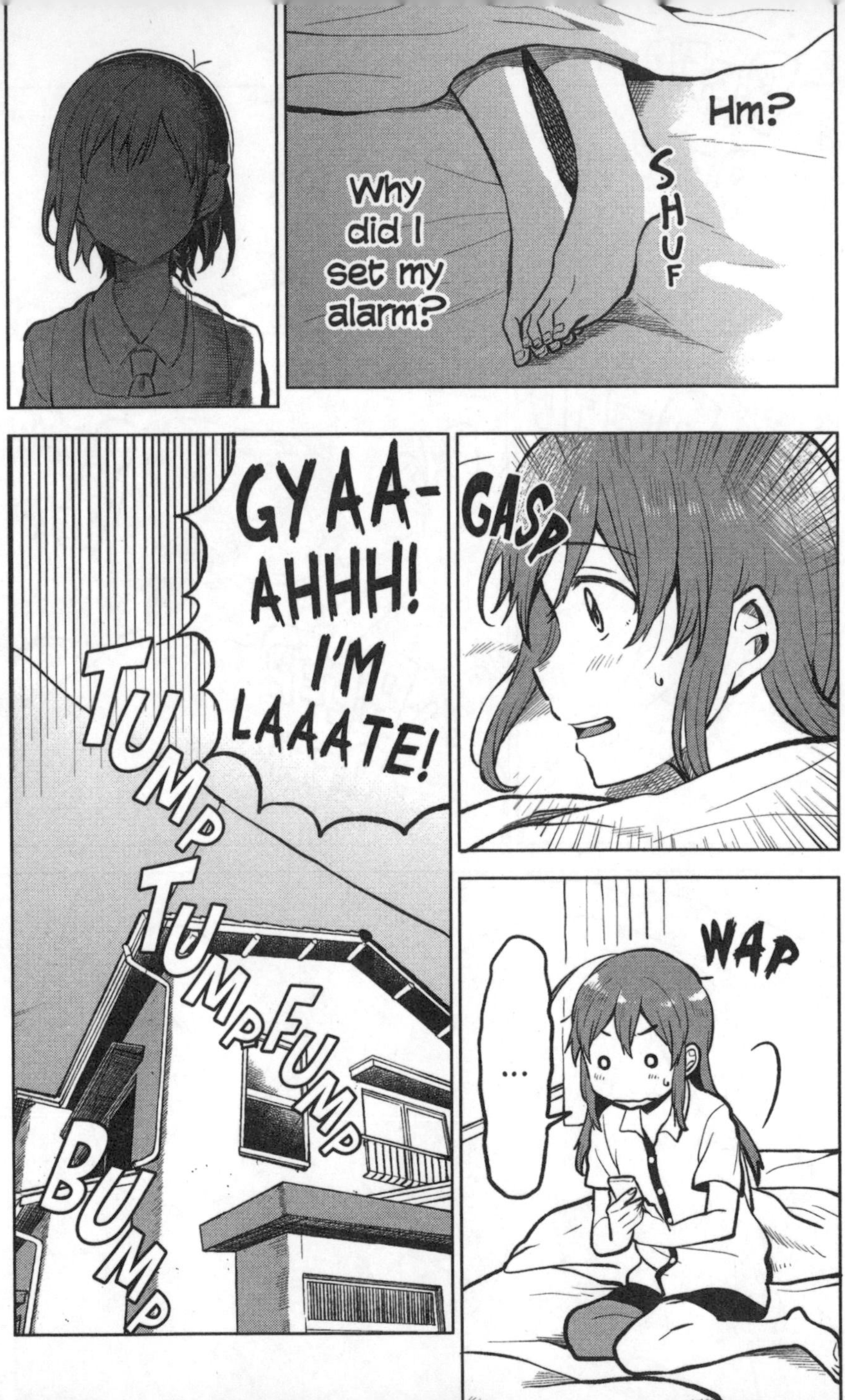
Hm?
SHUF
Why did I set my alarm?
GASP
WAP
...
GYAA-AHHH! I'M LAAATE!
TUMP
TUMP
TUMP
FUMP
BUMP

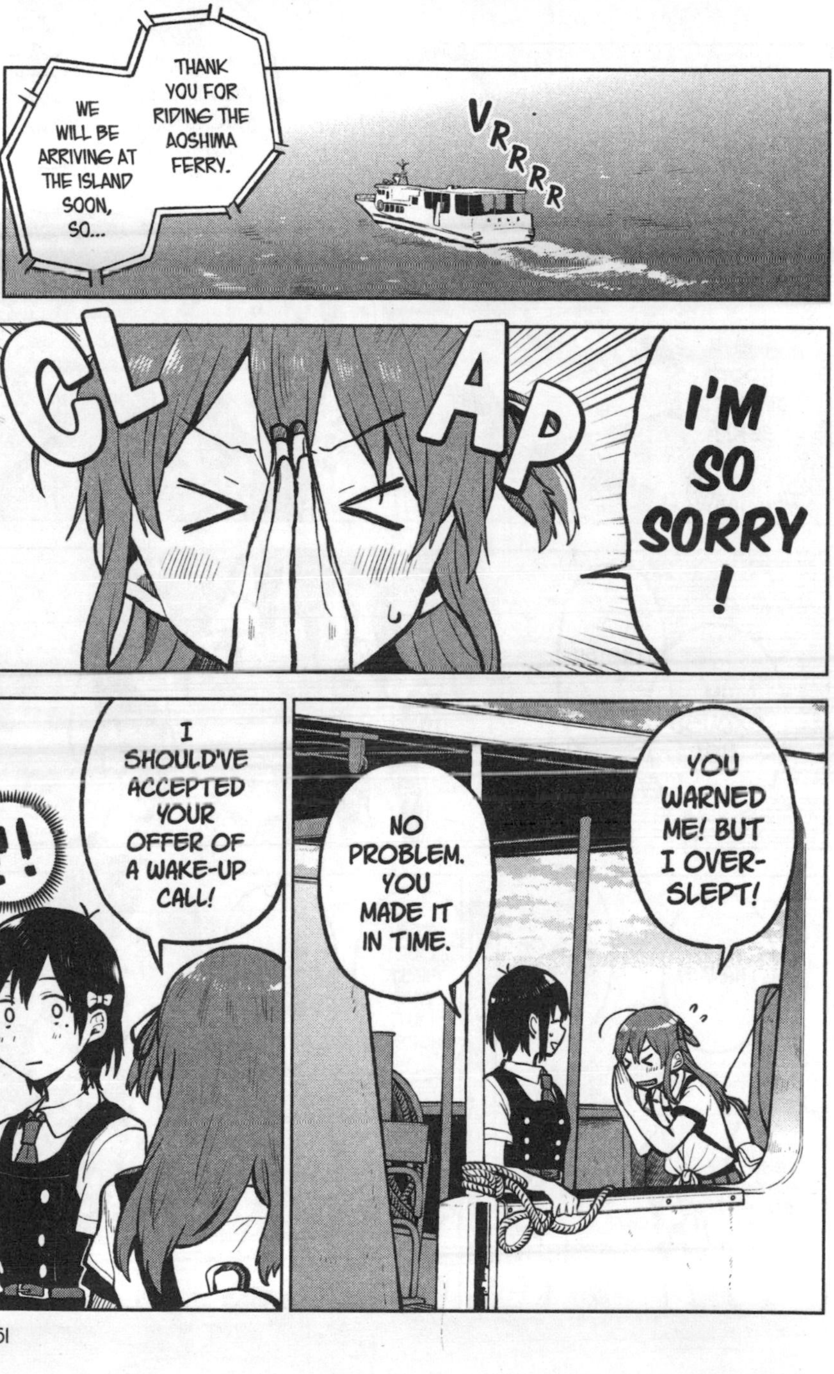
THANK YOU FOR RIDING THE AOSHIMA FERRY.
WE WILL BE ARRIVING AT THE ISLAND SOON, SO...
VRRRRR
CLAP
I'M SO SORRY!
YOU WARNED ME! BUT I OVER-SLEPT!
NO PROBLEM. YOU MADE IT IN TIME.
I SHOULD'VE ACCEPTED YOUR OFFER OF A WAKE-UP CALL!
?!

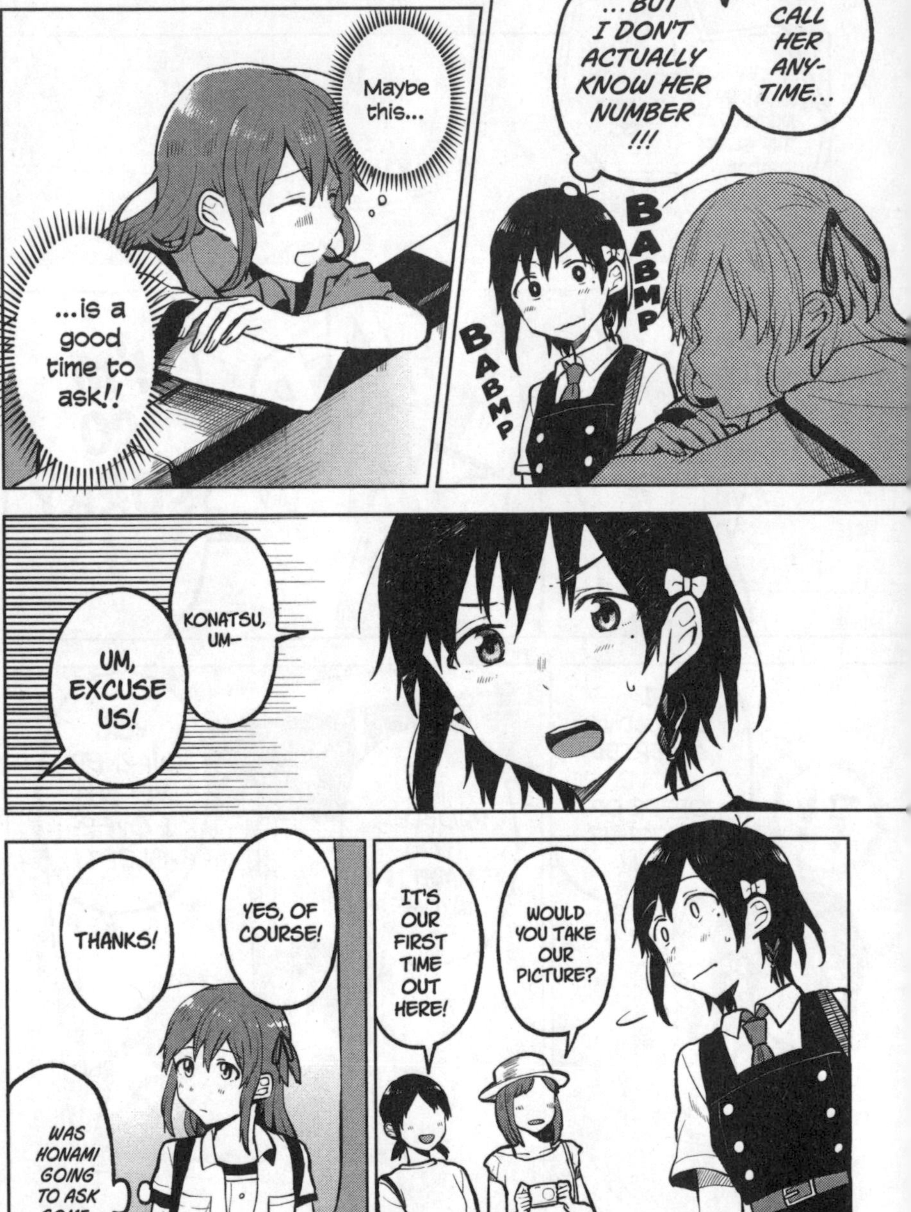
I'D CALL HER ANY-TIME...
...BUT I DON'T ACTUALLY KNOW HER NUMBER!!!
BABMP
BABMP
Maybe this...
...is a good time to ask!!
KONATSU, UM-
UM, EXCUSE US!
WOULD YOU TAKE OUR PICTURE?
IT'S OUR FIRST TIME OUT HERE!
YES, OF COURSE!
THANKS!
WAS HONAMI GOING TO ASK SOME-THING?

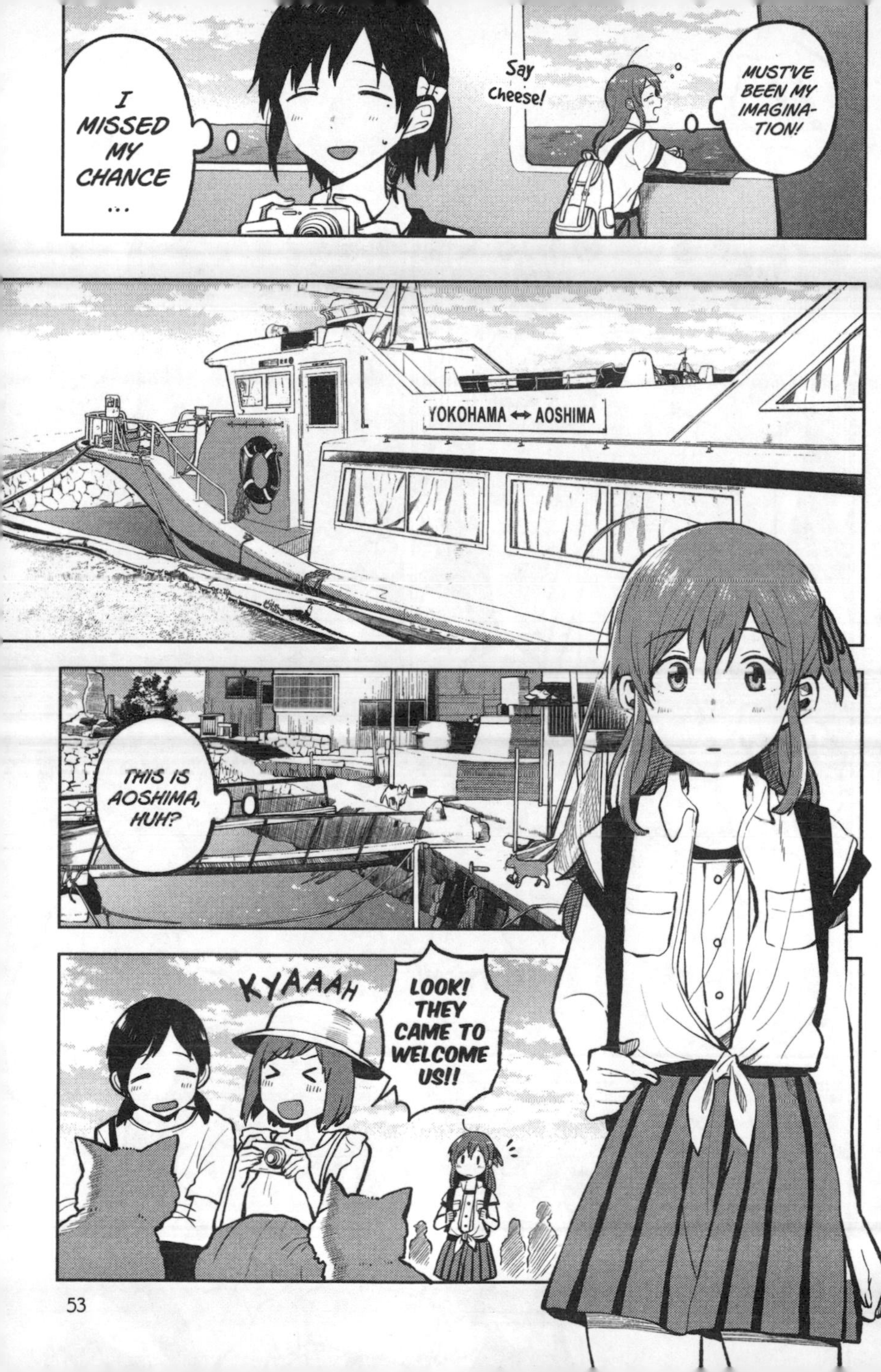
MUST'VE BEEN MY IMAGINATION!
Say Cheese!
I MISSED MY CHANCE ...
YOKOHAMA ↔ AOSHIMA
THIS IS AOSHIMA, HUH?
LOOK! THEY CAME TO WELCOME US!!
KYAAAH

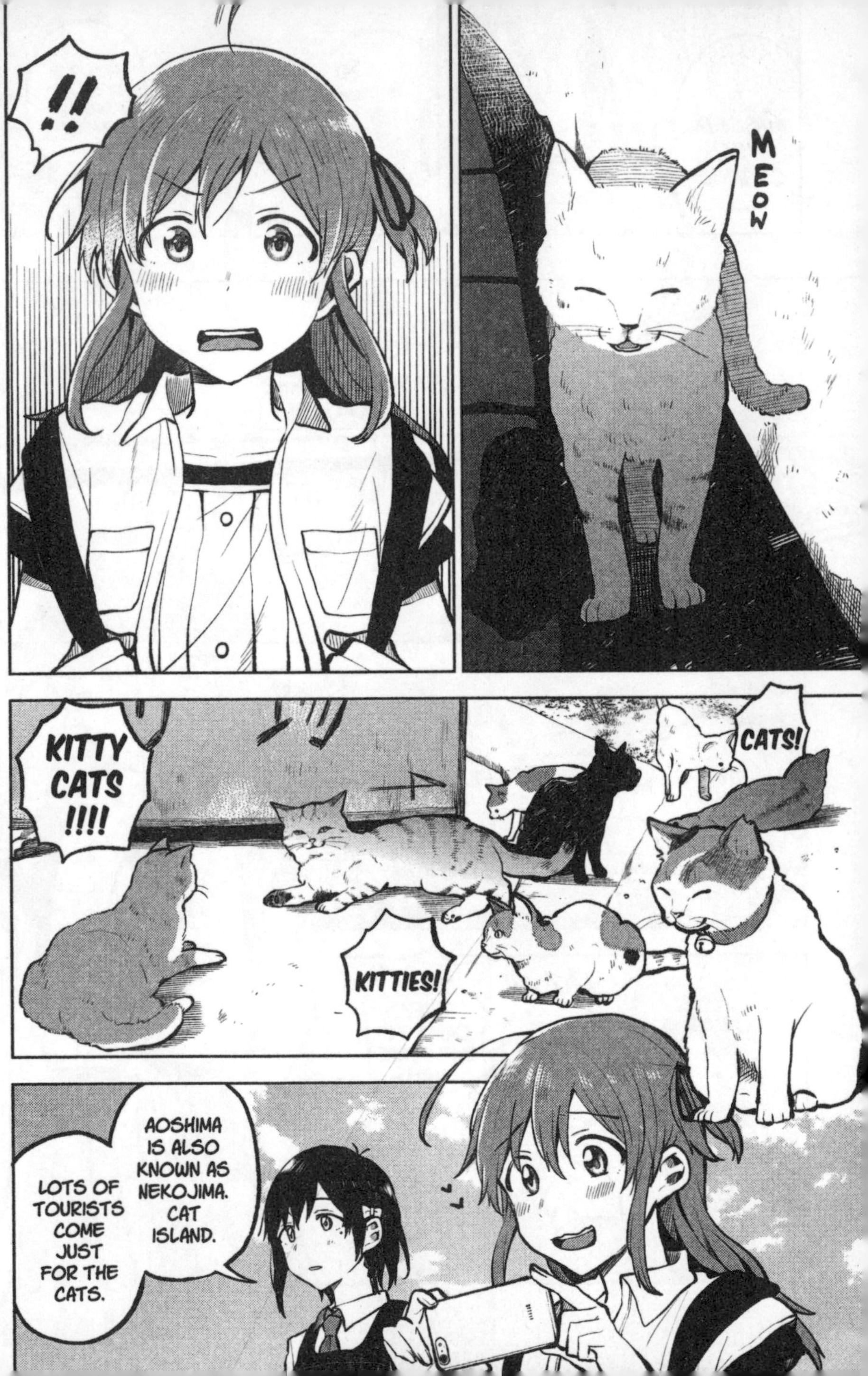
MEOW
!!
CATS!
KITTIES!
KITTY CATS !!!!
AOSHIMA IS ALSO KNOWN AS NEKOJIMA. CAT ISLAND.
LOTS OF TOURISTS COME JUST FOR THE CATS.

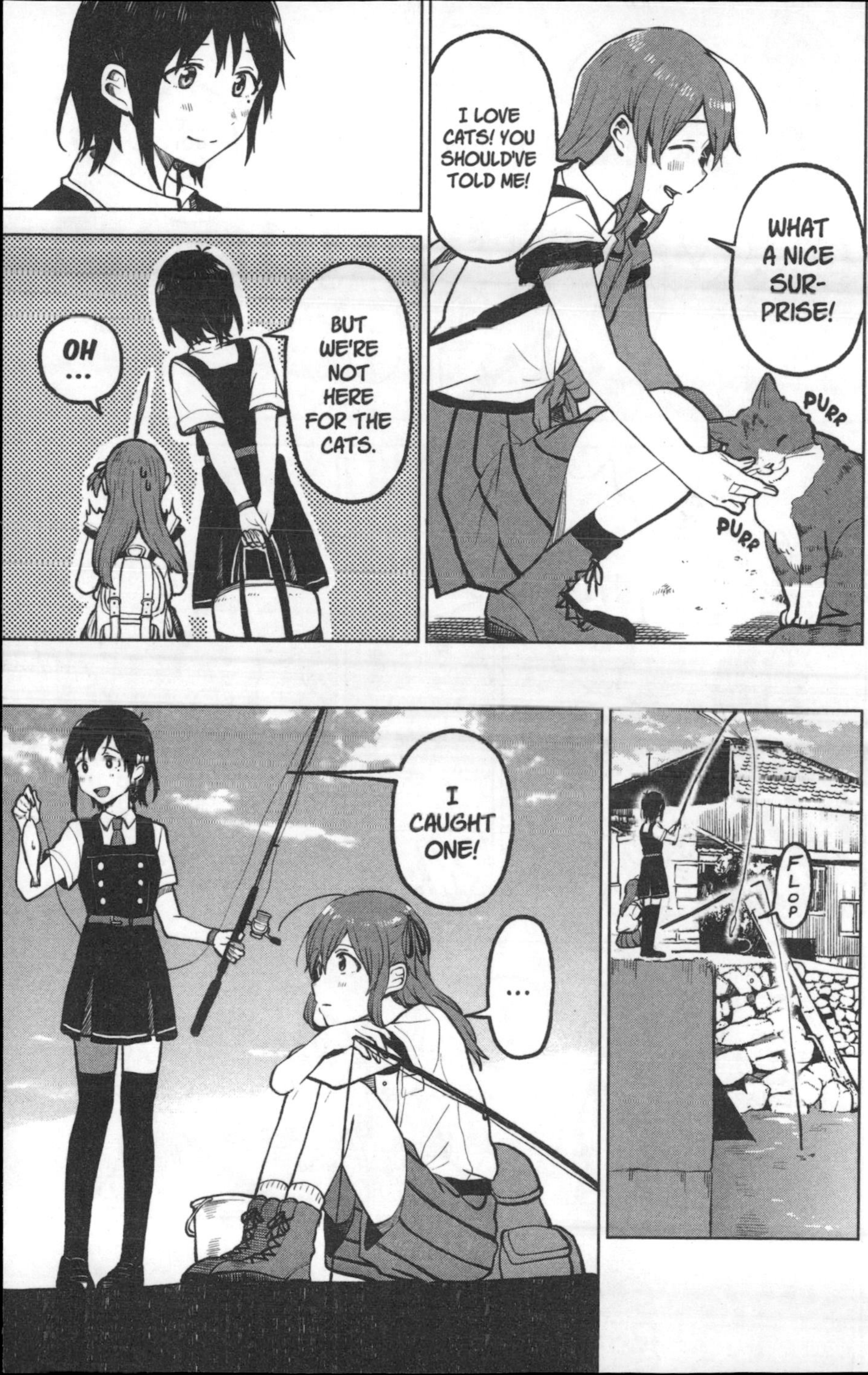
I LOVE CATS! YOU SHOULD'VE TOLD ME!
WHAT A NICE SUR-PRISE!
PURR
PURR
BUT WE'RE NOT HERE FOR THE CATS.
OH ...
FLOP
I CAUGHT ONE!
...

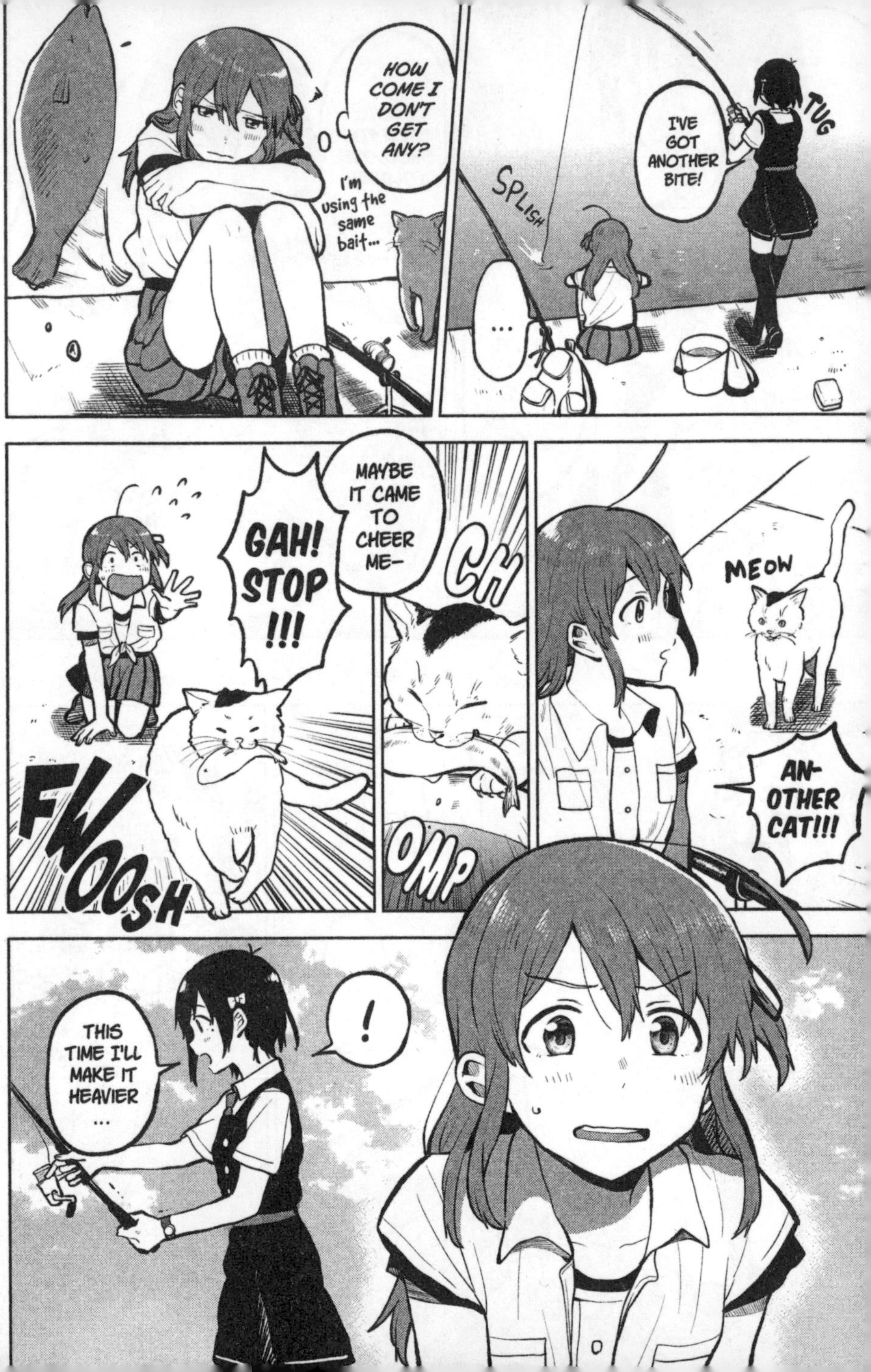
TUG
I'VE GOT ANOTHER BITE!
SPLISH
...
HOW COME I DON'T GET ANY?
I'm using the same bait...
MEOW
AN-OTHER CAT!!!
MAYBE IT CAME TO CHEER ME-
CH
OMP
GAH! STOP!!!
FWOOSH
!
THIS TIME I'LL MAKE IT HEAVIER ...

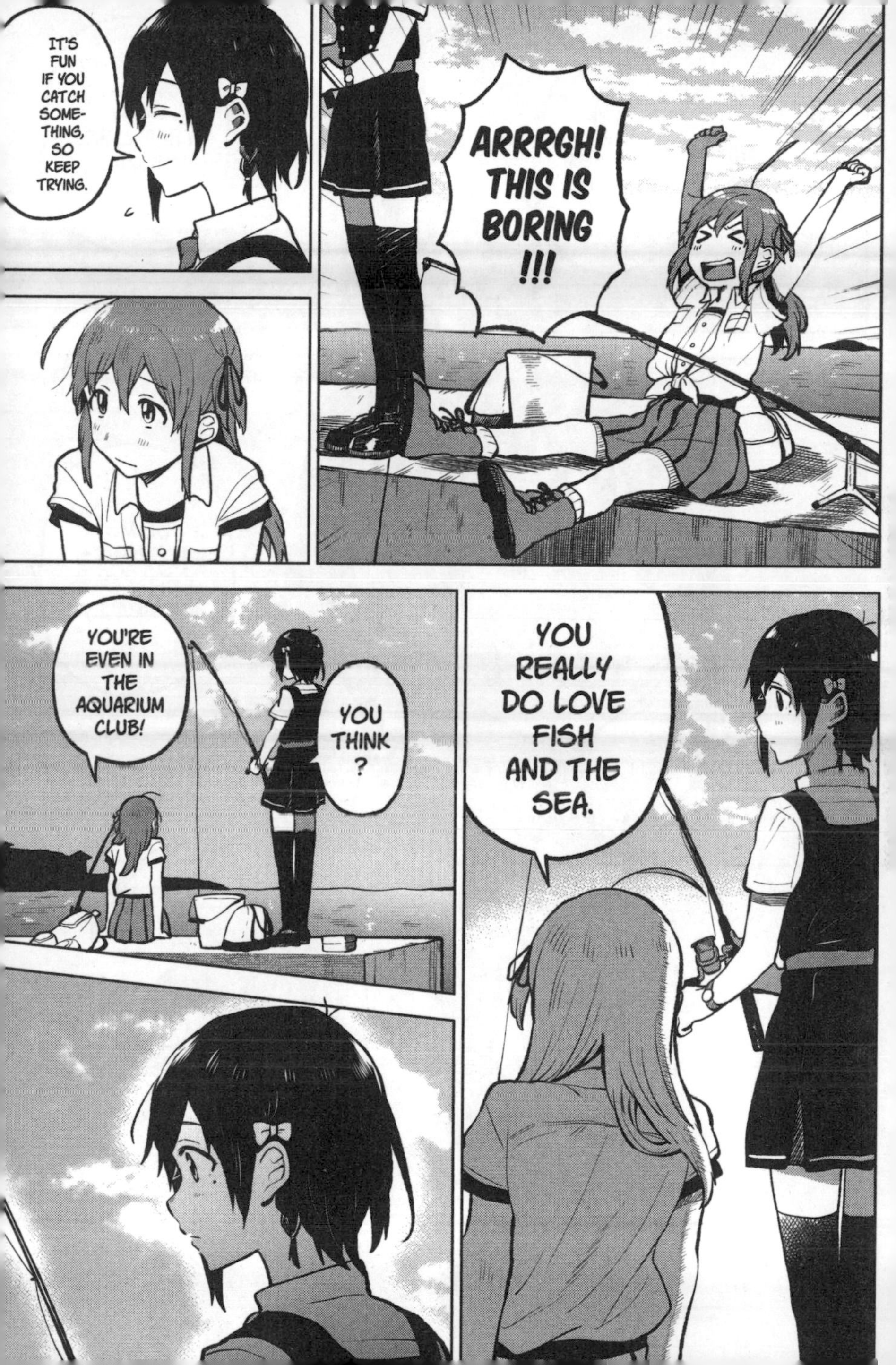
ARRRGH! THIS IS BORING!!!
IT'S FUN IF YOU CATCH SOMETHING, SO KEEP TRYING.
YOU REALLY DO LOVE FISH AND THE SEA.
YOU THINK?
YOU'RE EVEN IN THE AQUARIUM CLUB!

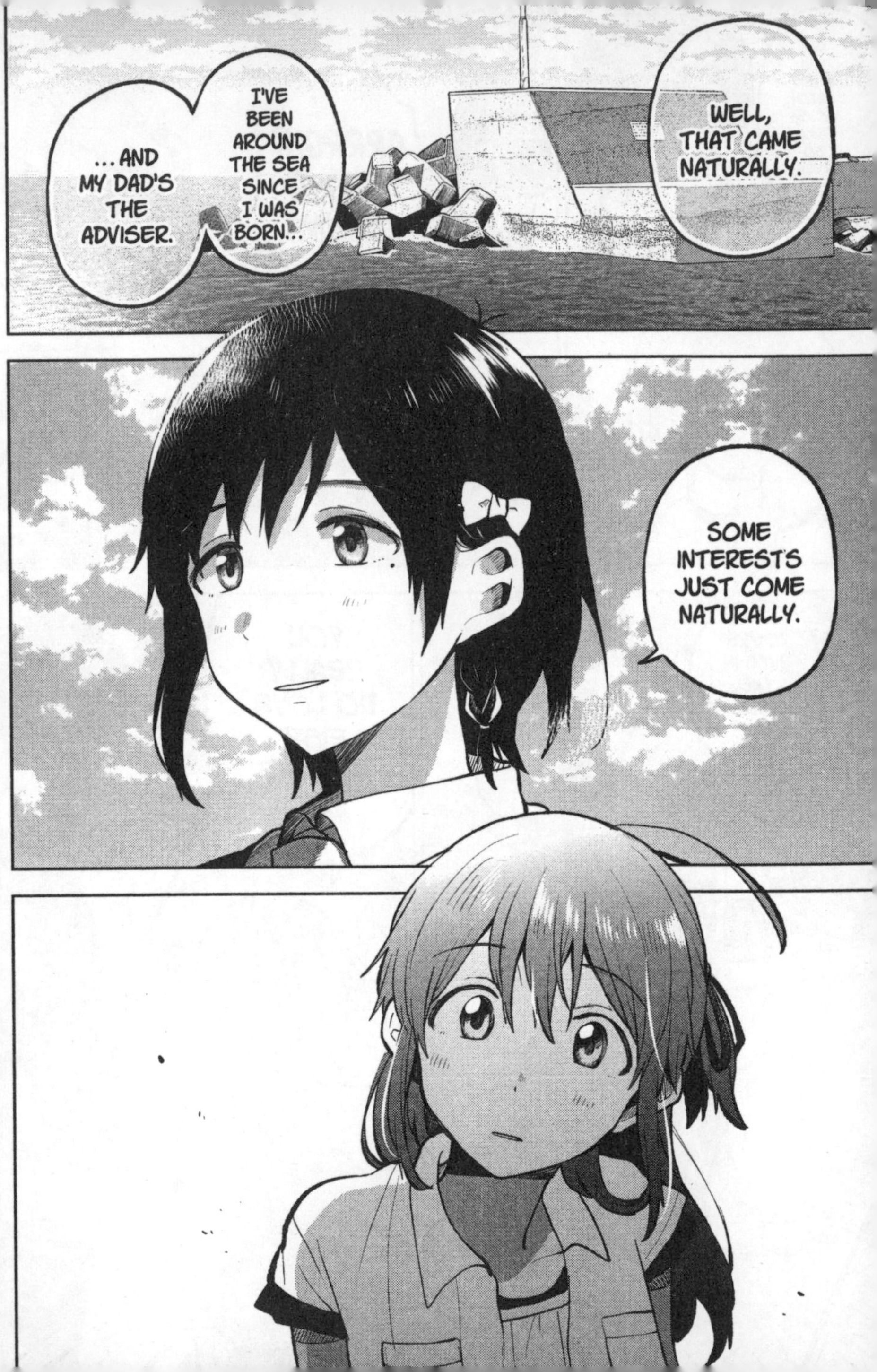
WELL, THAT CAME NATURALLY.
I'VE BEEN AROUND THE SEA SINCE I WAS BORN...
...AND MY DAD'S THE ADVISER.
SOME INTERESTS JUST COME NATURALLY.

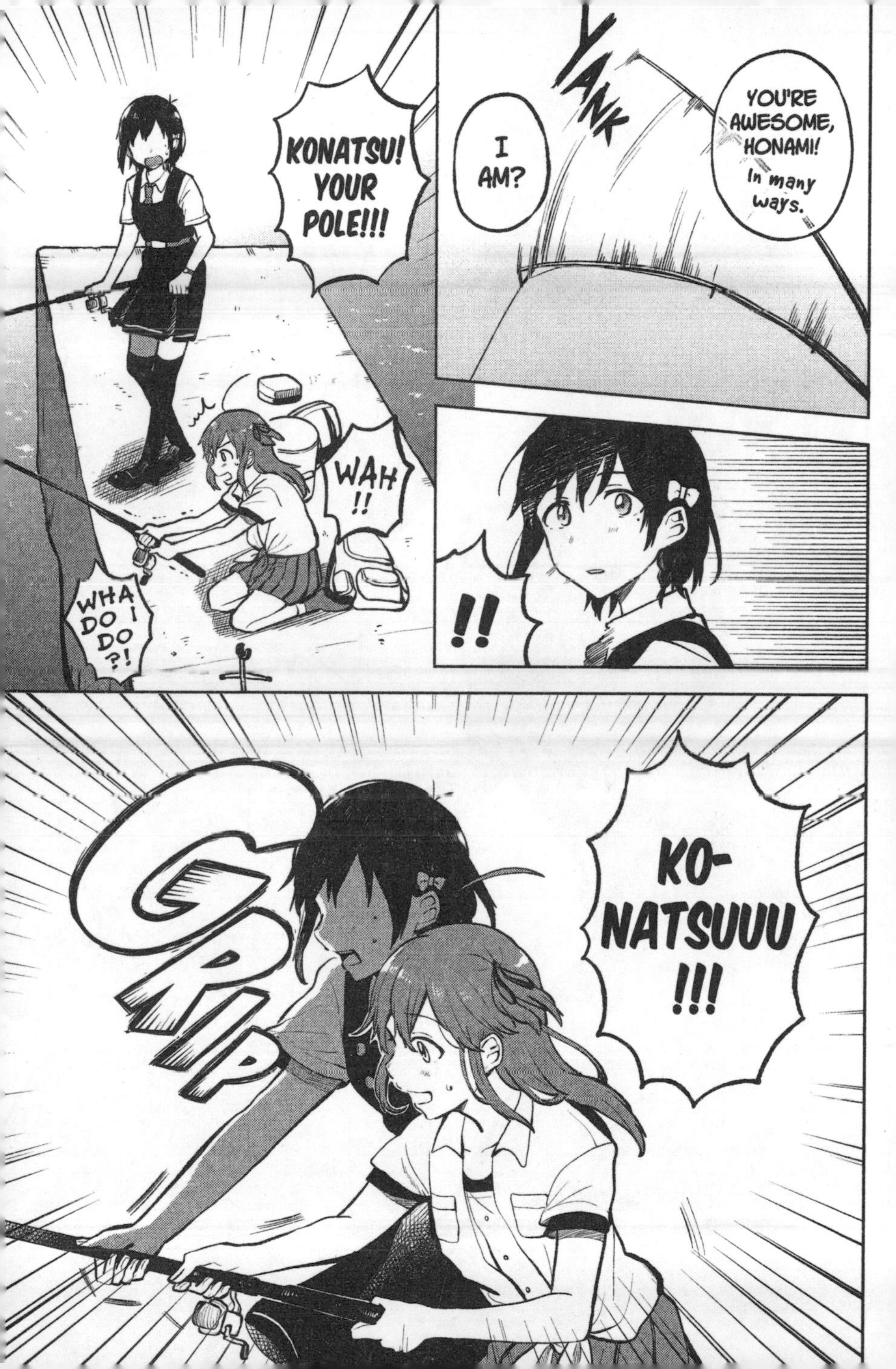
YANK
YOU'RE AWESOME, HONAMI! In many ways.
I AM?
!!
KONATSU! YOUR POLE!!!
WAH!!
WHA DO I DO?!
KO-NATSUUU!!!
GRIP

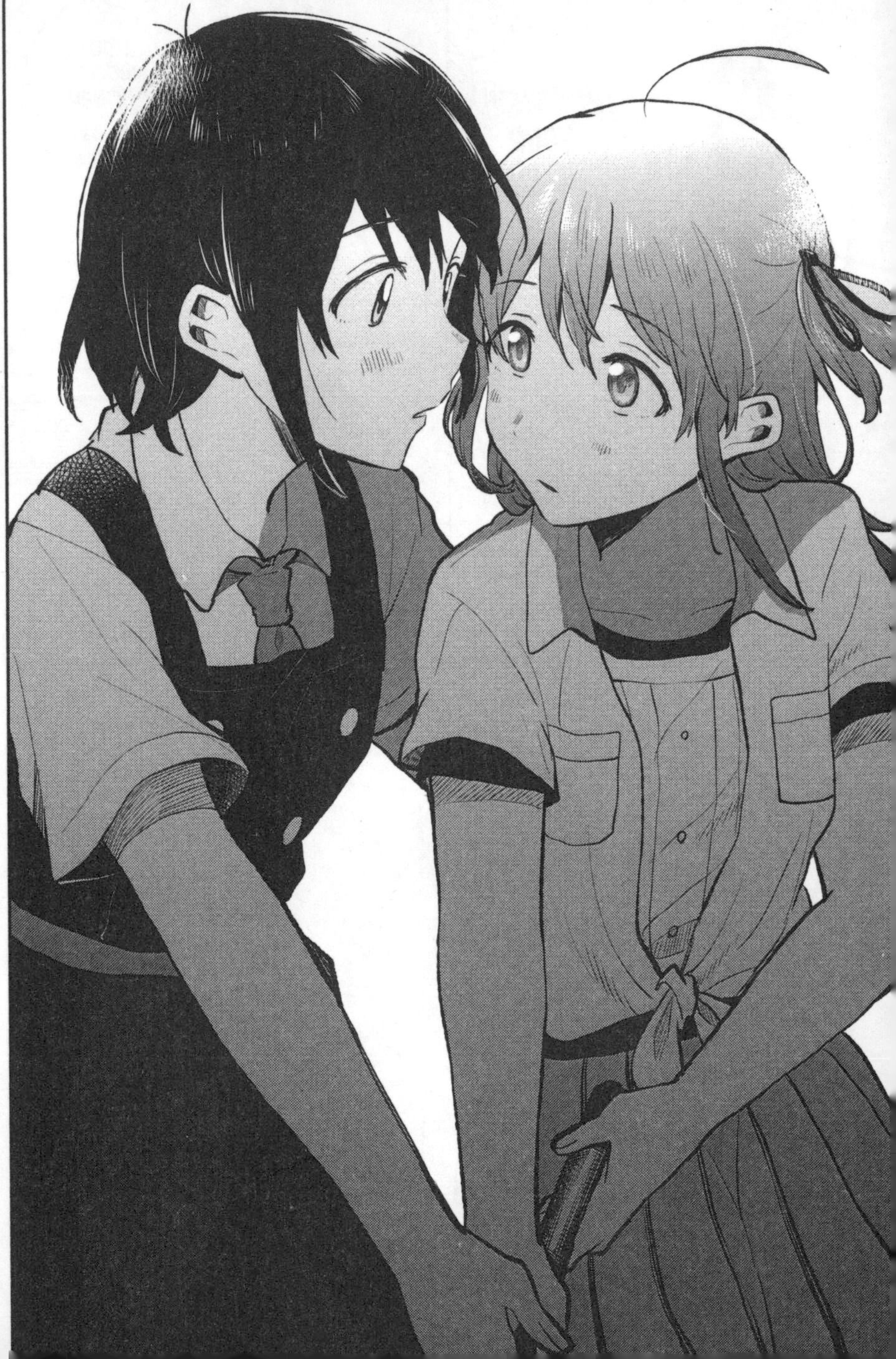

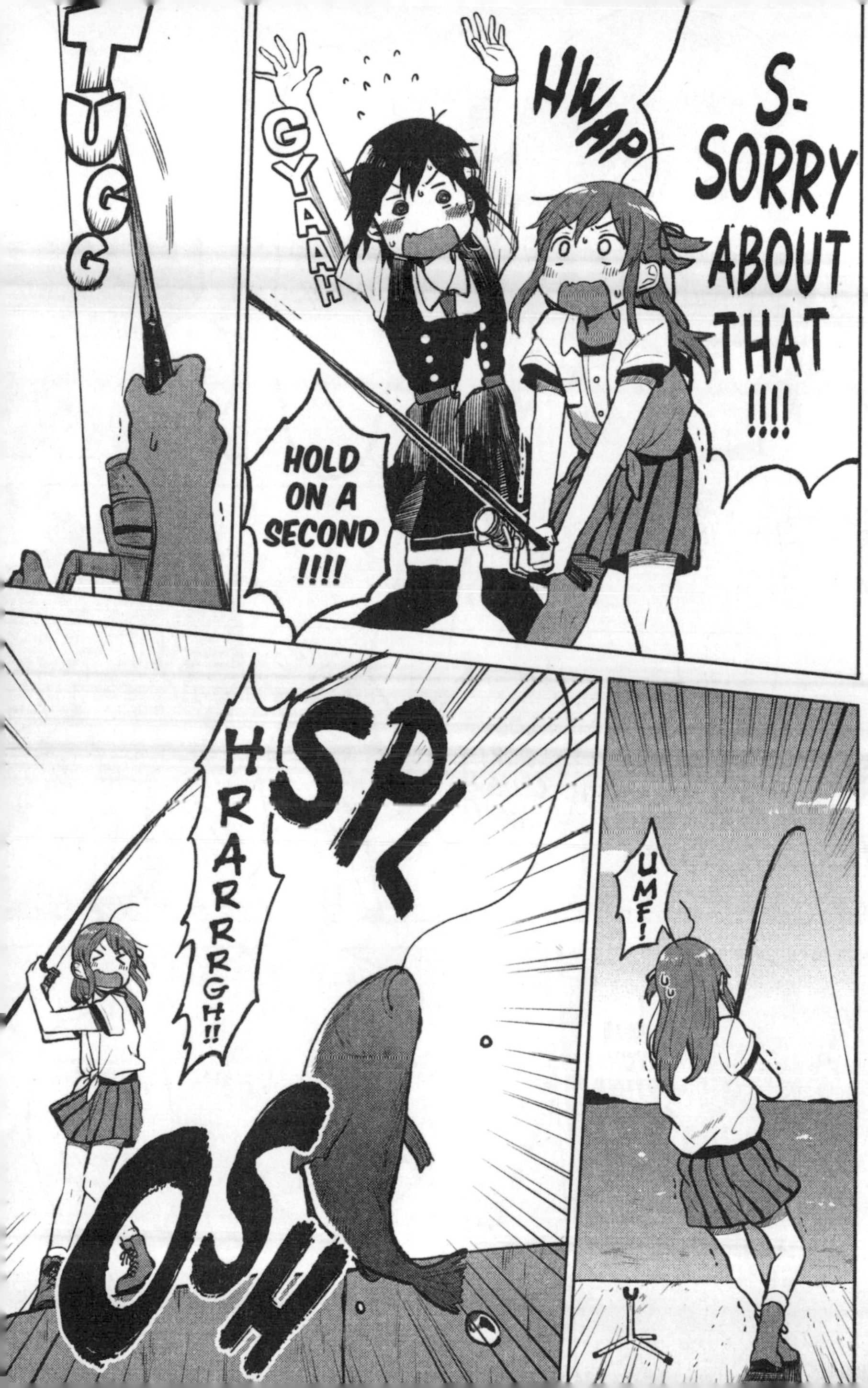
S-SORRY ABOUT THAT!!!!
HWAP
GYAAAH
HOLD ON A SECOND!!!!
TUG TUG
UMF!
SPL
HRARRRGH!!
OSH

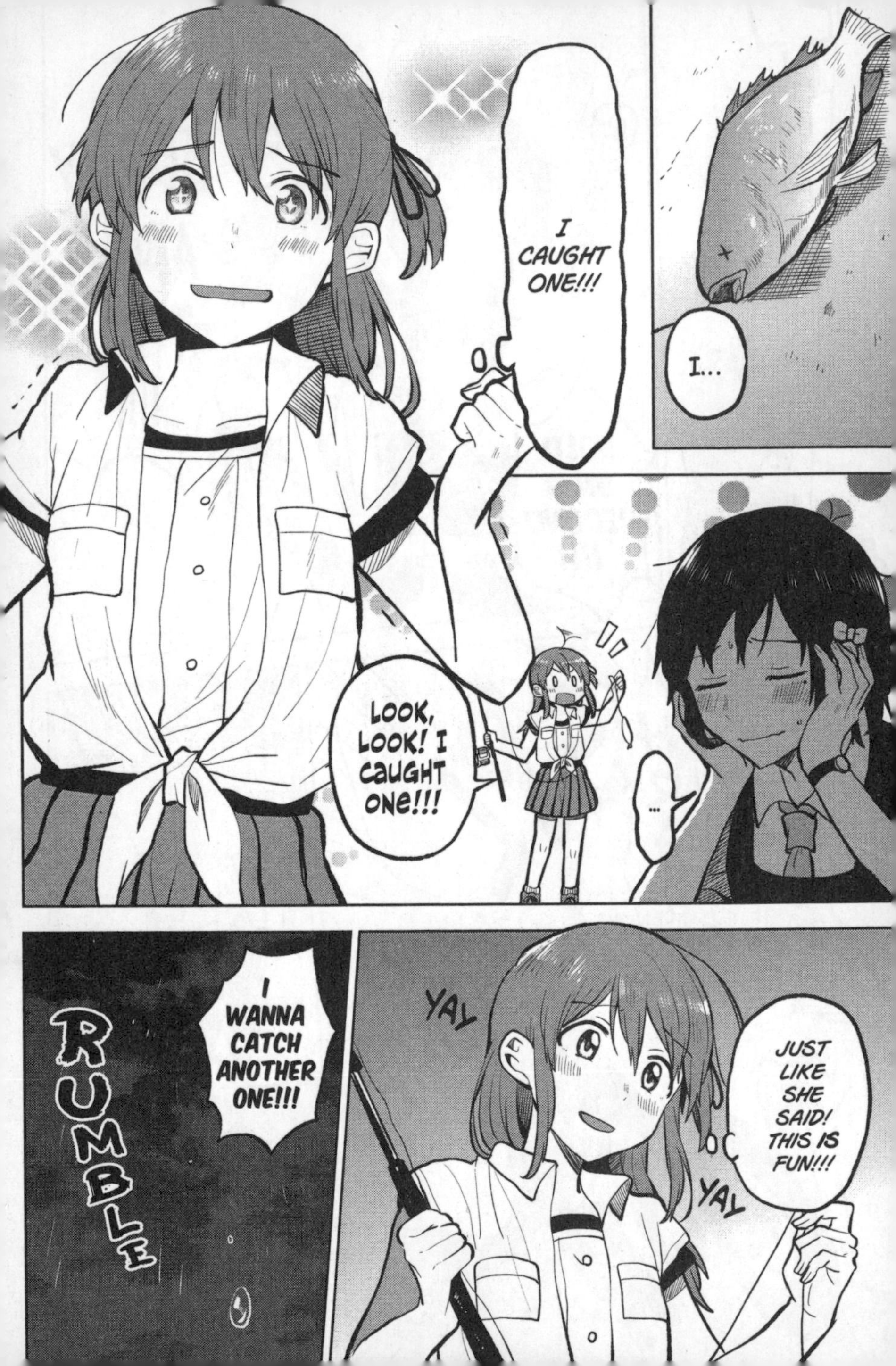
I...
I CAUGHT ONE!!!
LOOK, LOOK! I CAUGHT ONE!!!
...
YAY
JUST LIKE SHE SAID! THIS IS FUN!!!
YAY
I WANNA CATCH ANOTHER ONE!!!
RUMBLE

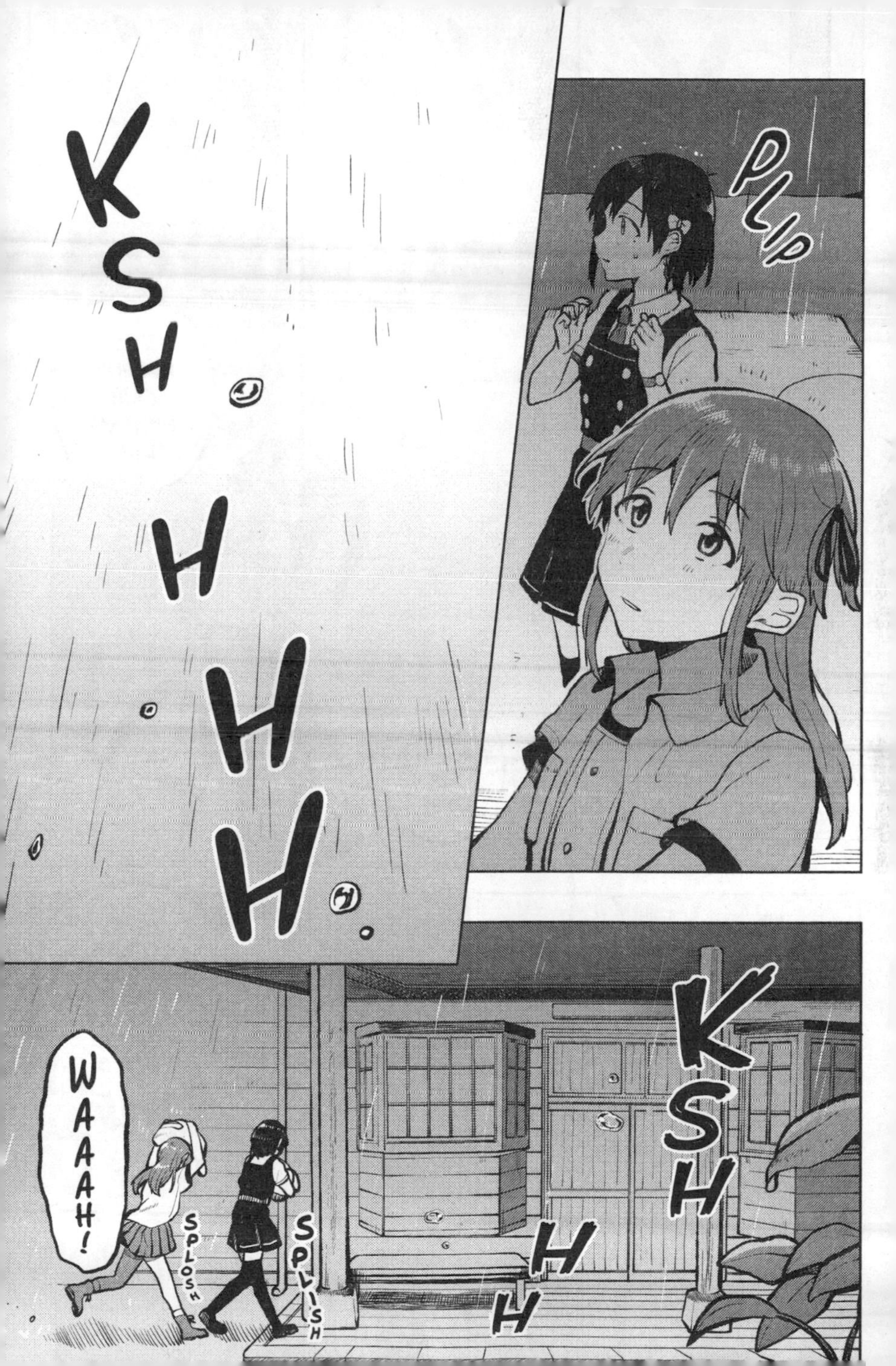
PLIP
KSHHHH
KSHHH
SPLISH
SPLOSH
WAAAAH!

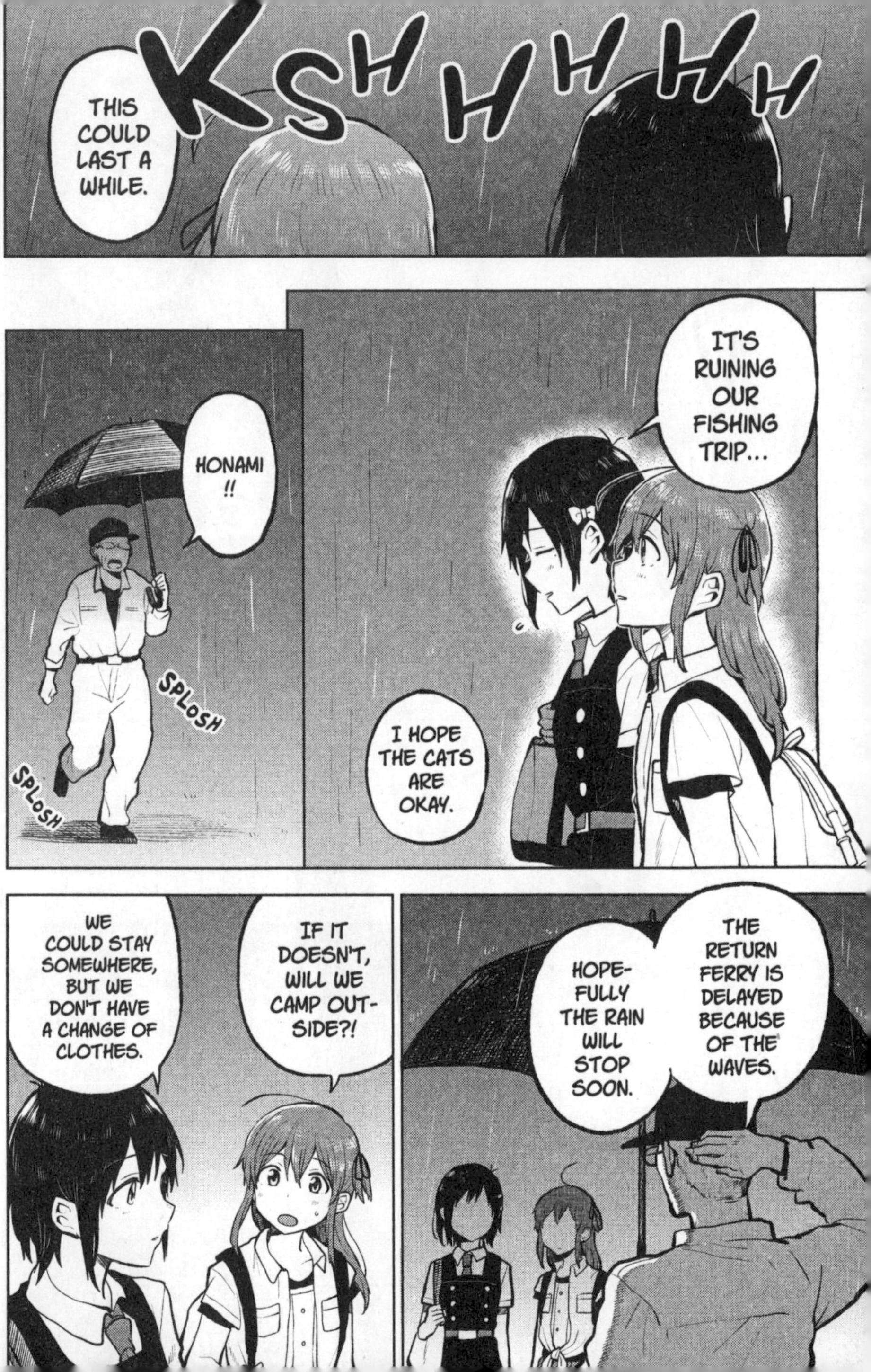
KSHHHHHH
THIS COULD LAST A WHILE.
IT'S RUINING OUR FISHING TRIP...
I HOPE THE CATS ARE OKAY.
HONAMI!!
SPLOSH
SPLOSH
THE RETURN FERRY IS DELAYED BECAUSE OF THE WAVES.
HOPE-FULLY THE RAIN WILL STOP SOON.
IF IT DOESN'T, WILL WE CAMP OUT-SIDE?!
WE COULD STAY SOMEWHERE, BUT WE DON'T HAVE A CHANGE OF CLOTHES.

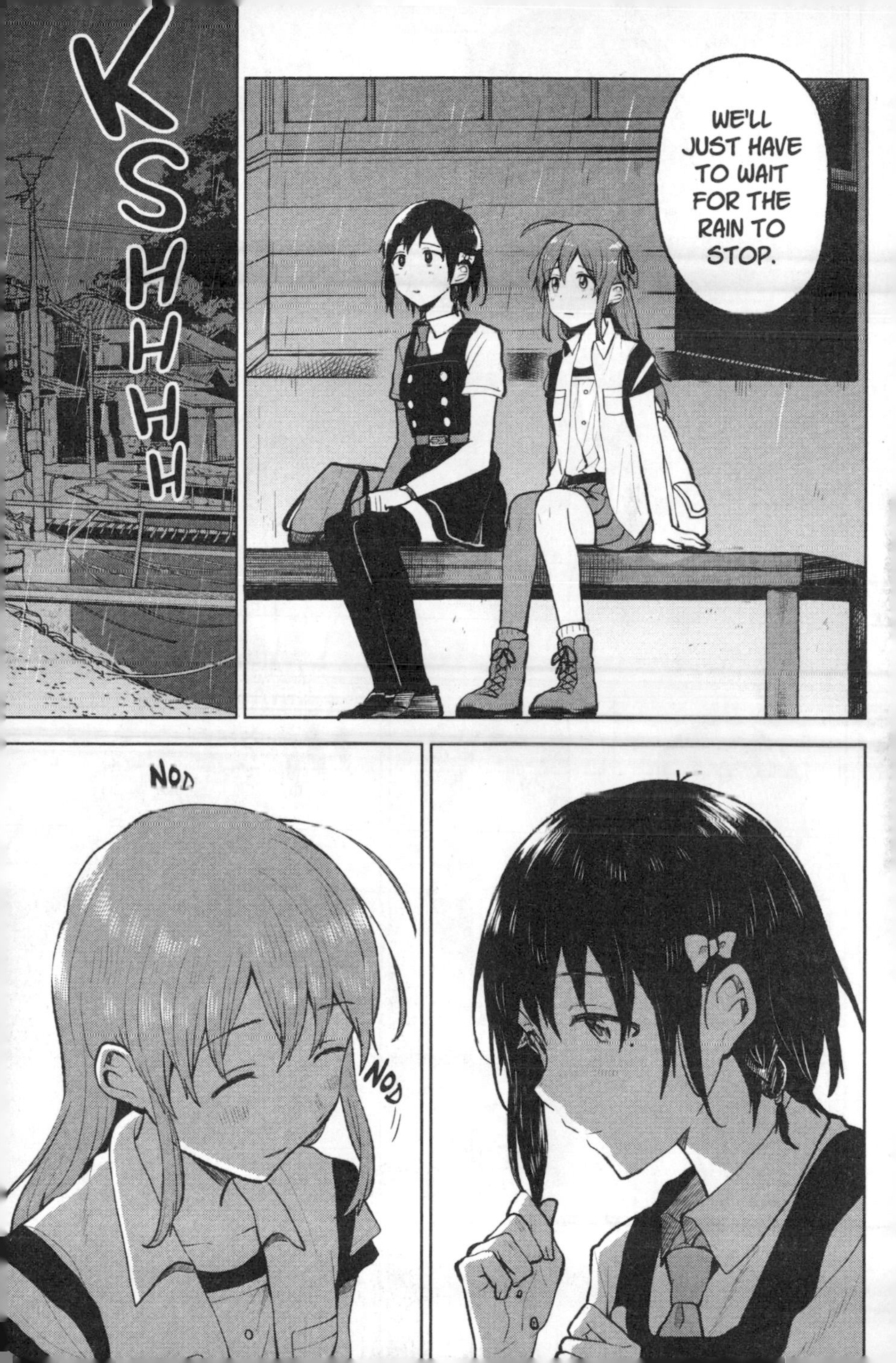
WE'LL JUST HAVE TO WAIT FOR THE RAIN TO STOP.
KSHHHHH
NOD
NOD

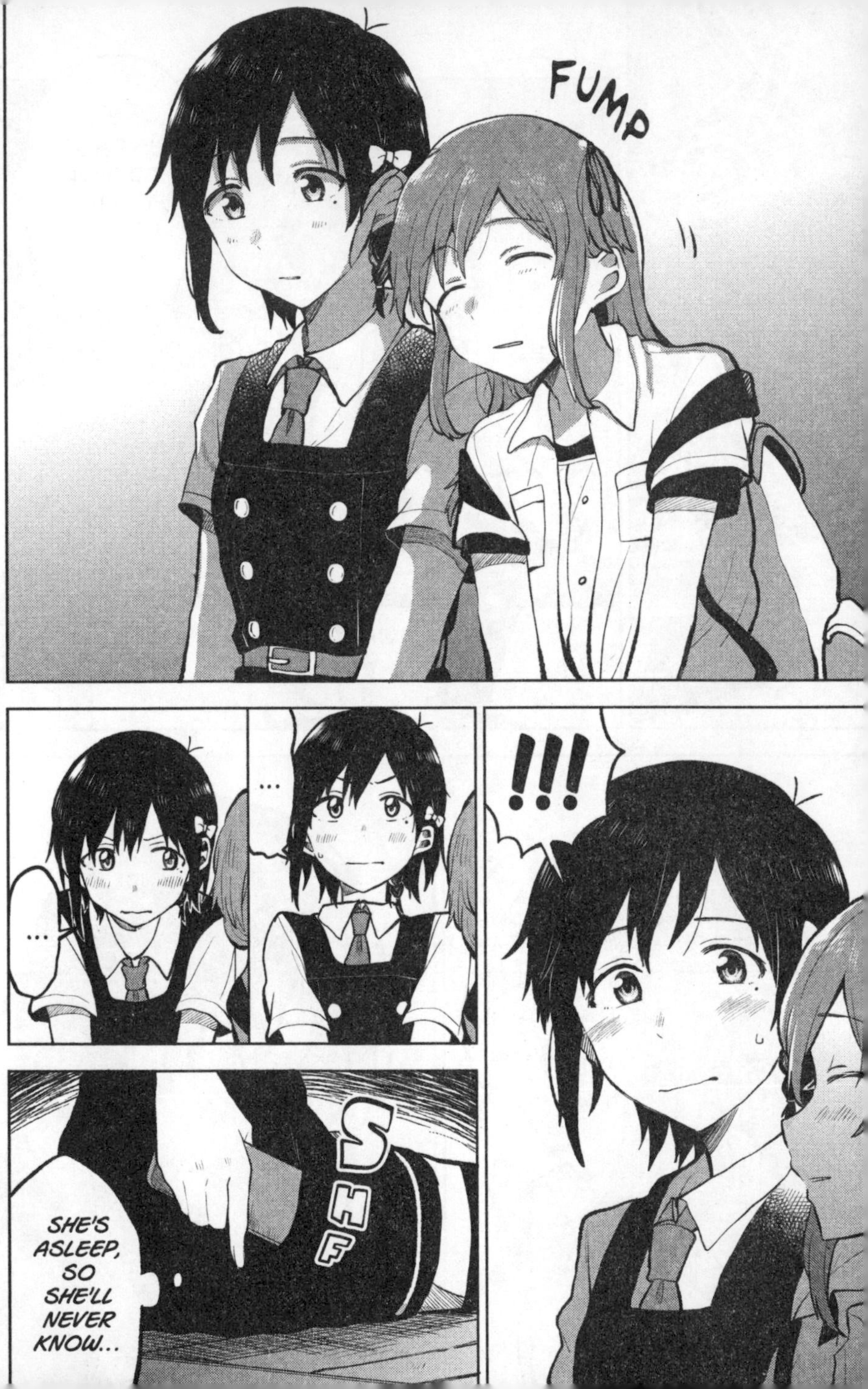
FUMP
!!!
...
...
SHF
SHE'S ASLEEP, SO SHE'LL NEVER KNOW...

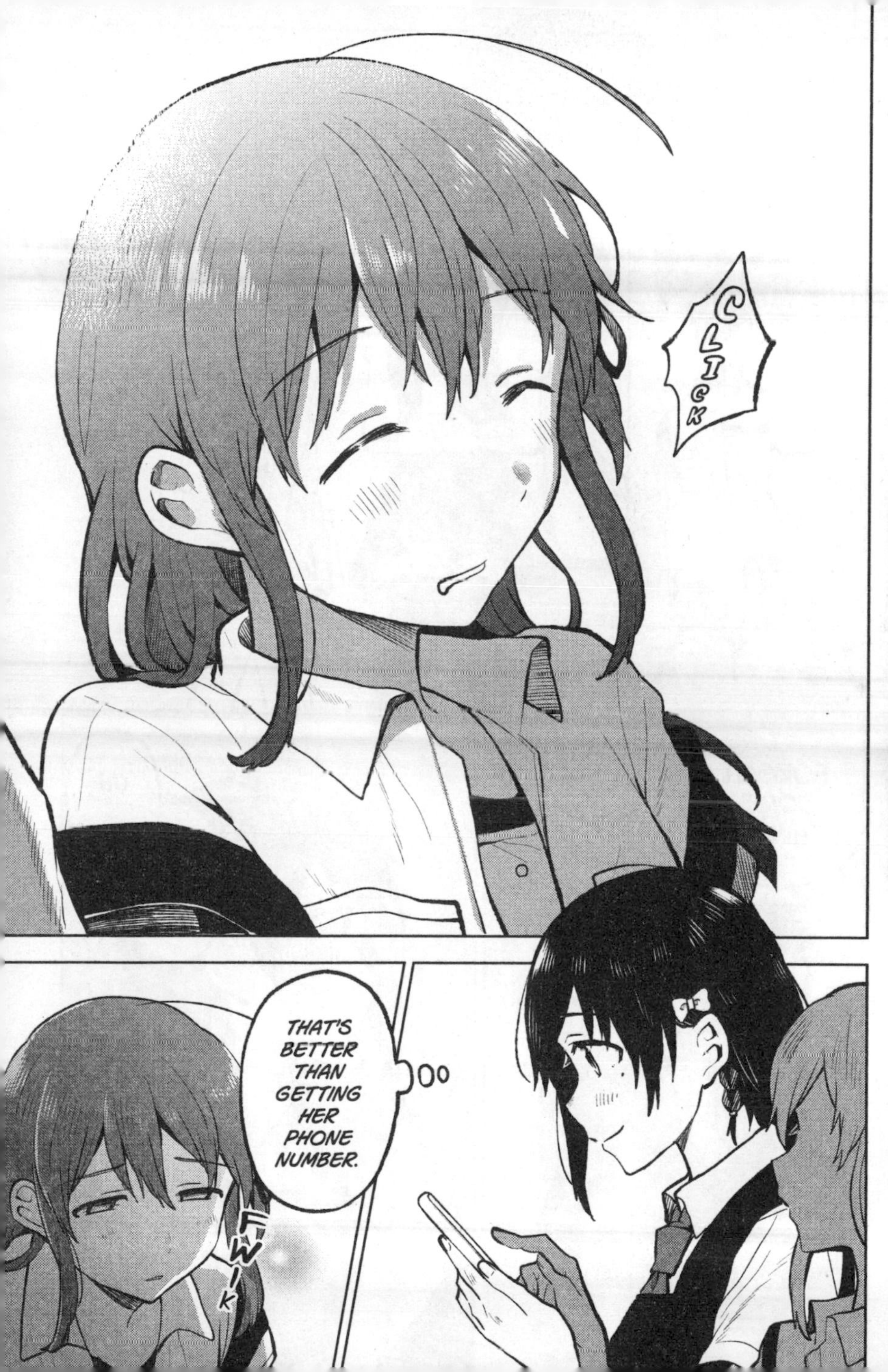
CLICK
THAT'S BETTER THAN GETTING HER PHONE NUMBER.
FWIK

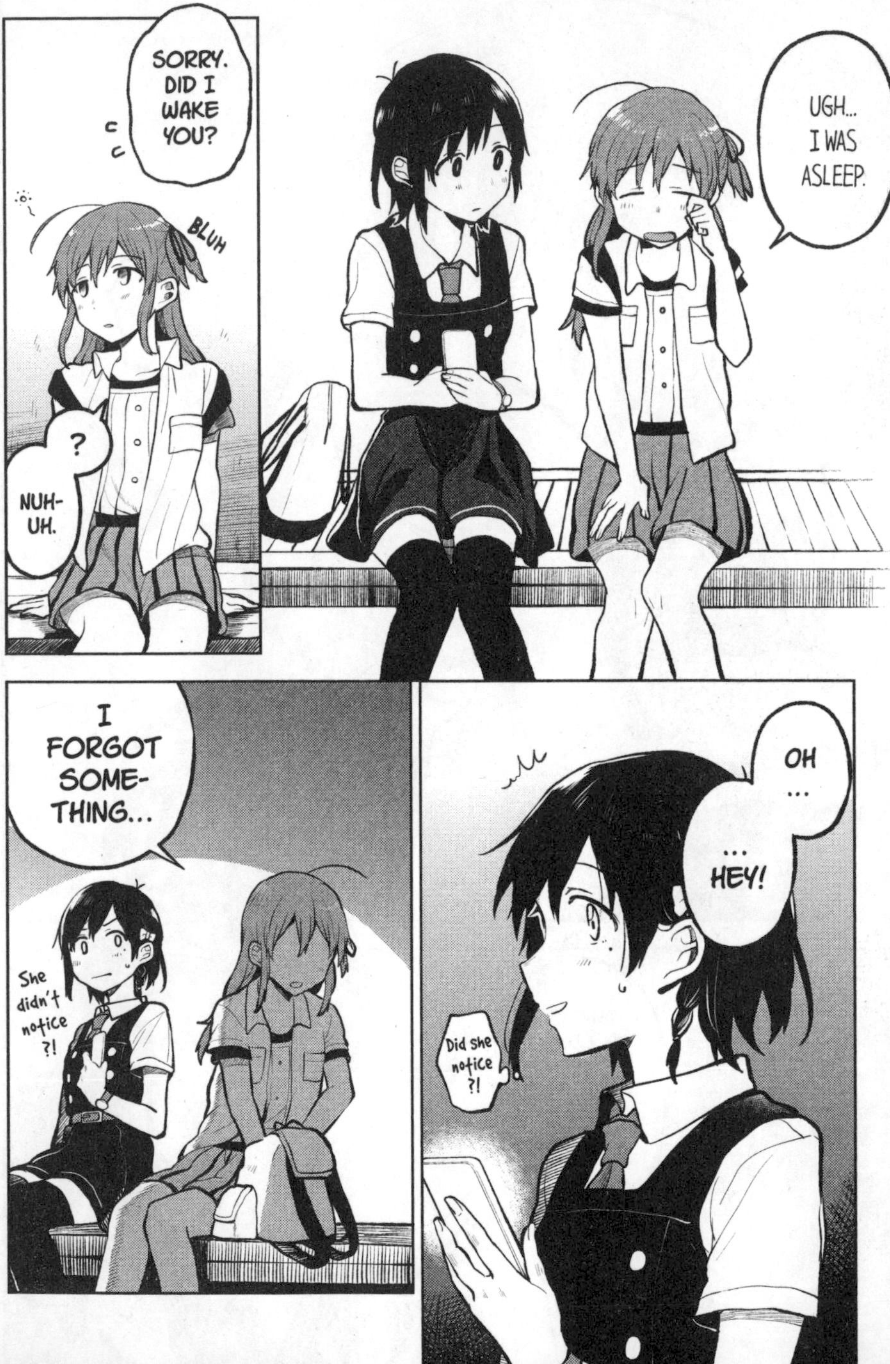
UGH... I WAS ASLEEP.
SORRY. DID I WAKE YOU?
BLUH
?
NUH-UH.
OH ...
... HEY!
Did she notice ?!
I FORGOT SOME-THING...
She didn't notice ?!

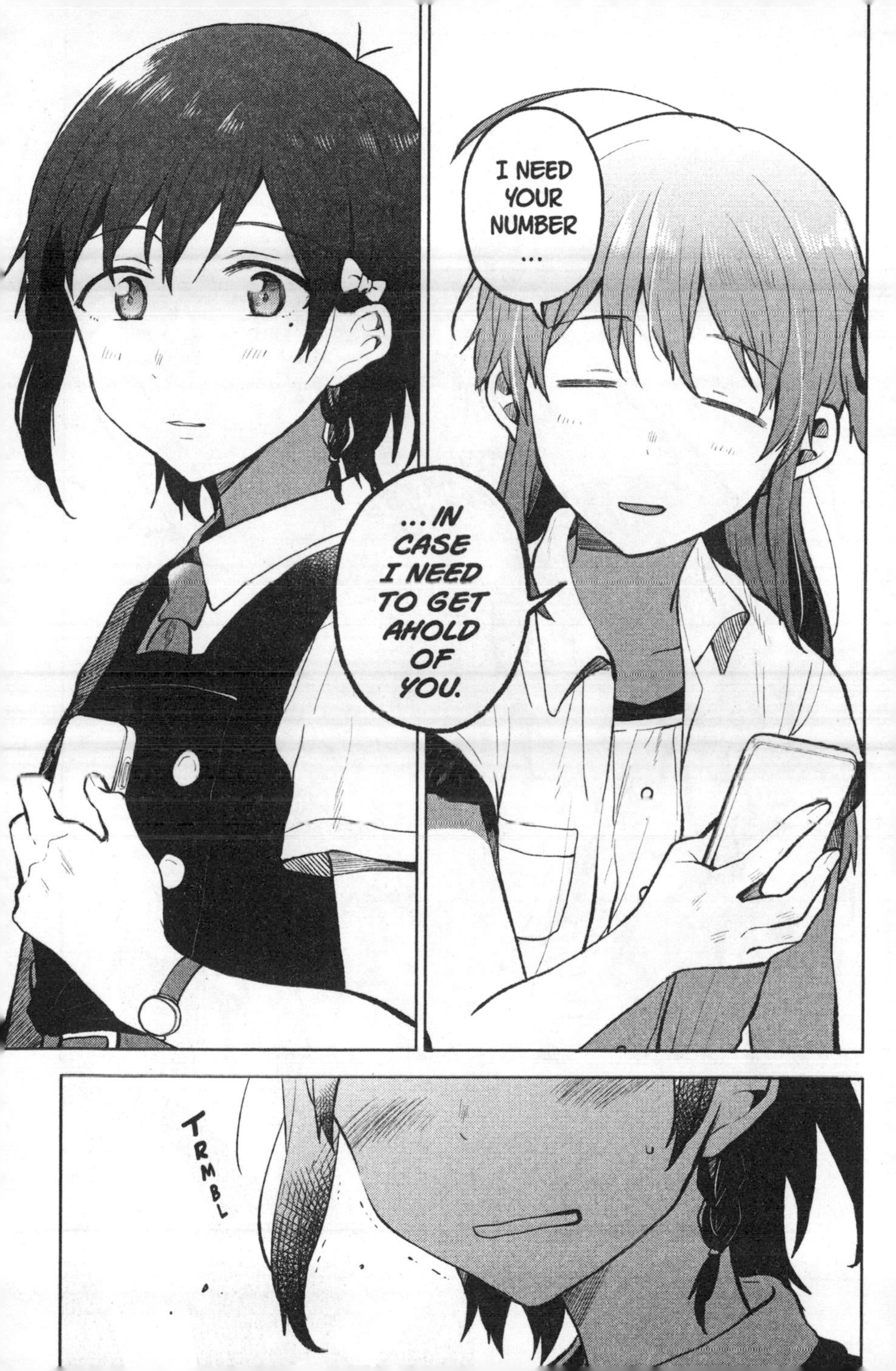
I NEED YOUR NUMBER ...
...IN CASE I NEED TO GET AHOLD OF YOU.
TRMBL

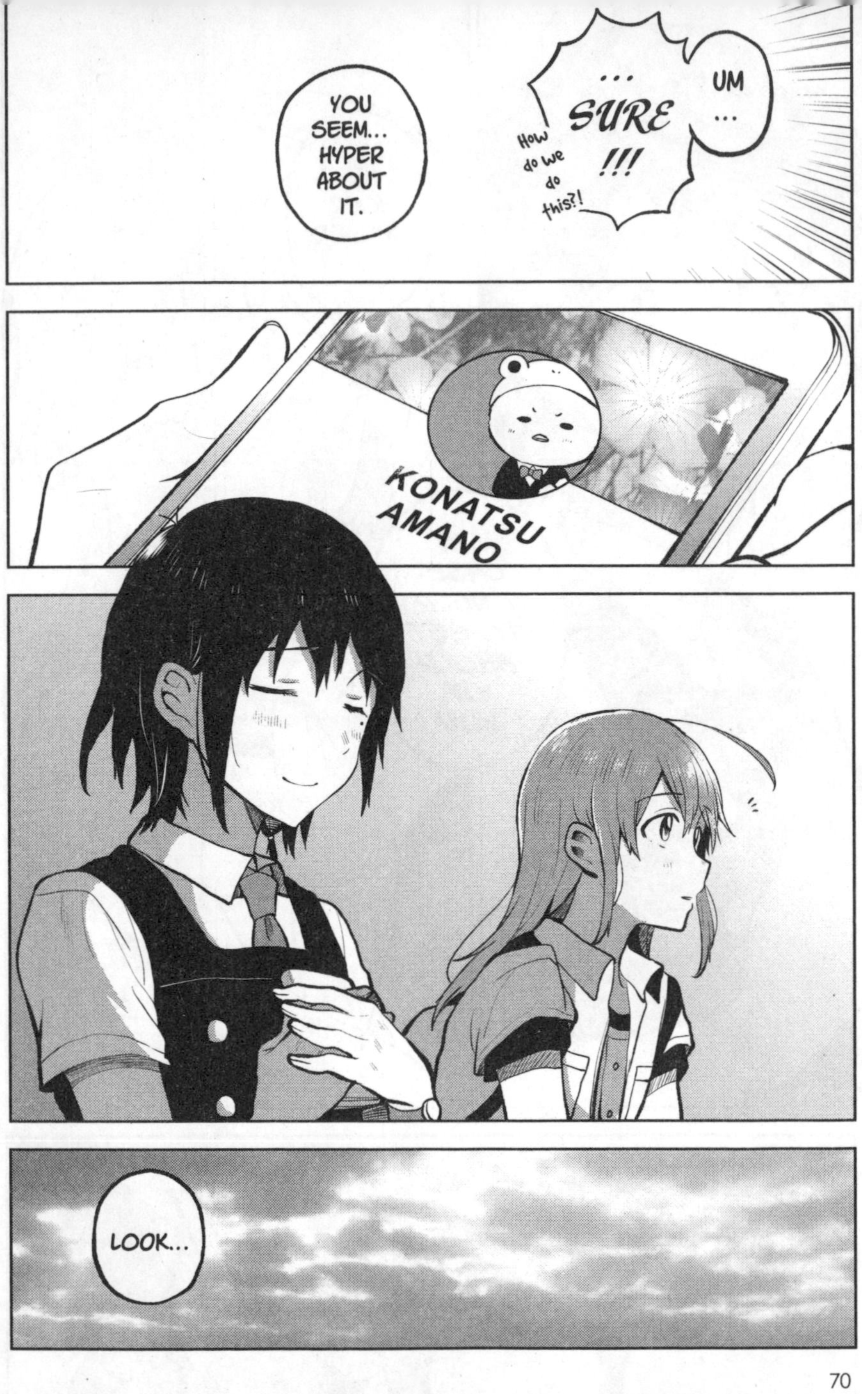
UM ...
... SURE !!!
How do we do this?!
YOU SEEM... HYPER ABOUT IT.
KONATSU AMANO
LOOK...

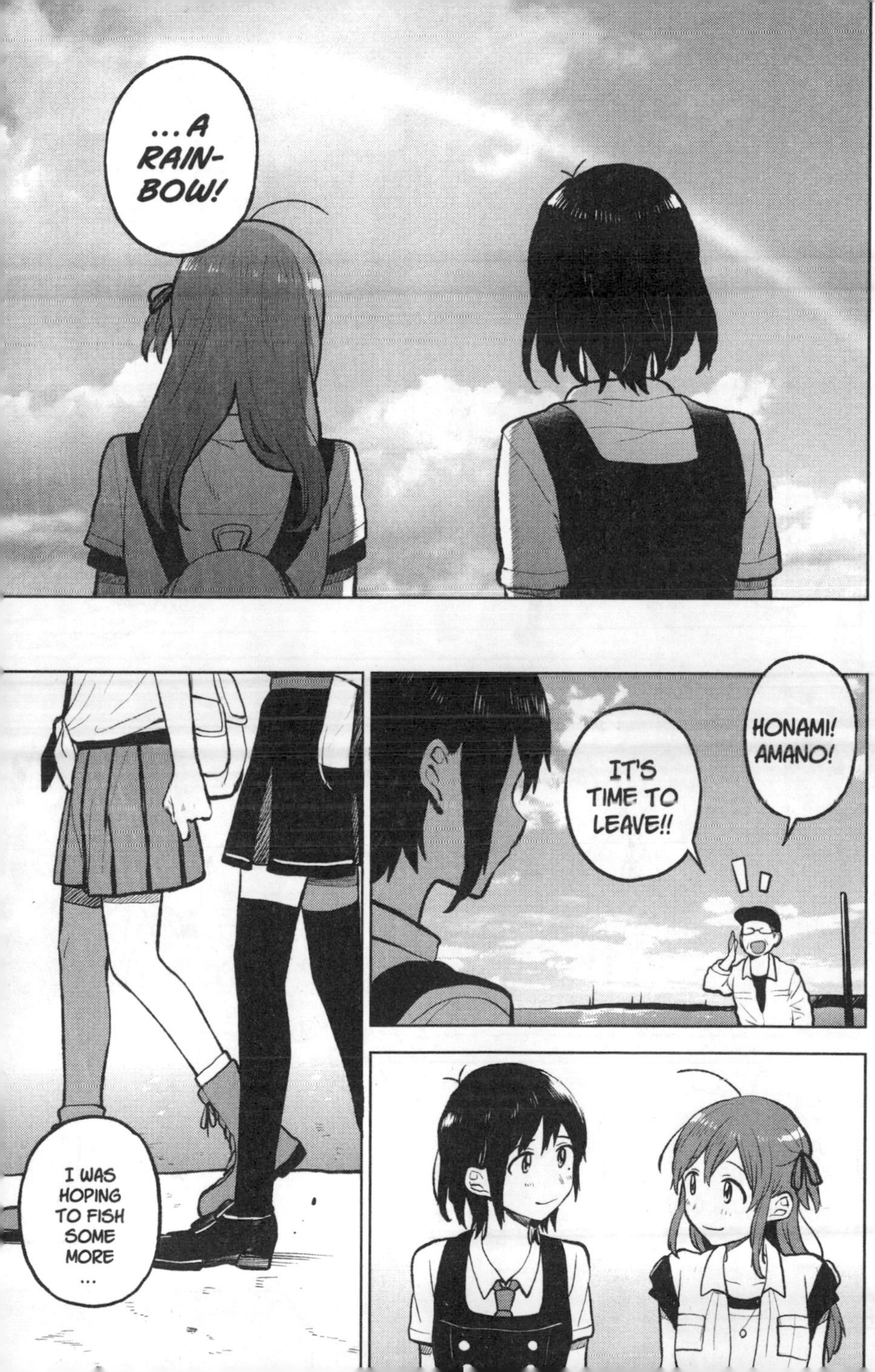
...A RAIN-BOW!
HONAMI! AMANO!
IT'S TIME TO LEAVE!!
I WAS HOPING TO FISH SOME MORE ...

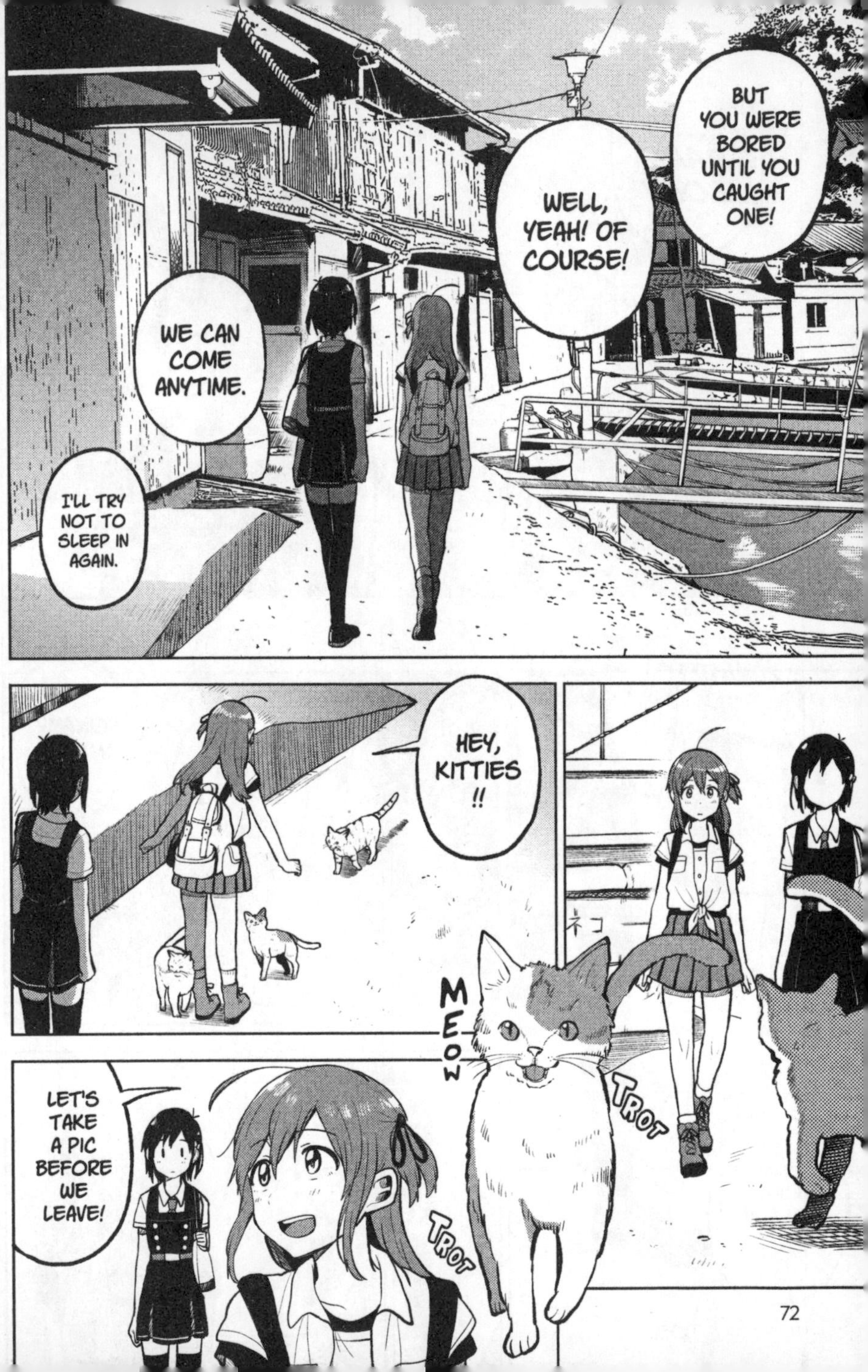
BUT YOU WERE BORED UNTIL YOU CAUGHT ONE!
WELL, YEAH! OF COURSE!
WE CAN COME ANYTIME.
I'LL TRY NOT TO SLEEP IN AGAIN.
ネコ
MEOW
TROT
TROT
HEY, KITTIES!!
LET'S TAKE A PIC BEFORE WE LEAVE!

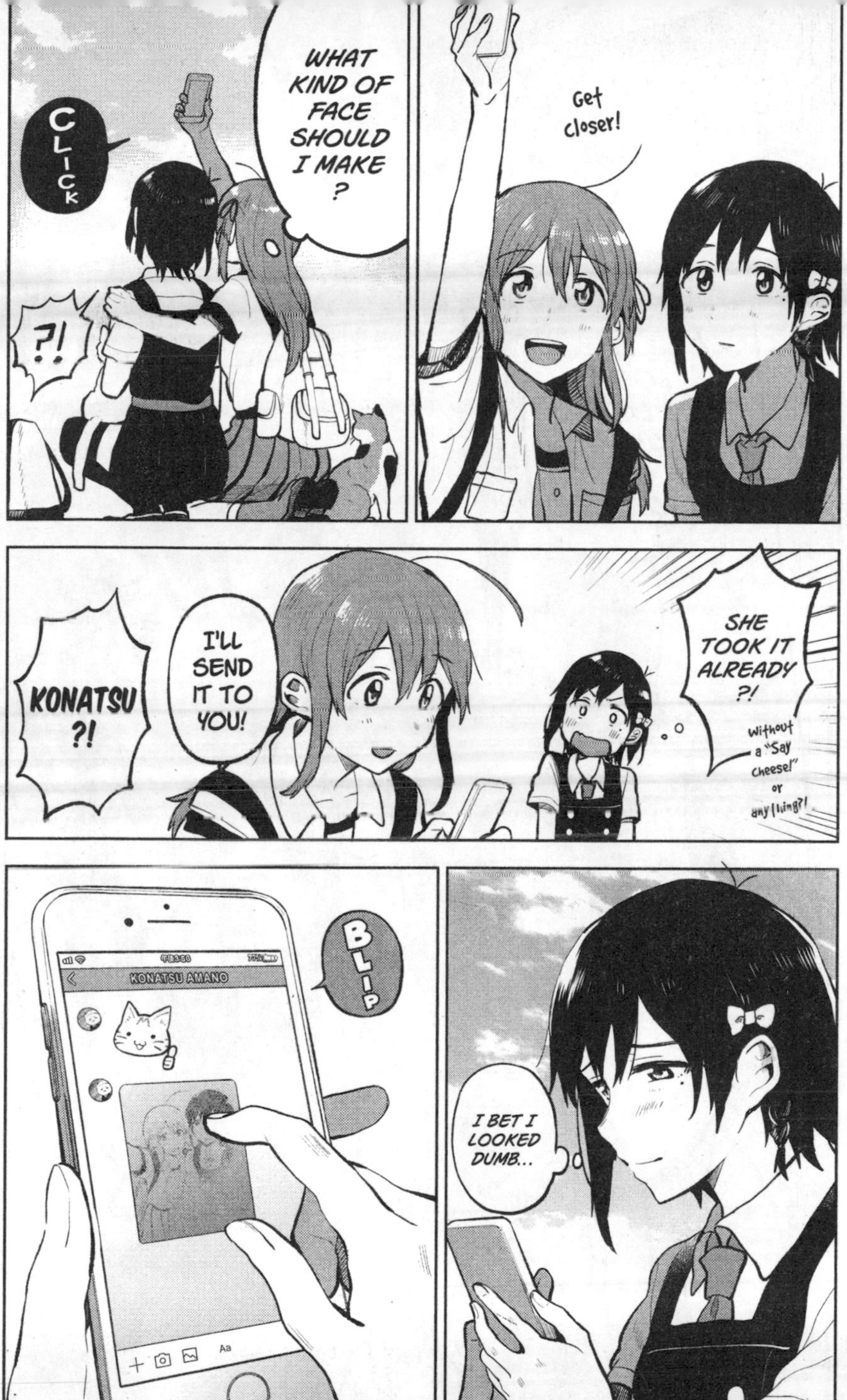
Get closer!
WHAT KIND OF FACE SHOULD I MAKE?
CLICK
?!
SHE TOOK IT ALREADY?!
Without a "Say cheese!" or anything?!
I'LL SEND IT TO YOU!
KONATSU?!
I BET I LOOKED DUMB...
BLIP
KONATSU AMANO
Aa

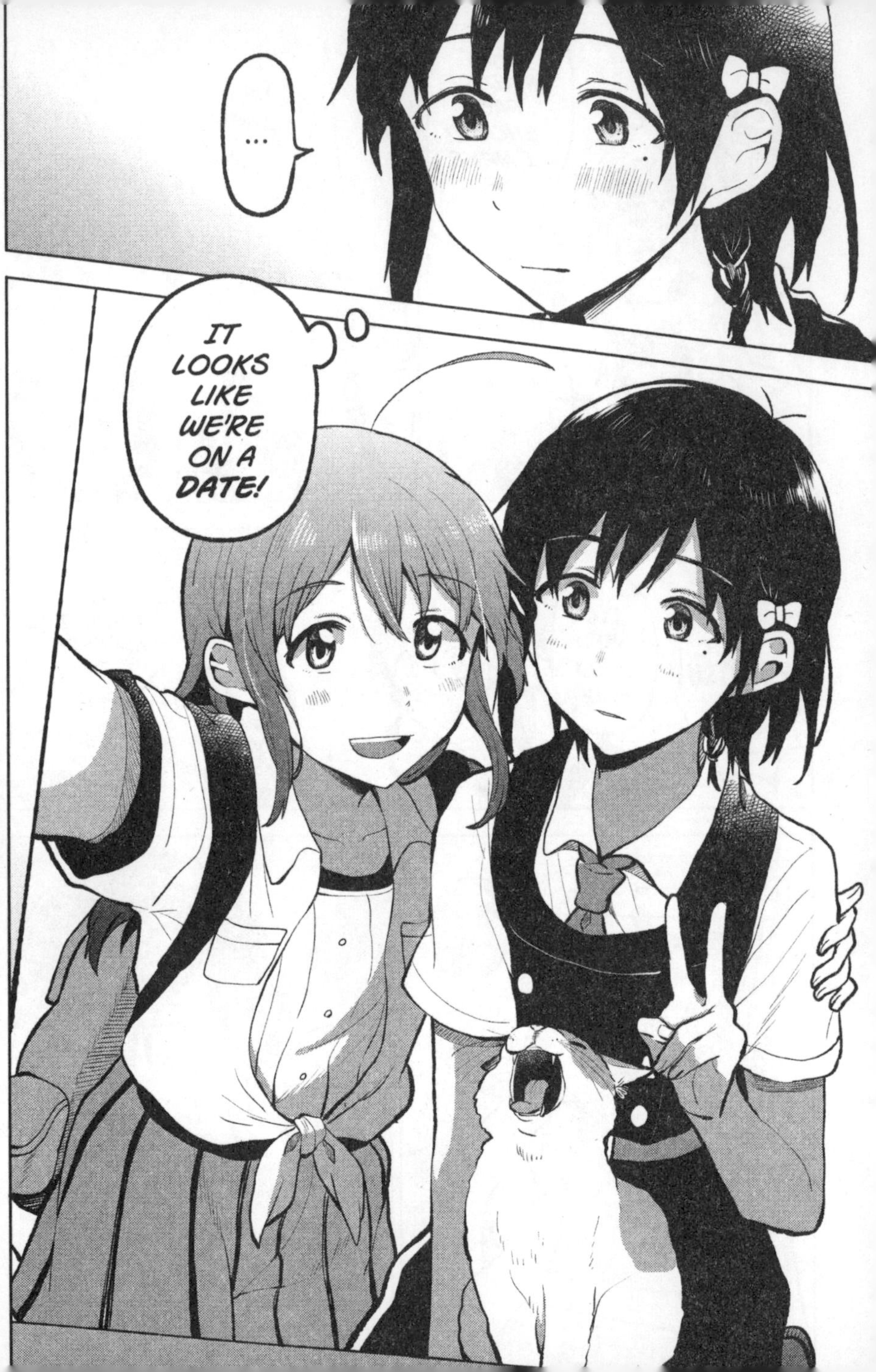
...
IT LOOKS LIKE WE'RE ON A DATE!

A Tropical Fish
Yearns for Snow

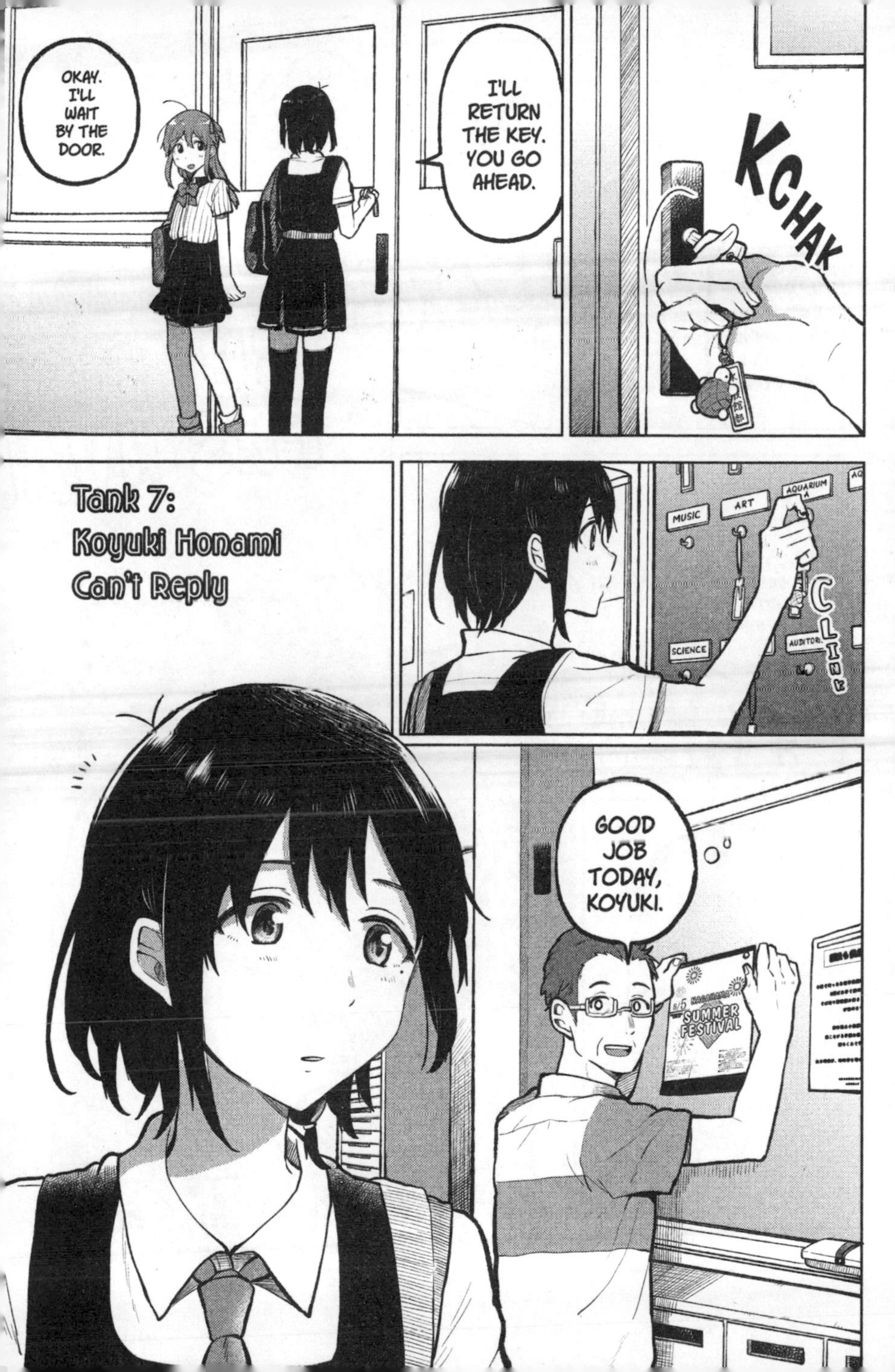
KCHAK
I'LL RETURN THE KEY. YOU GO AHEAD.
OKAY. I'LL WAIT BY THE DOOR.
AQUARIUM A
ART
MUSIC
SCIENCE
CLINK
Tank 7: Koyuki Honami Can't Reply
GOOD JOB TODAY, KOYUKI.
8/5 NAGAHAMA SUMMER FESTIVAL

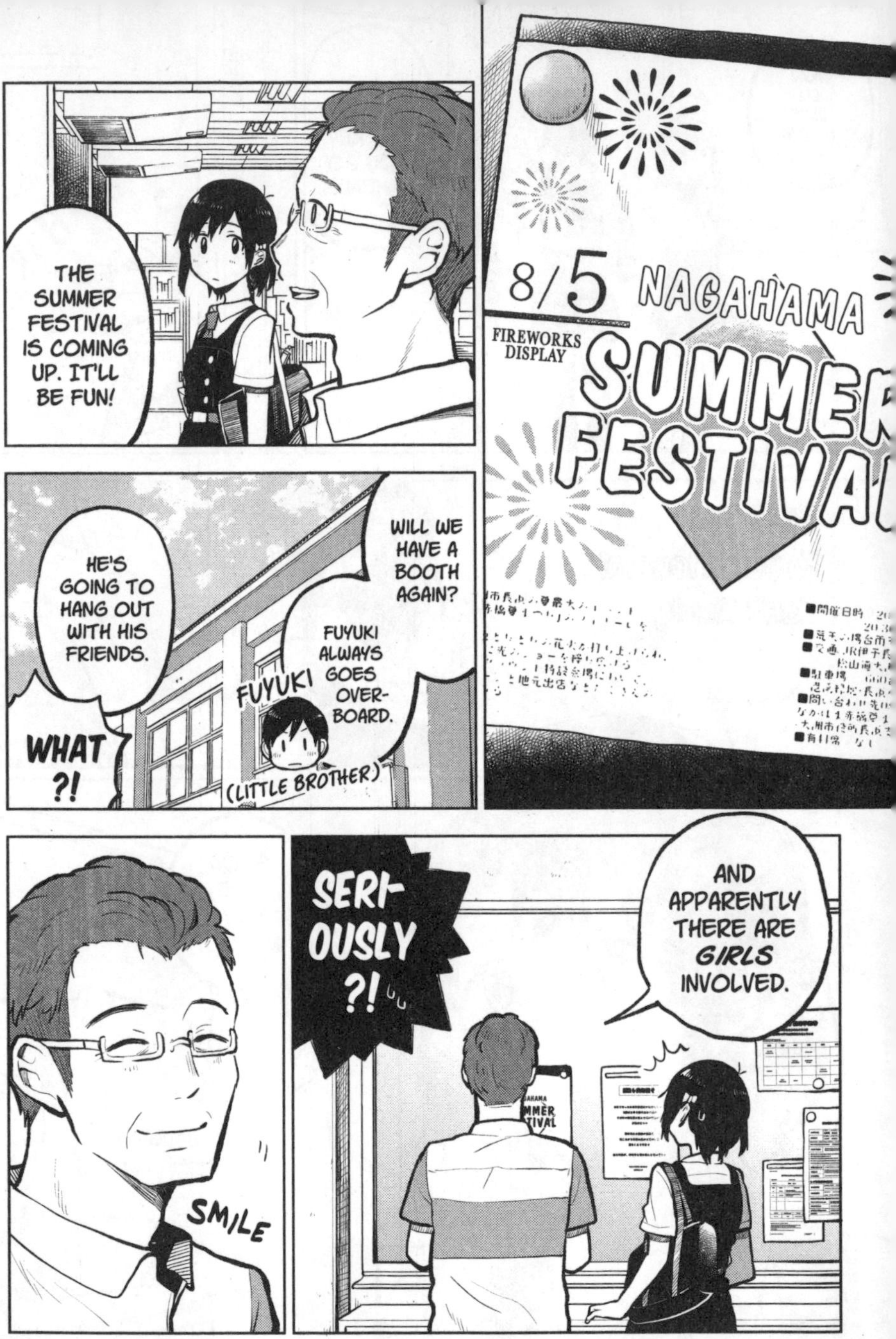
8/5
NAGAHAMA
SUMMER FESTIVAL
FIREWORKS DISPLAY
THE SUMMER FESTIVAL IS COMING UP. IT'LL BE FUN!
WILL WE HAVE A BOOTH AGAIN?
HE'S GOING TO HANG OUT WITH HIS FRIENDS.
FUYUKI ALWAYS GOES OVER-BOARD.
FUYUKI
(LITTLE BROTHER)
WHAT?!
AND APPARENTLY THERE ARE *GIRLS* INVOLVED.
SERI-OUSLY?!
SMILE

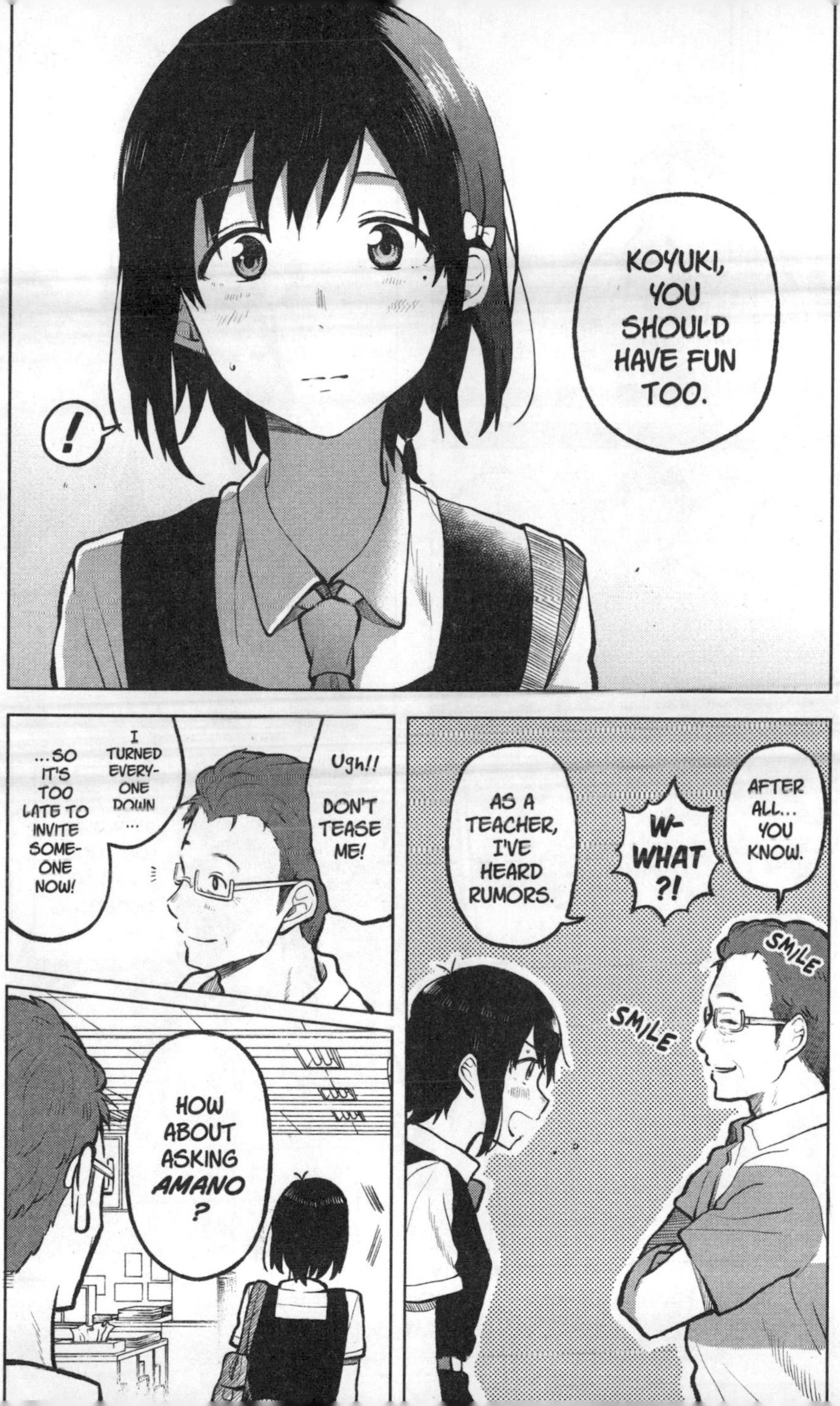

KOYUKI, YOU SHOULD HAVE FUN TOO.
!
AFTER ALL... YOU KNOW.
W-WHAT ?!
AS A TEACHER, I'VE HEARD RUMORS.
SMILE
SMILE
Ugh!!
DON'T TEASE ME!
I TURNED EVERY-ONE DOWN ...
...SO IT'S TOO LATE TO INVITE SOME-ONE NOW!
HOW ABOUT ASKING AMANO ?

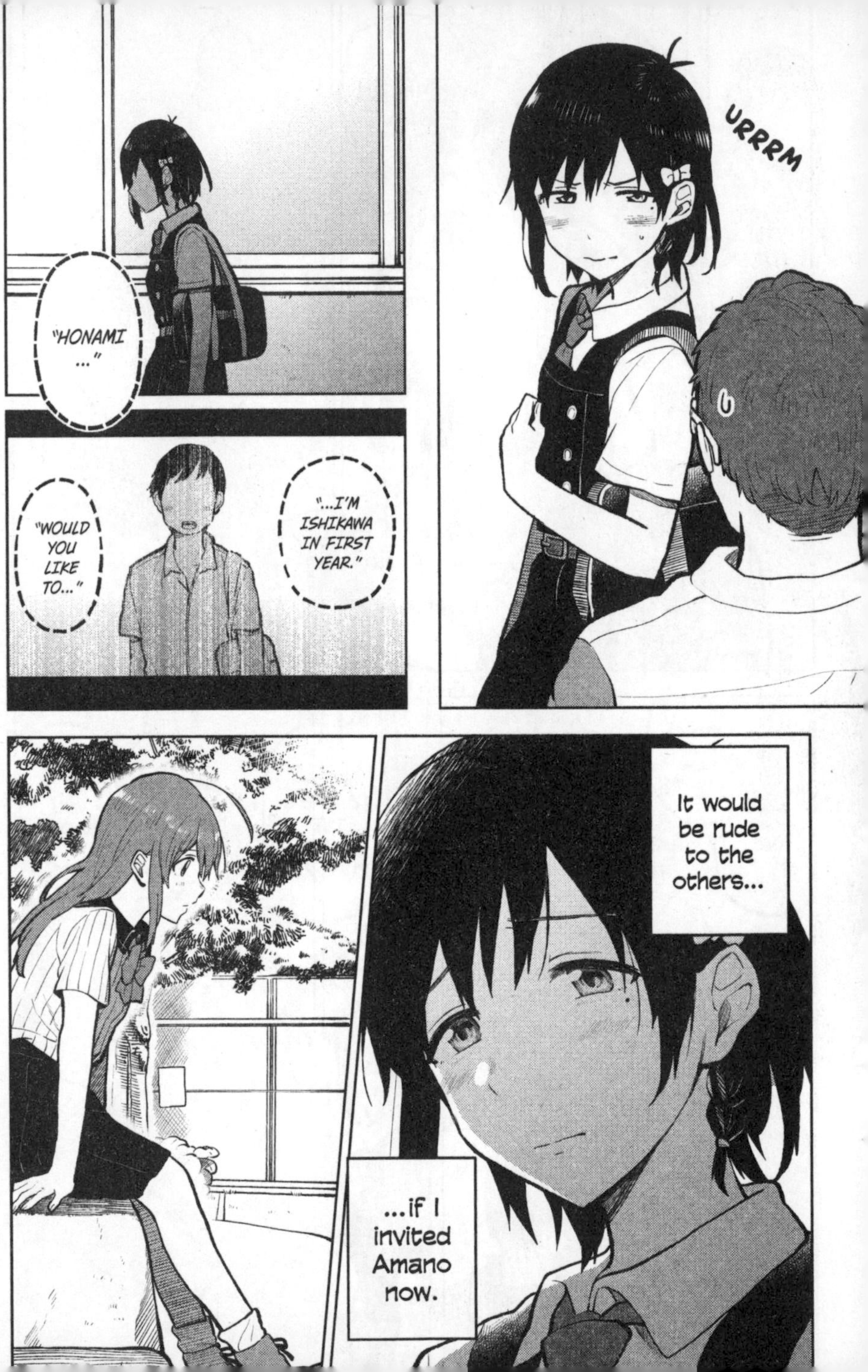
URRRM
"HONAMI ..."
"...I'M ISHIKAWA IN FIRST YEAR."
"WOULD YOU LIKE TO..."
It would be rude to the others...
...if I invited Amano now.

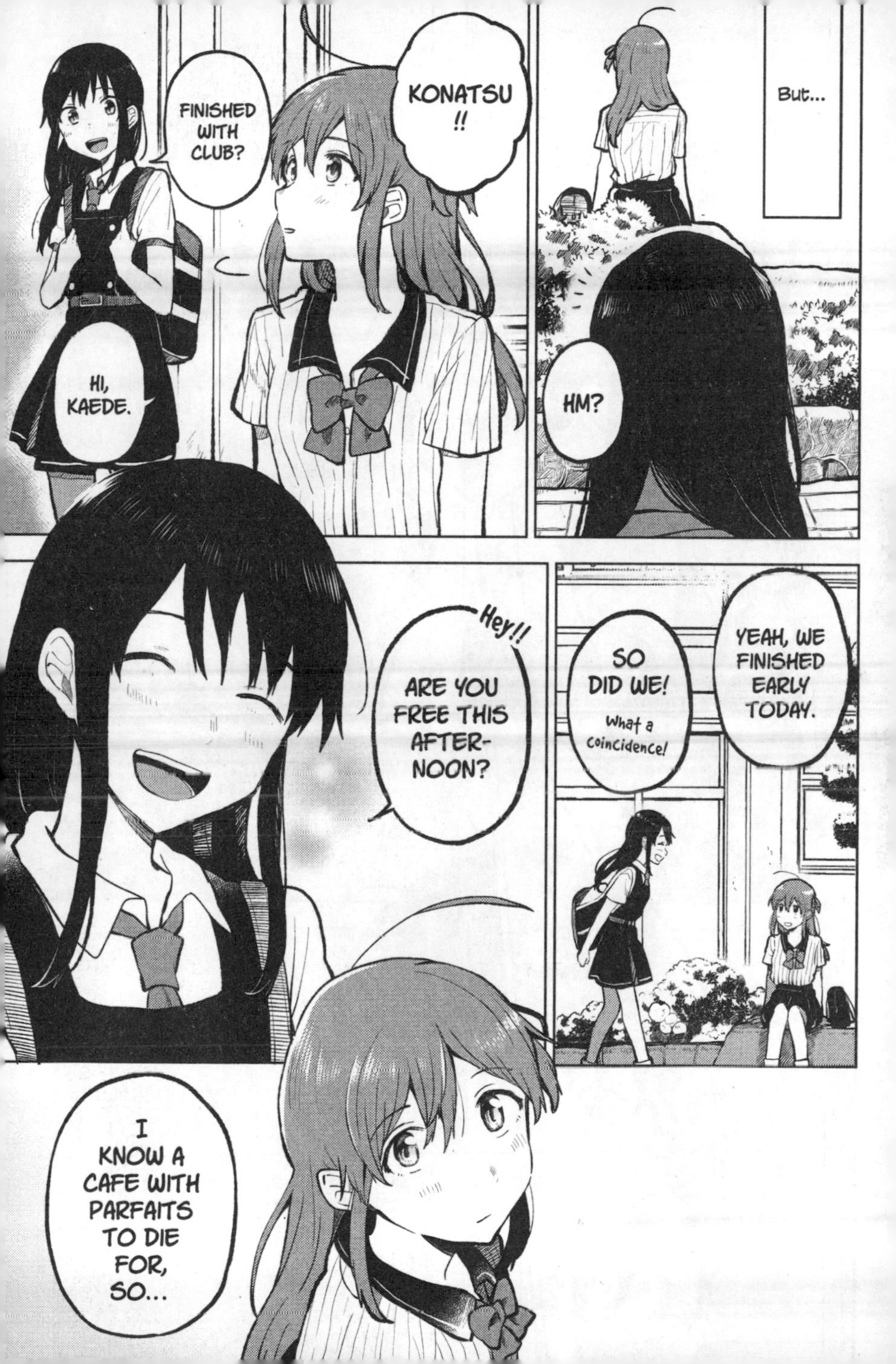
But...
HM?
KONATSU!!
FINISHED WITH CLUB?
HI, KAEDE.
YEAH, WE FINISHED EARLY TODAY.
SO DID WE! What a coincidence!
Hey!!
ARE YOU FREE THIS AFTERNOON?
I KNOW A CAFE WITH PARFAITS TO DIE FOR, SO...

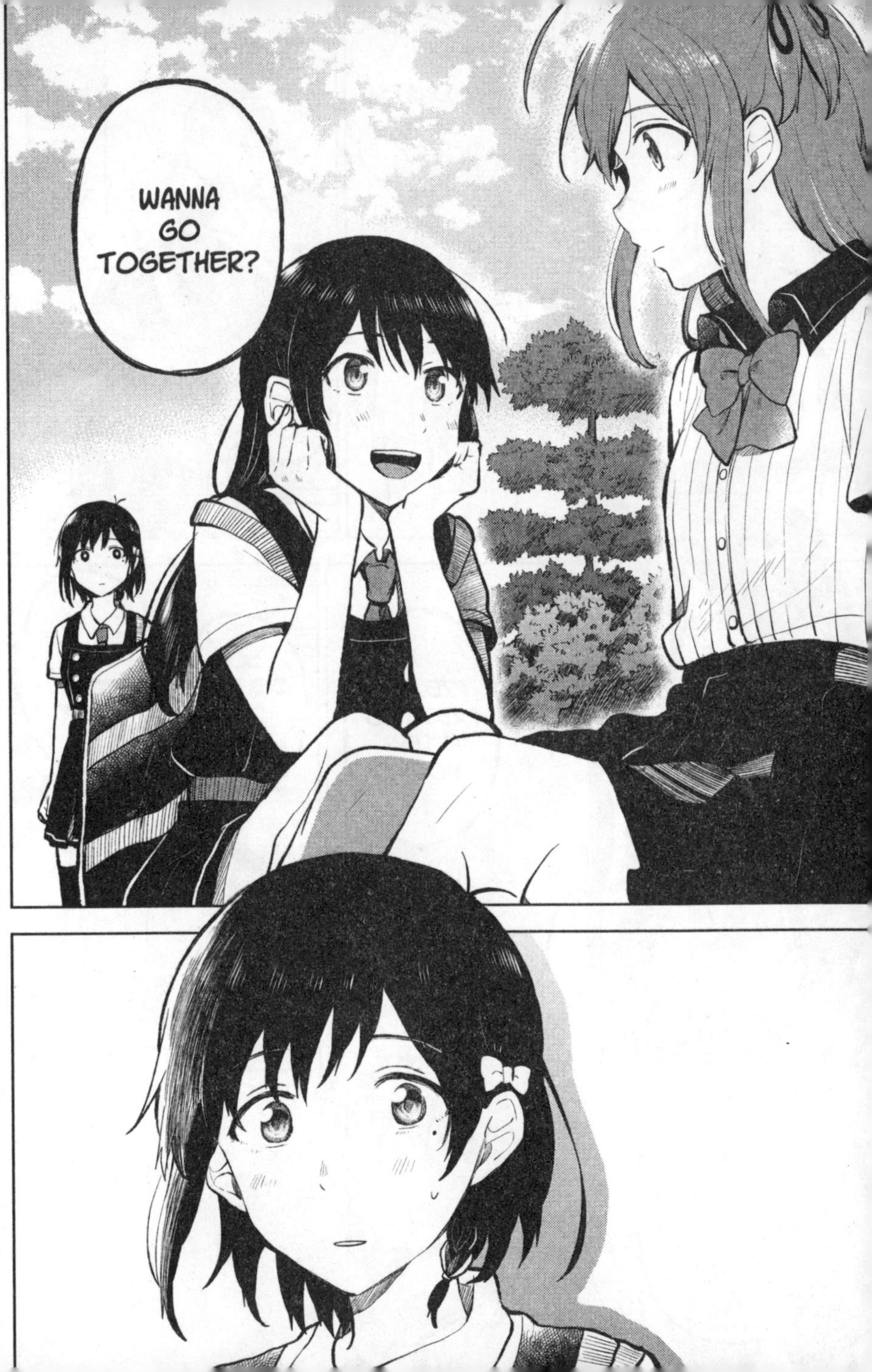
WANNA GO TOGETHER?

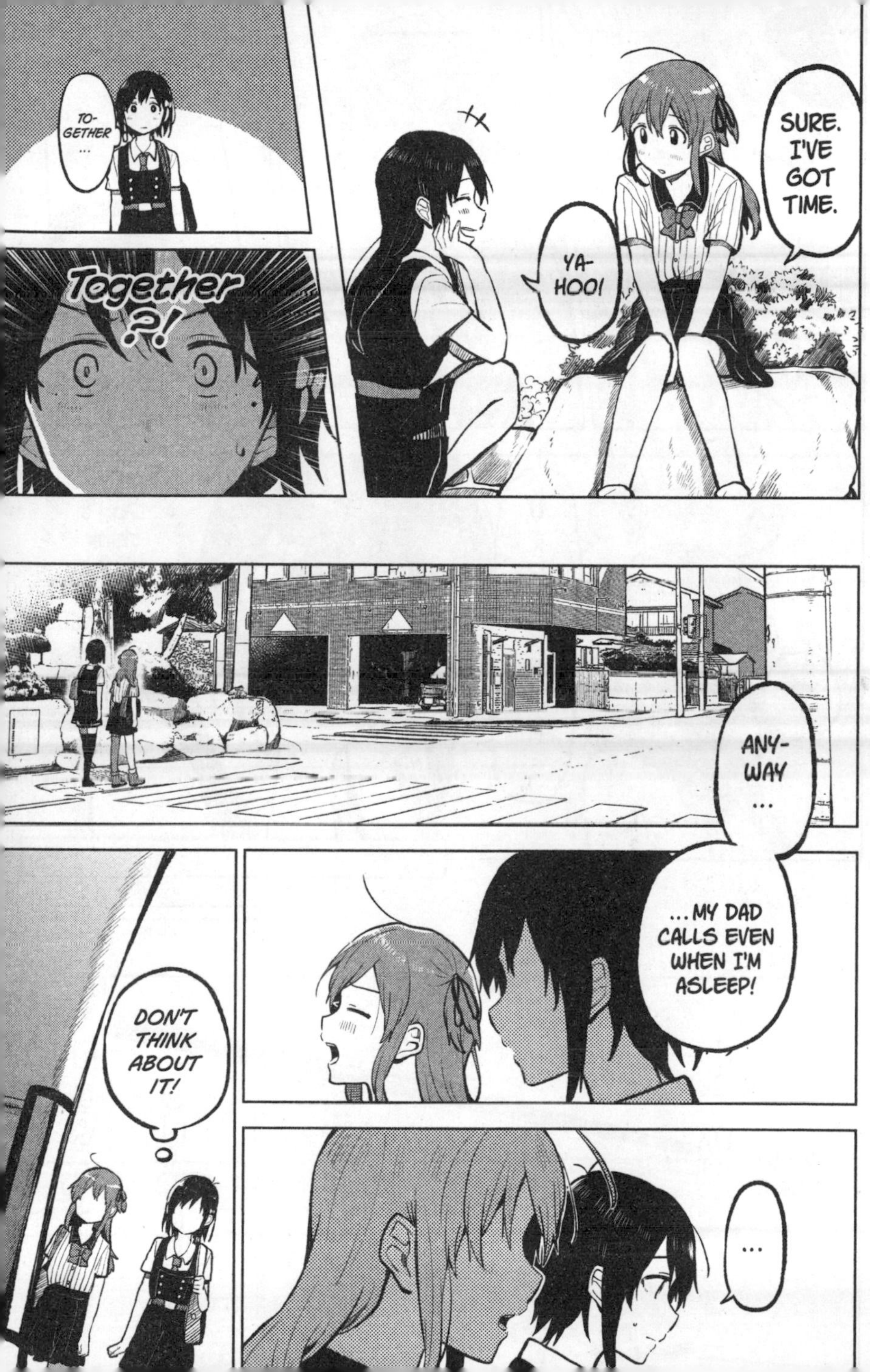
SURE. I'VE GOT TIME.
YA-HOO!
TO-GETHER ...
Together ?!
ANY-WAY ...
... MY DAD CALLS EVEN WHEN I'M ASLEEP!
...
DON'T THINK ABOUT IT!

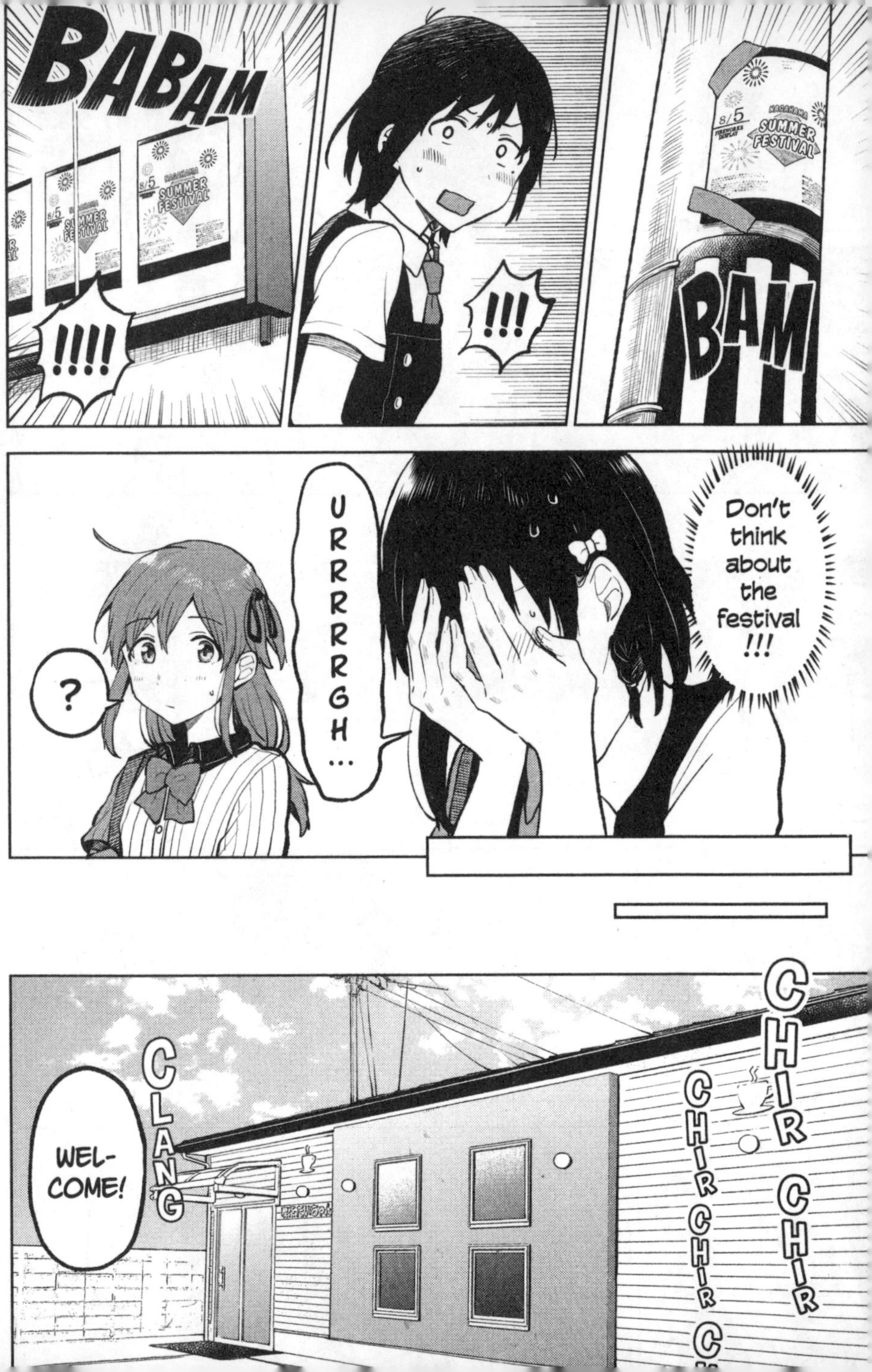
8/5
FIREWORKS DISPLAY
NAGAHAMA
SUMMER FESTIVAL
BAM
!!!
BABAM
NAGAHAMA
SUMMER FESTIVAL
!!!!
Don't think about the festival!!!
URRRRRGH...
?
CHIR CHIR
CHIR CHIR C...
CLANG
WEL-COME!

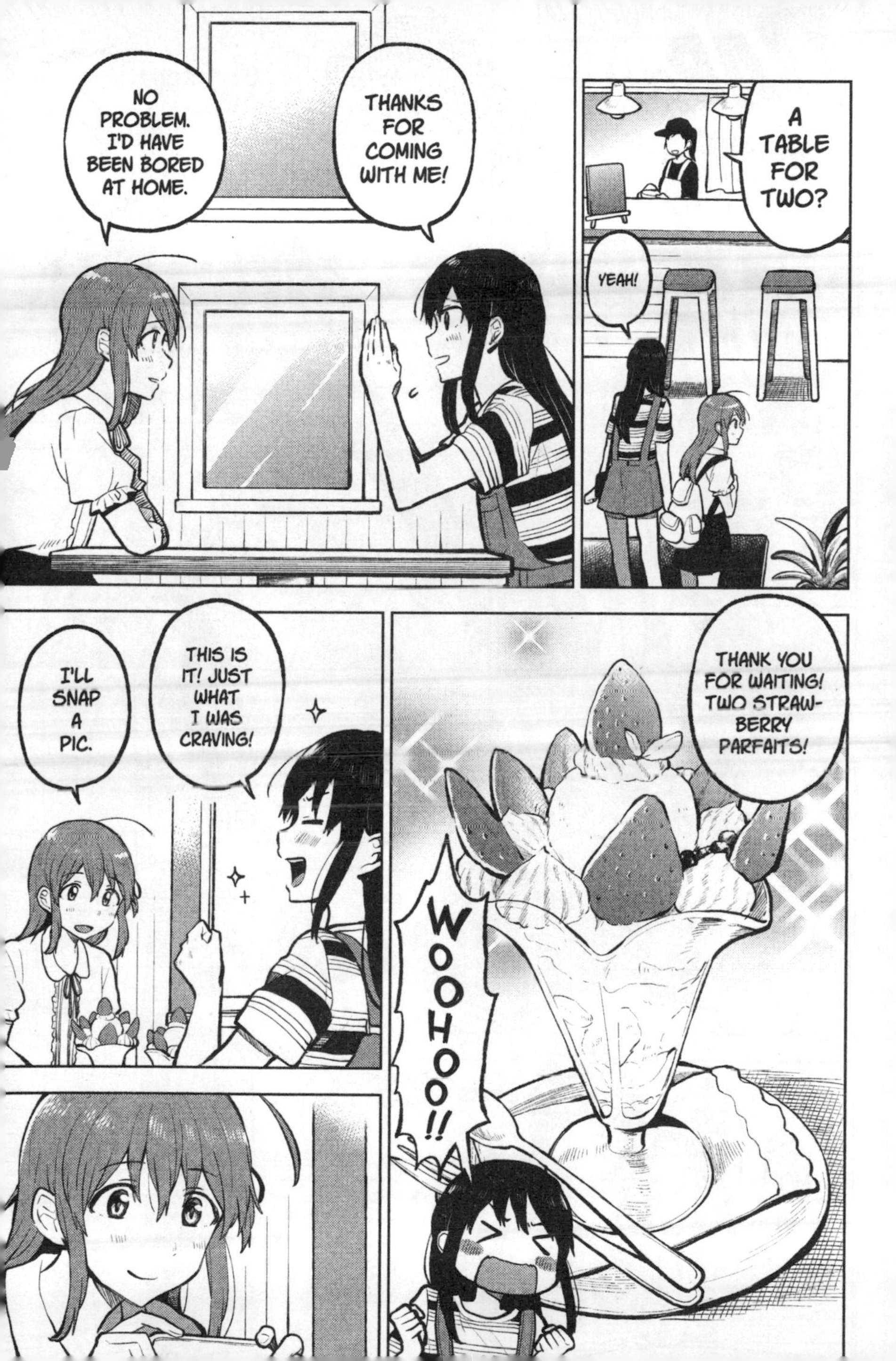
A TABLE FOR TWO?
YEAH!
THANKS FOR COMING WITH ME!
NO PROBLEM. I'D HAVE BEEN BORED AT HOME.
THANK YOU FOR WAITING! TWO STRAW-BERRY PARFAITS!
WOOHOO!!
THIS IS IT! JUST WHAT I WAS CRAVING!
I'LL SNAP A PIC.

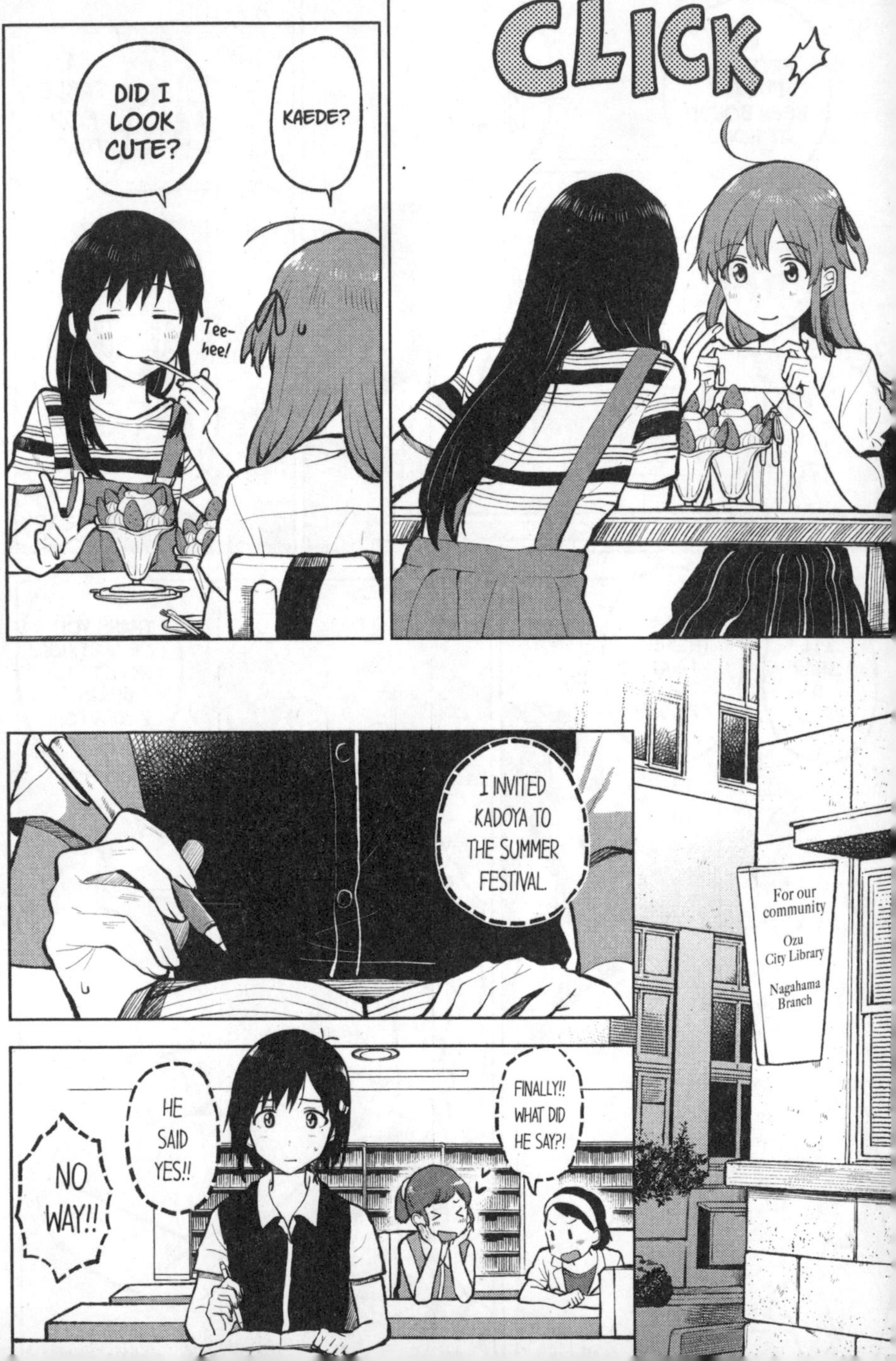
CLICK
KAEDE?
DID I LOOK CUTE?
Tee-hee!
For our community
Ozu City Library
Nagahama Branch
I INVITED KADOYA TO THE SUMMER FESTIVAL.
FINALLY!! WHAT DID HE SAY?!
HE SAID YES!!
NO WAY!!

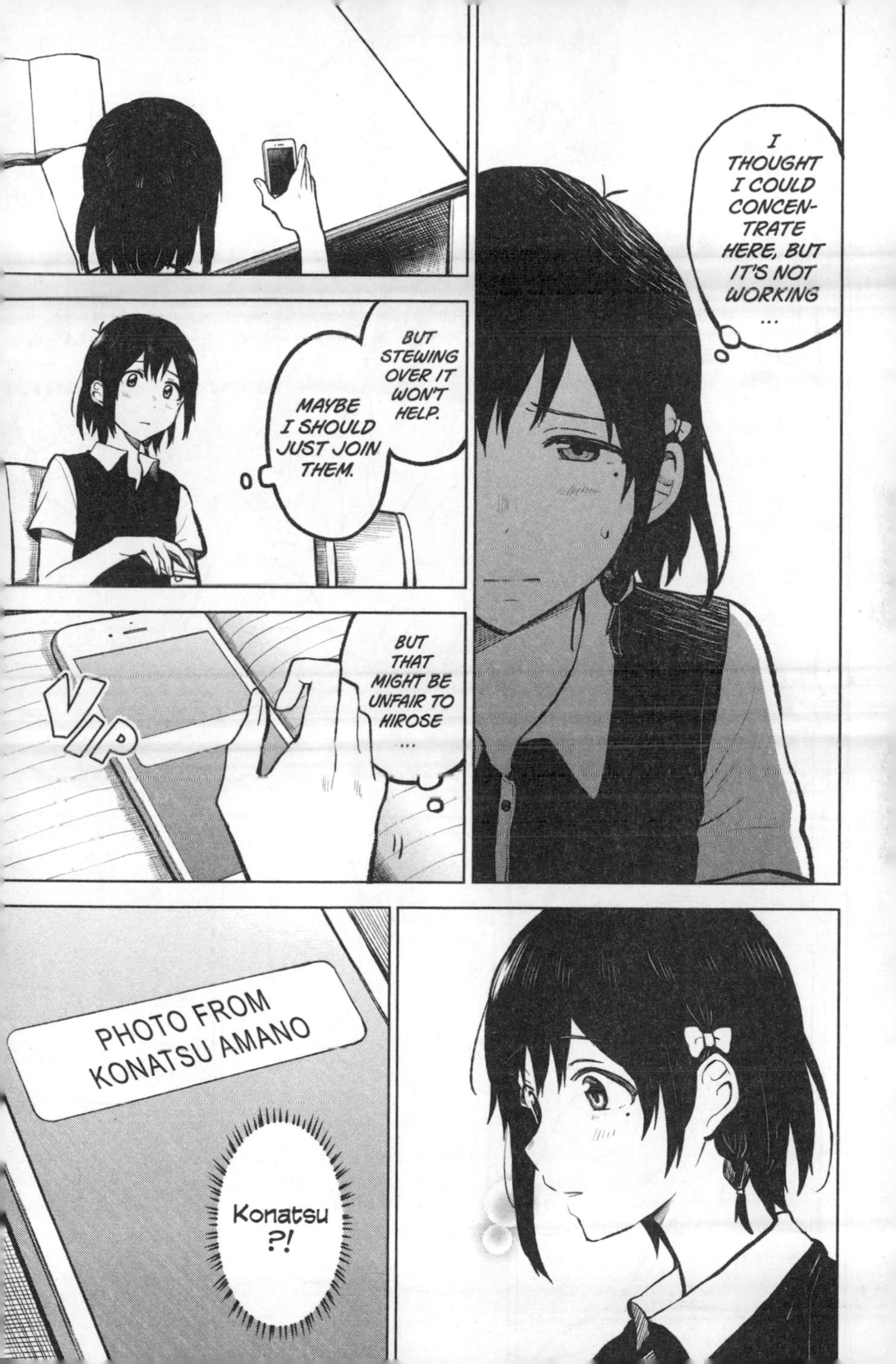
I THOUGHT I COULD CONCENTRATE HERE, BUT IT'S NOT WORKING ...
BUT STEWING OVER IT WON'T HELP.
MAYBE I SHOULD JUST JOIN THEM.
BUT THAT MIGHT BE UNFAIR TO HIROSE ...
VIP
PHOTO FROM KONATSU AMANO
Konatsu ?!

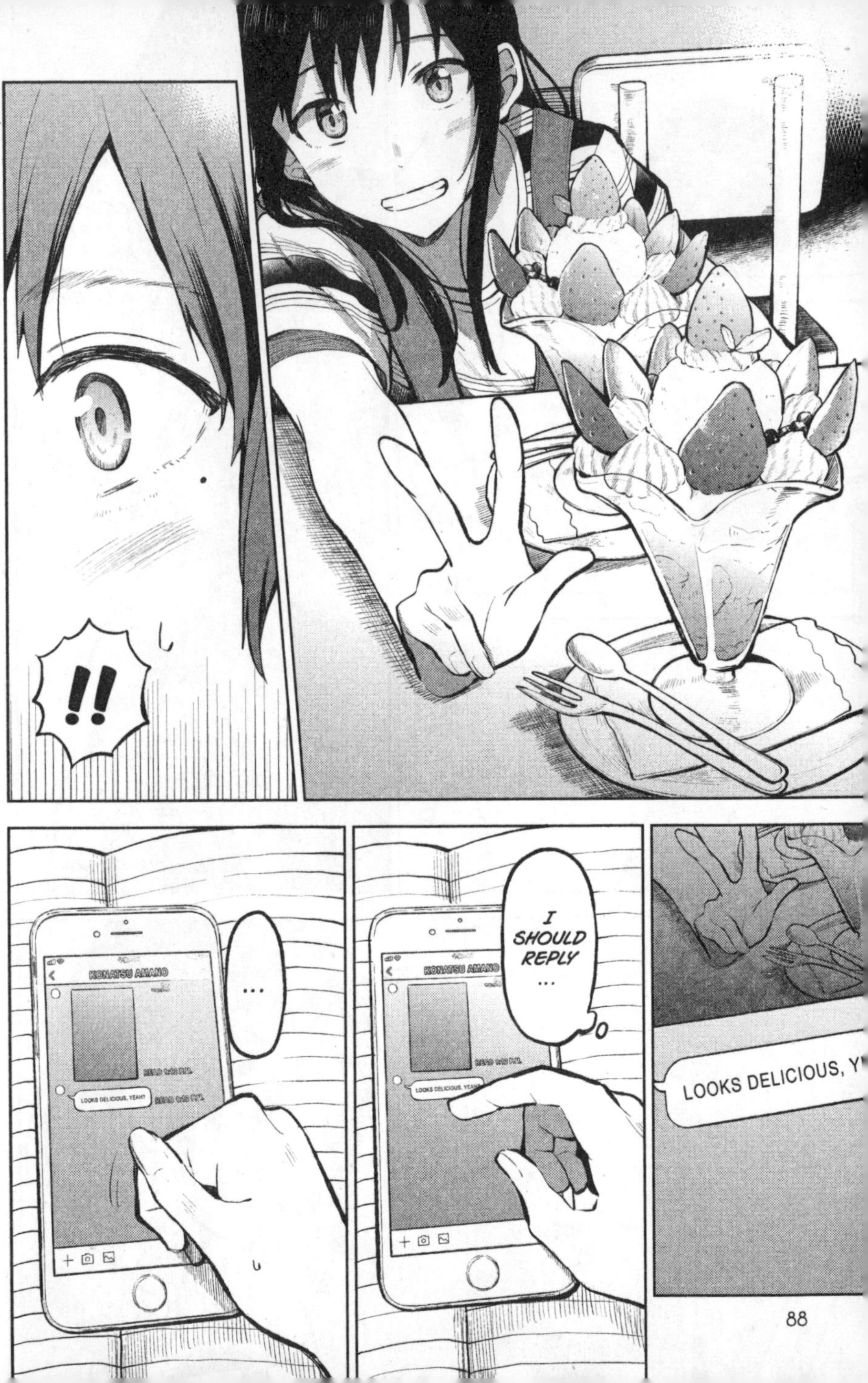
!!
LOOKS DELICIOUS, Y
I SHOULD REPLY ...
KONATSU AMANO
LOOKS DELICIOUS, YEAH?
...
KONATSU AMANO
LOOKS DELICIOUS, YEAH?

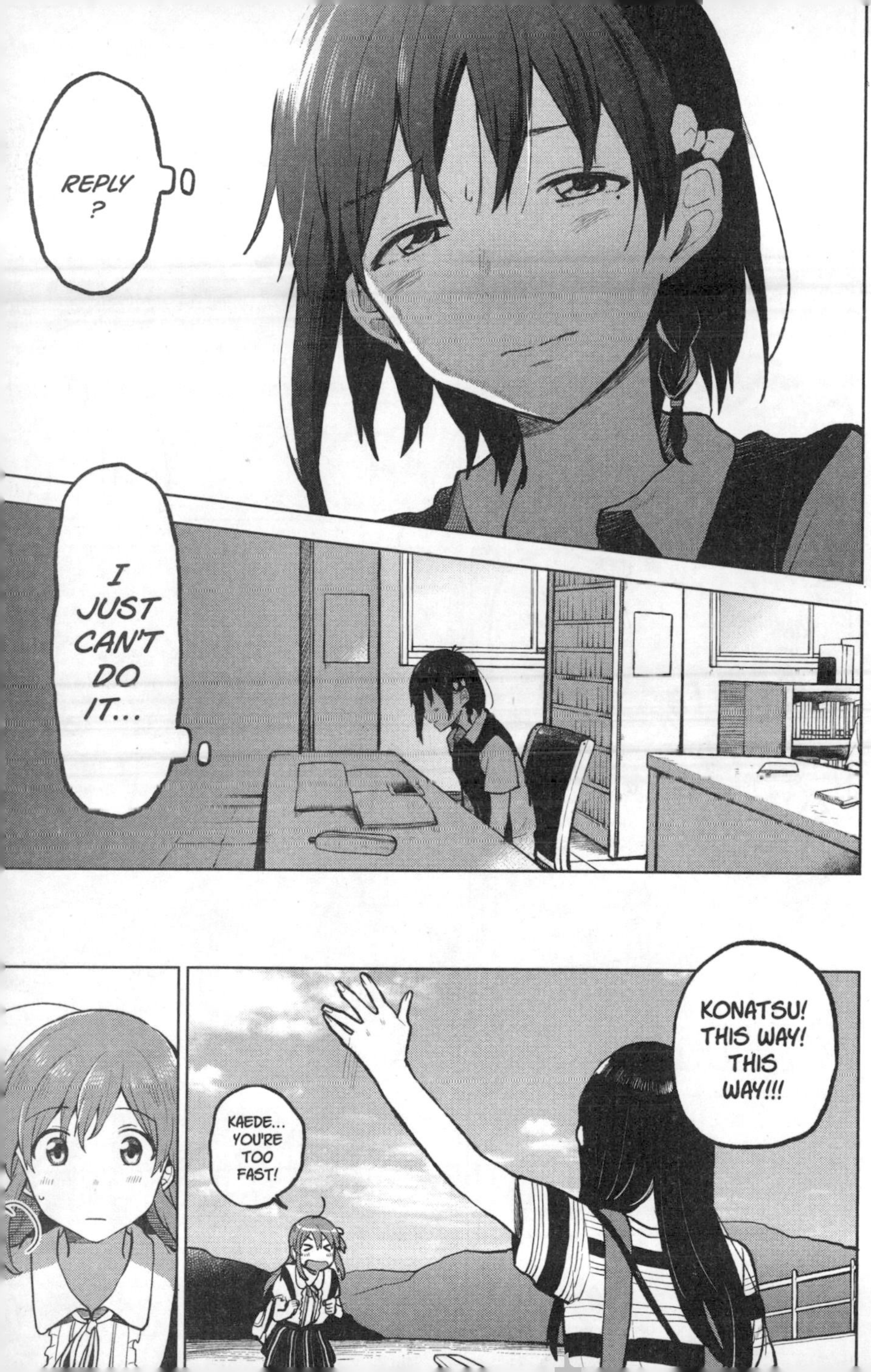
REPLY?
I JUST CAN'T DO IT...
KONATSU! THIS WAY! THIS WAY!!!
KAEDE... YOU'RE TOO FAST!

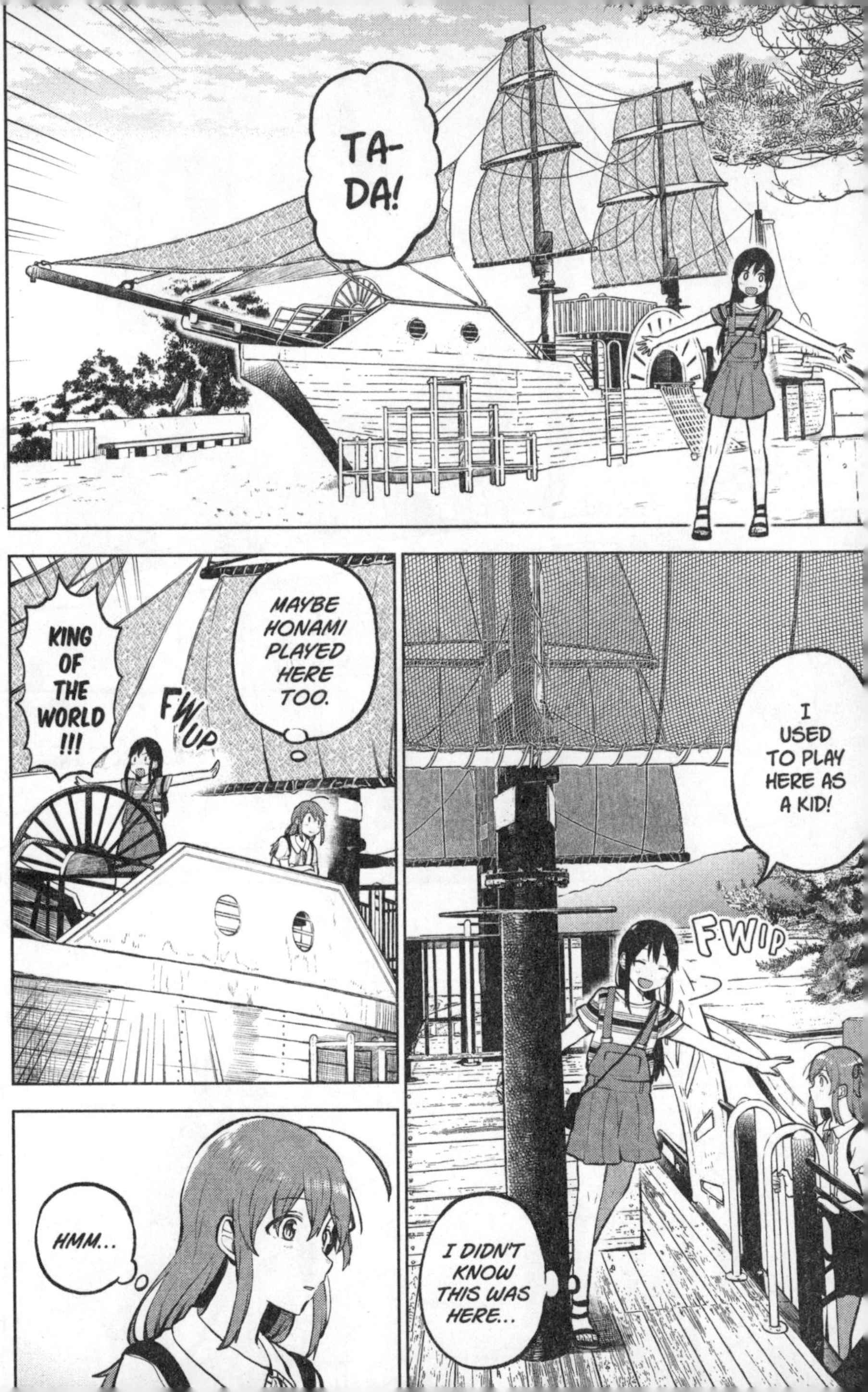
TA-DA!
I USED TO PLAY HERE AS A KID!
FWIP
I DIDN'T KNOW THIS WAS HERE...
MAYBE HONAMI PLAYED HERE TOO.
KING OF THE WORLD!!!
FWUP
HMM...

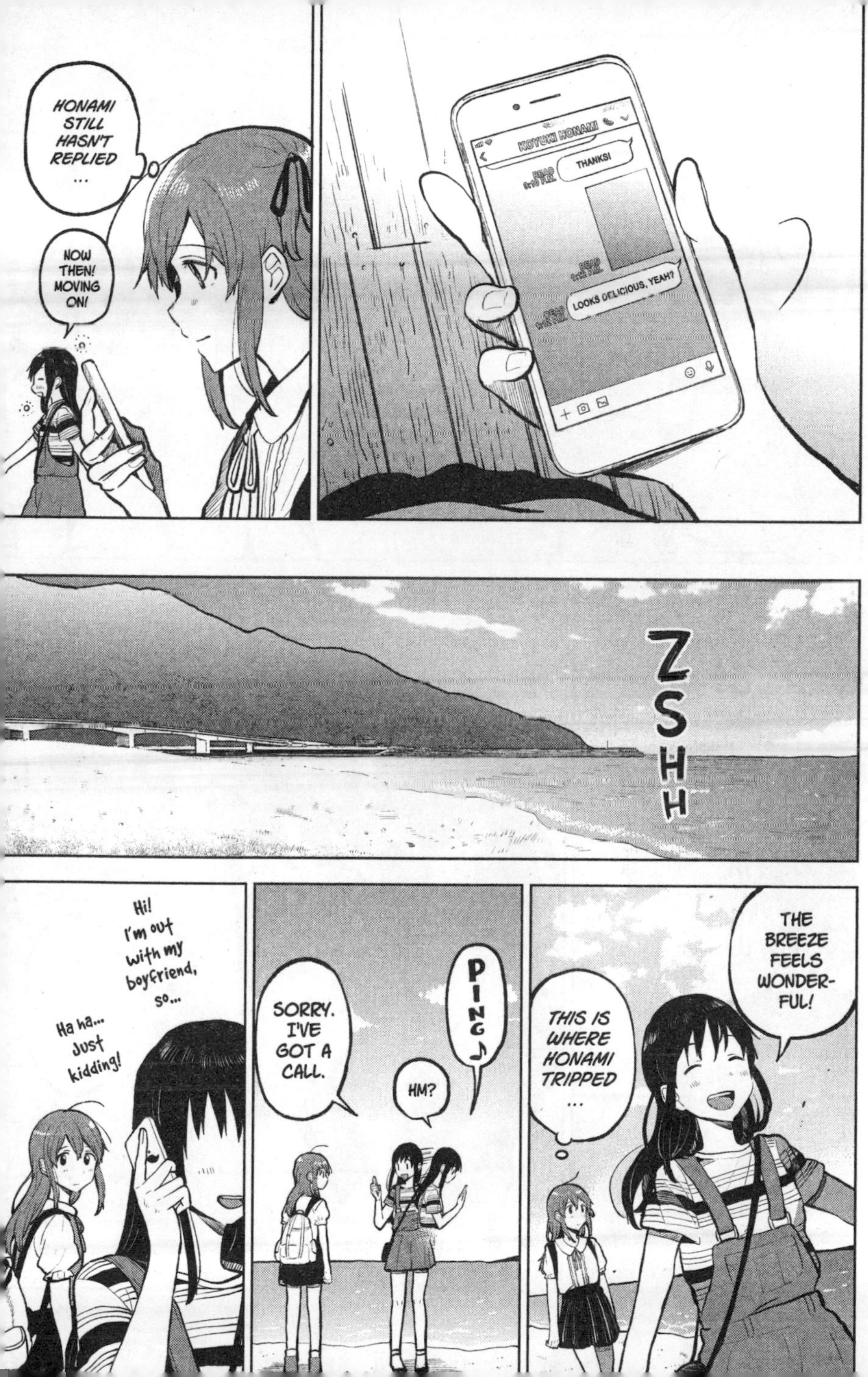
KOYUKI HONAMI
THANKS!
LOOKS DELICIOUS, YEAH?
HONAMI STILL HASN'T REPLIED ...
NOW THEN! MOVING ON!
ZSHH
THE BREEZE FEELS WONDER-FUL!
THIS IS WHERE HONAMI TRIPPED ...
PING♪
HM?
SORRY. I'VE GOT A CALL.
Hi! I'm out with my boyfriend, so...
Ha ha... Just kidding!

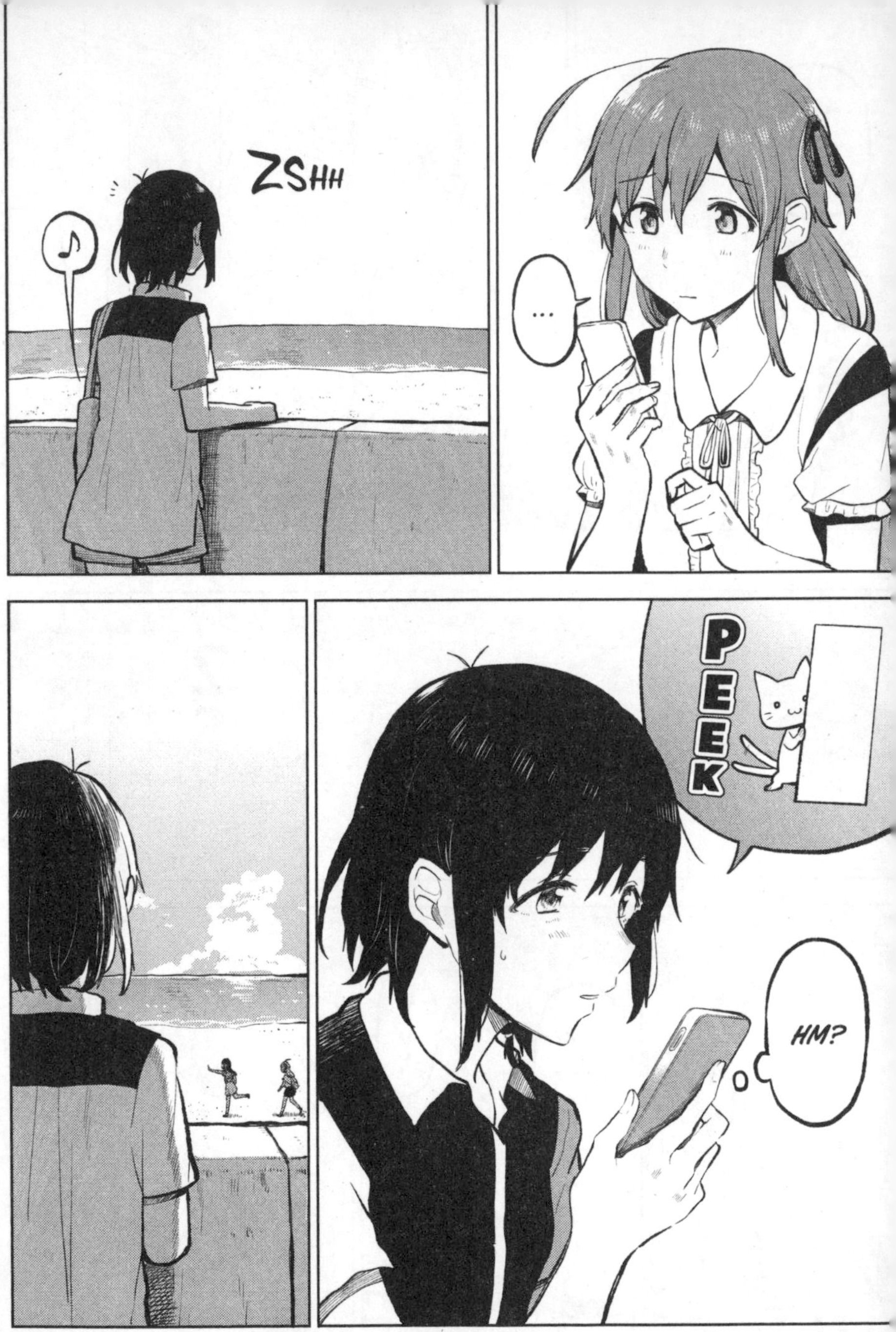
...
ZSHH
♪
PEEK
HM?

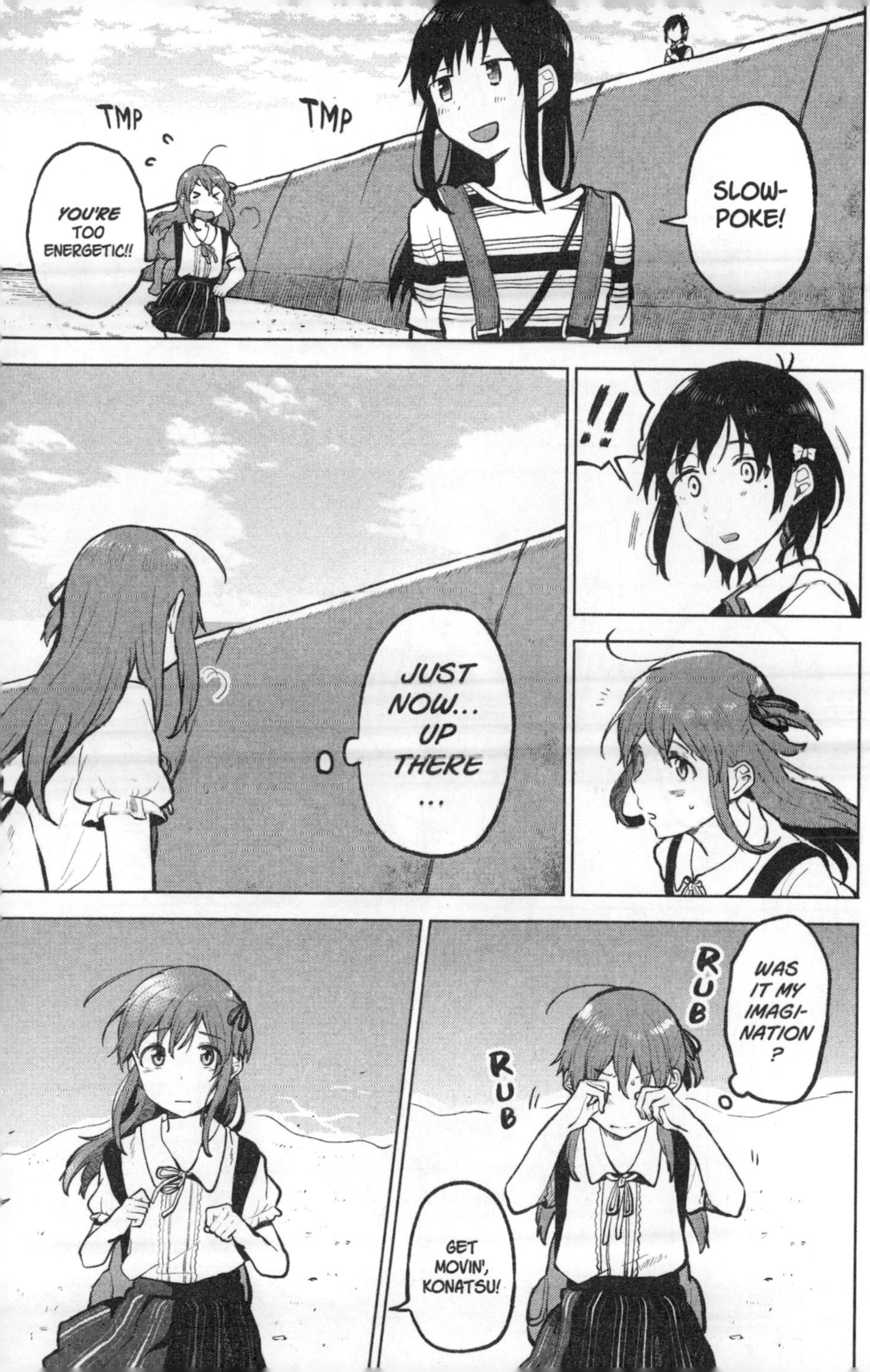
SLOW-POKE!
TMP
TMP
YOU'RE TOO ENERGETIC!!
!!
JUST NOW... UP THERE ...
WAS IT MY IMAGINATION?
RUB
RUB
GET MOVIN', KONATSU!

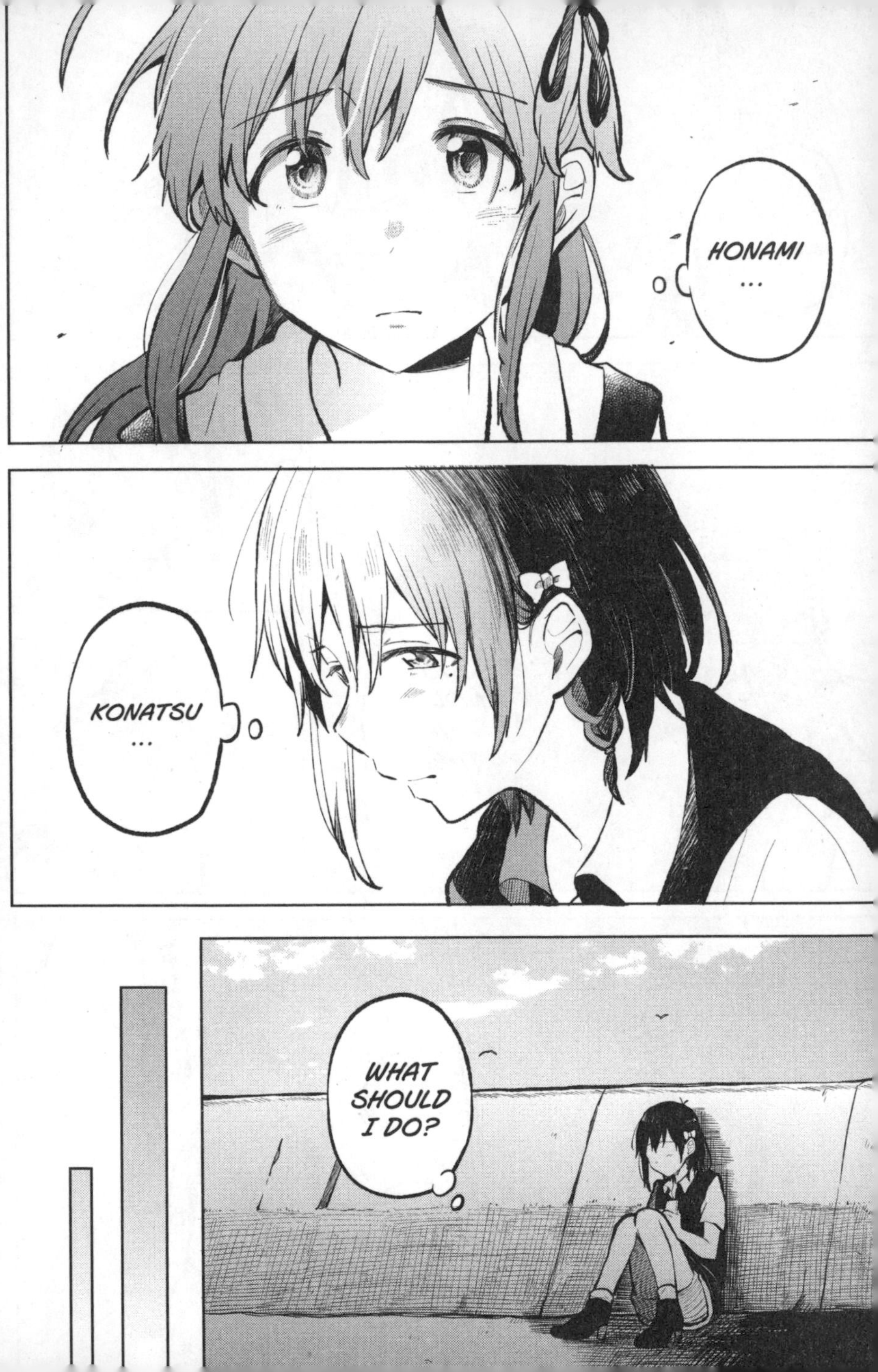
HONAMI ...
KONATSU ...
WHAT SHOULD I DO?

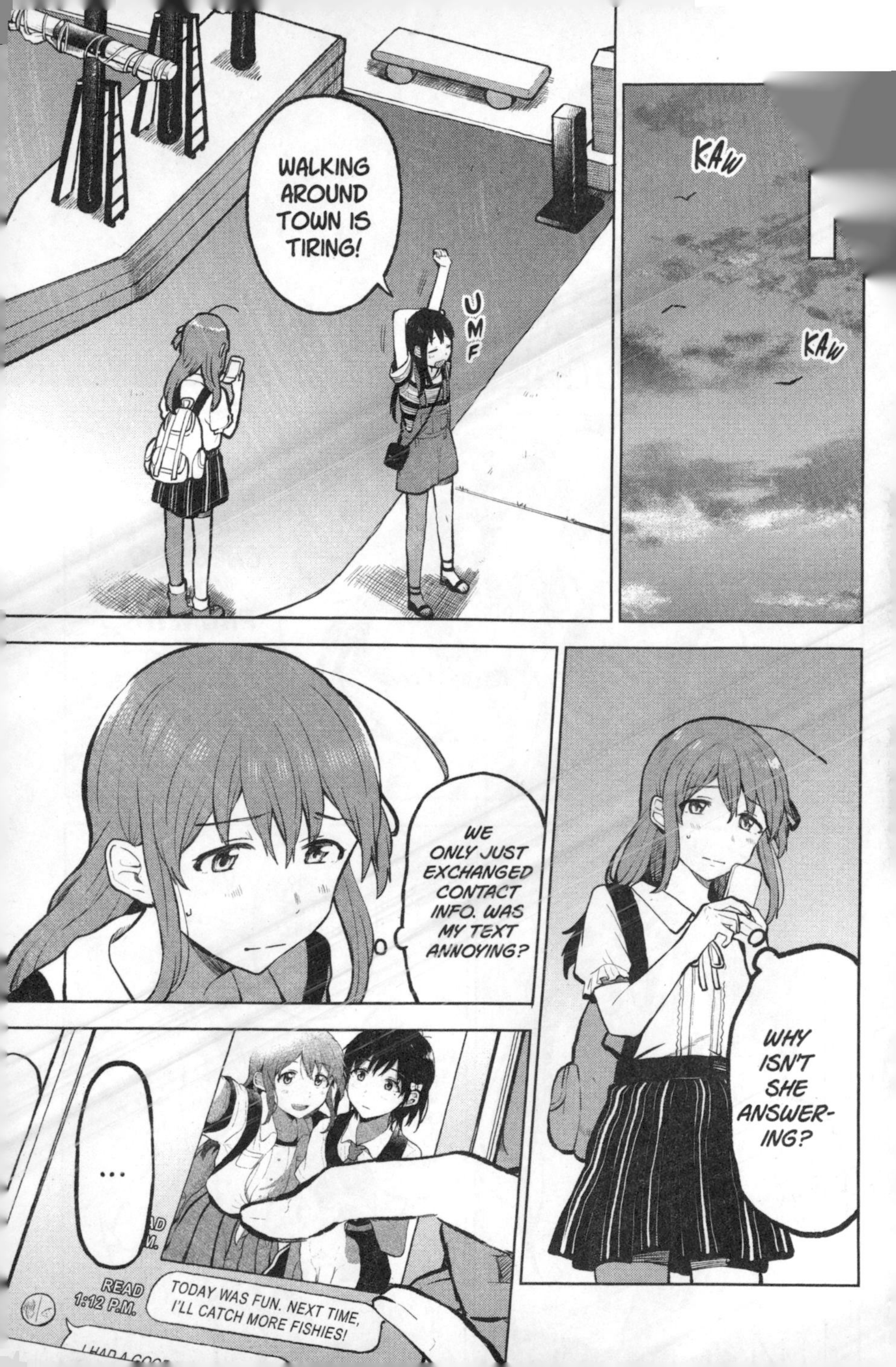
KAW
KAW
WALKING AROUND TOWN IS TIRING!
UMF
WHY ISN'T SHE ANSWER-ING?
WE ONLY JUST EXCHANGED CONTACT INFO. WAS MY TEXT ANNOYING?
...
READ 1:12 P.M.
TODAY WAS FUN. NEXT TIME, I'LL CATCH MORE FISHIES!

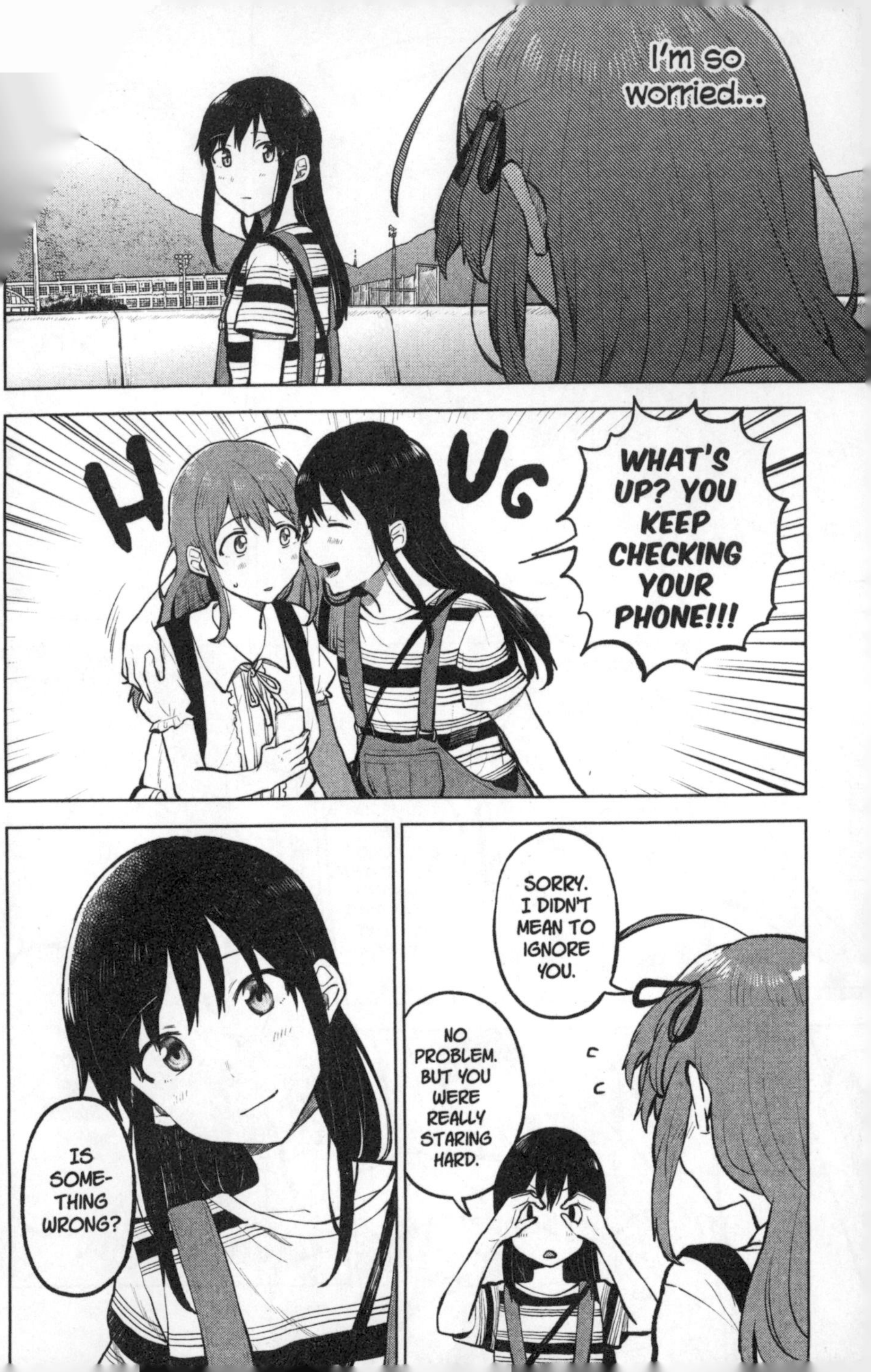
I'm so worried...
HUG
WHAT'S UP? YOU KEEP CHECKING YOUR PHONE!!!
SORRY. I DIDN'T MEAN TO IGNORE YOU.
NO PROBLEM. BUT YOU WERE REALLY STARING HARD.
IS SOME-THING WRONG?

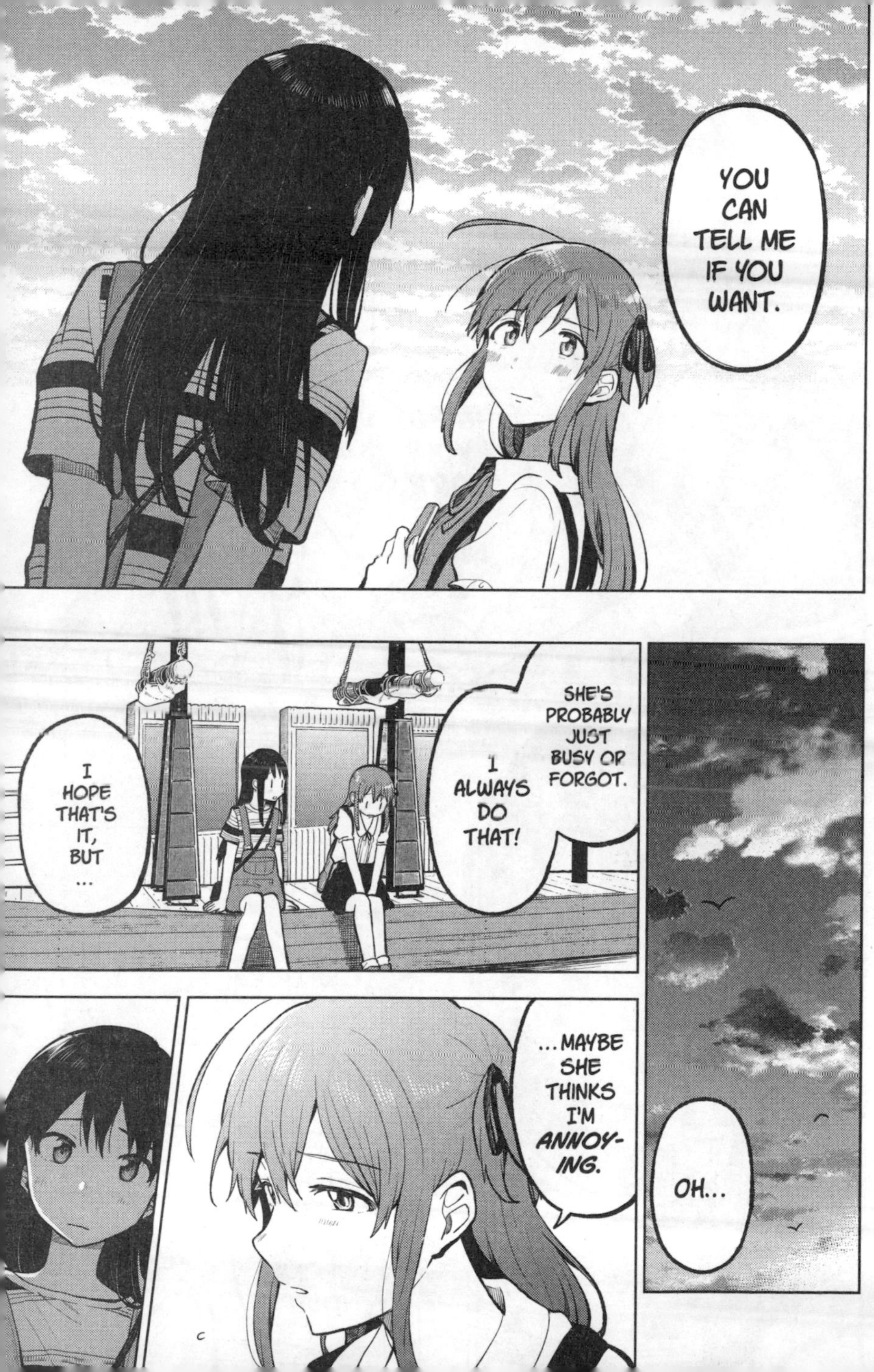
YOU CAN TELL ME IF YOU WANT.
OH...
SHE'S PROBABLY JUST BUSY OR FORGOT.
I ALWAYS DO THAT!
I HOPE THAT'S IT, BUT ...
...MAYBE SHE THINKS I'M *ANNOYING.*

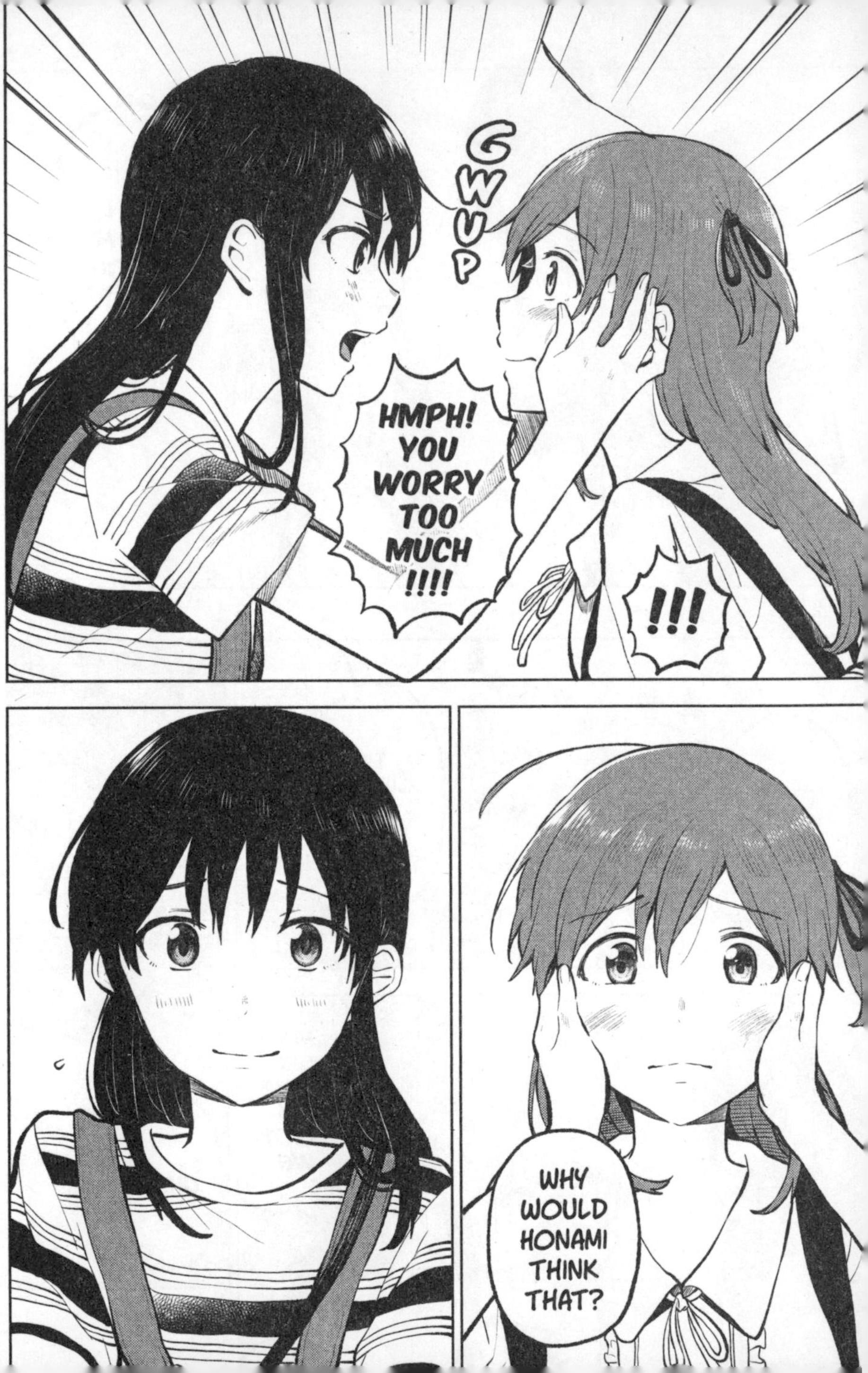
GWUP
HMPH! YOU WORRY TOO MUCH!!!!
!!!
WHY WOULD HONAMI THINK THAT?

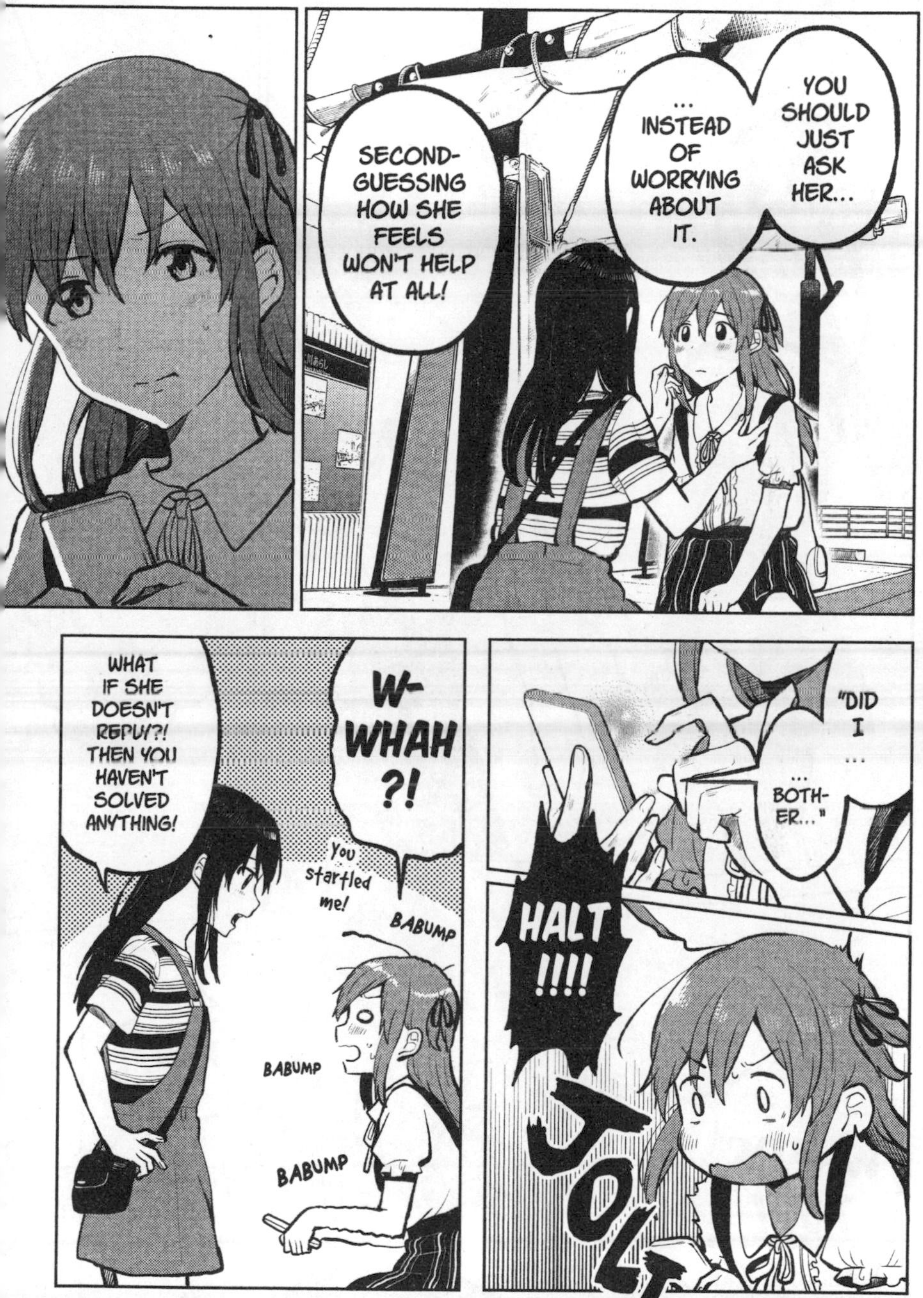
YOU SHOULD JUST ASK HER...
... INSTEAD OF WORRYING ABOUT IT.
SECOND-GUESSING HOW SHE FEELS WON'T HELP AT ALL!
"DID I ... ... BOTHER-ER..."
HALT !!!!
JOLT
W-WHAH?!
You startled me!
BABUMP
BABUMP
BABUMP
WHAT IF SHE DOESN'T REPLY?! THEN YOU HAVEN'T SOLVED ANYTHING!

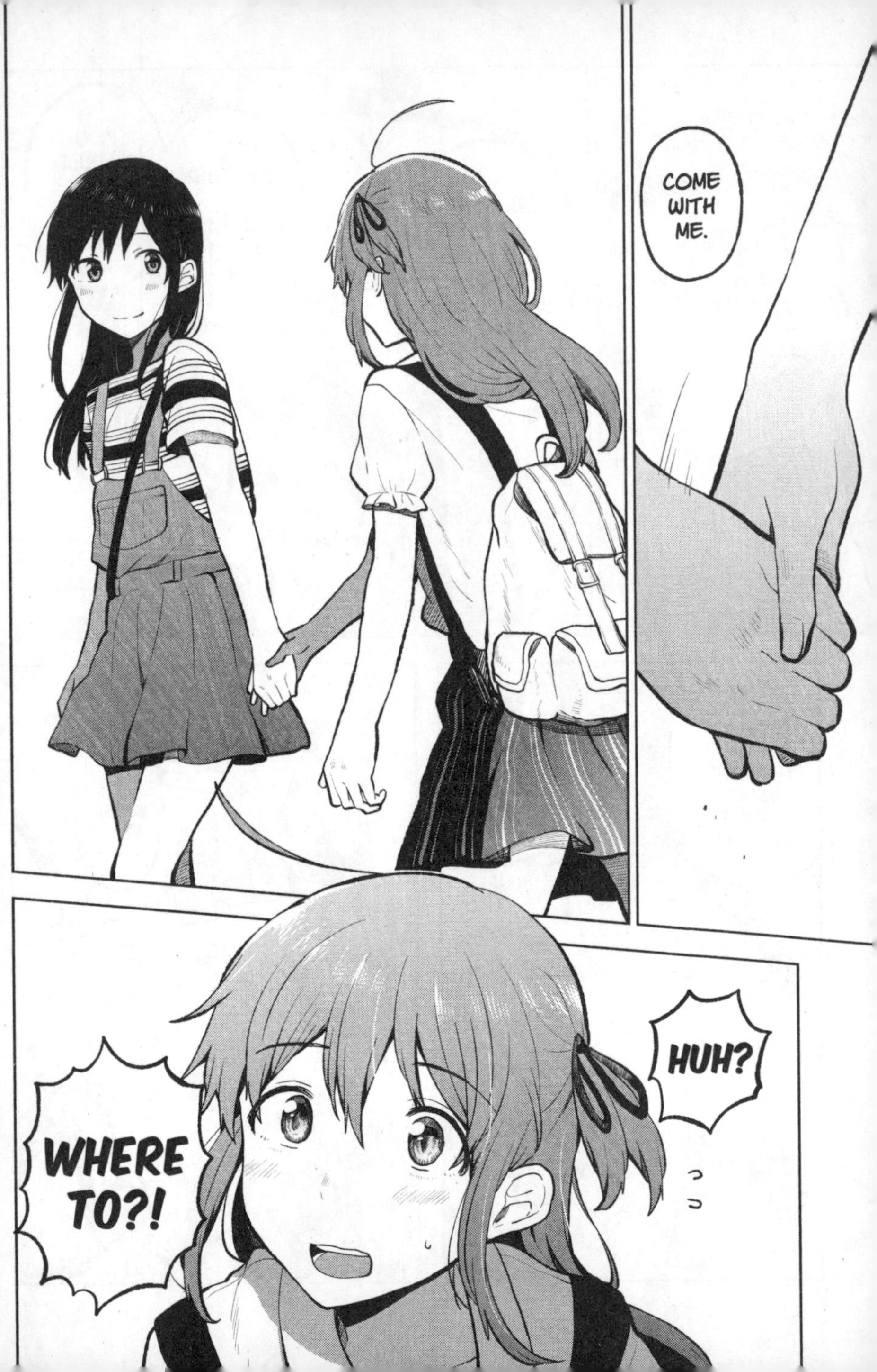
COME WITH ME.
HUH?
WHERE TO?!

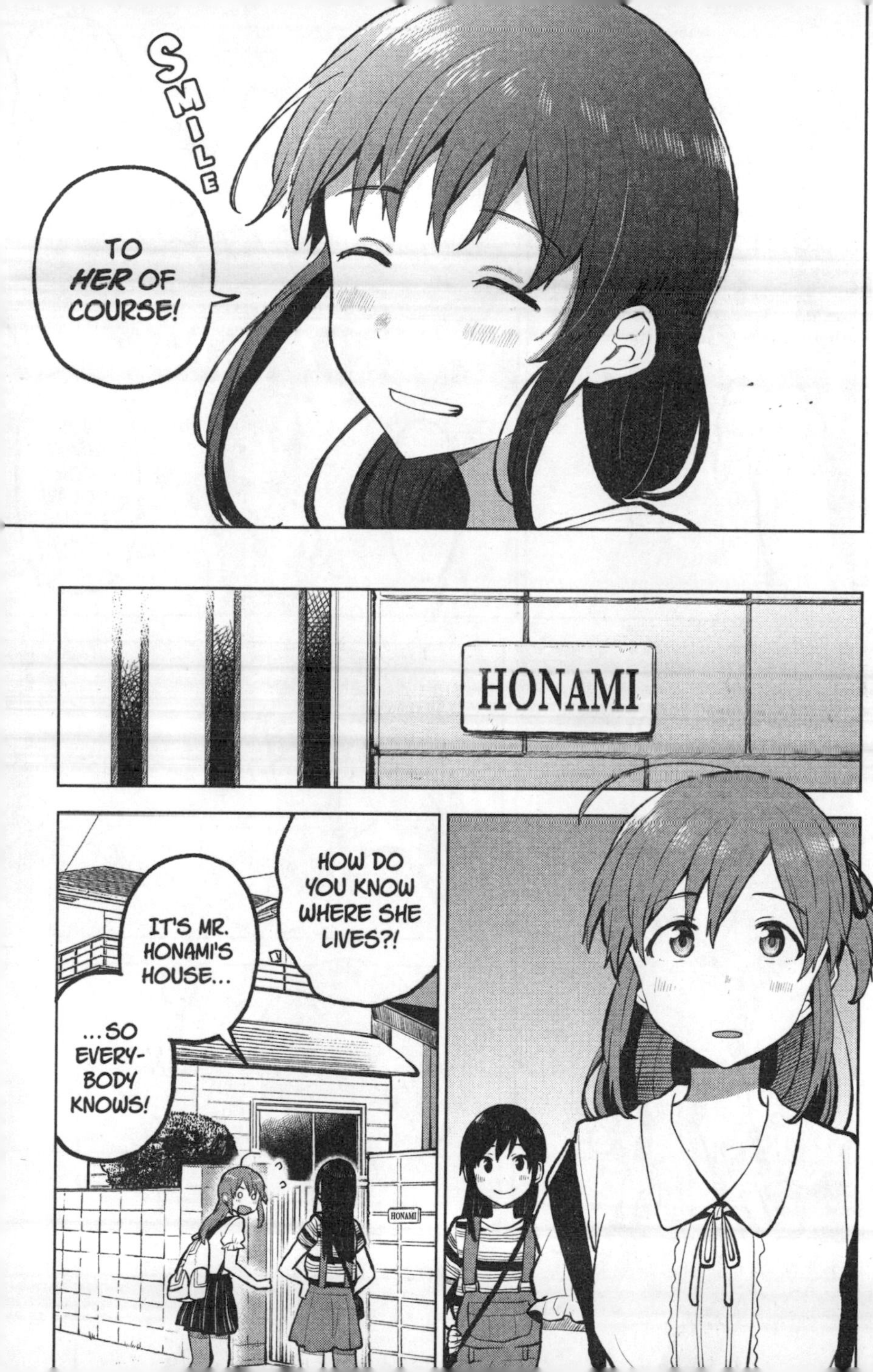
SMILE
TO *HER* OF COURSE!
HONAMI
HOW DO YOU KNOW WHERE SHE LIVES?!
IT'S MR. HONAMI'S HOUSE...
...SO EVERY-BODY KNOWS!
HONAMI

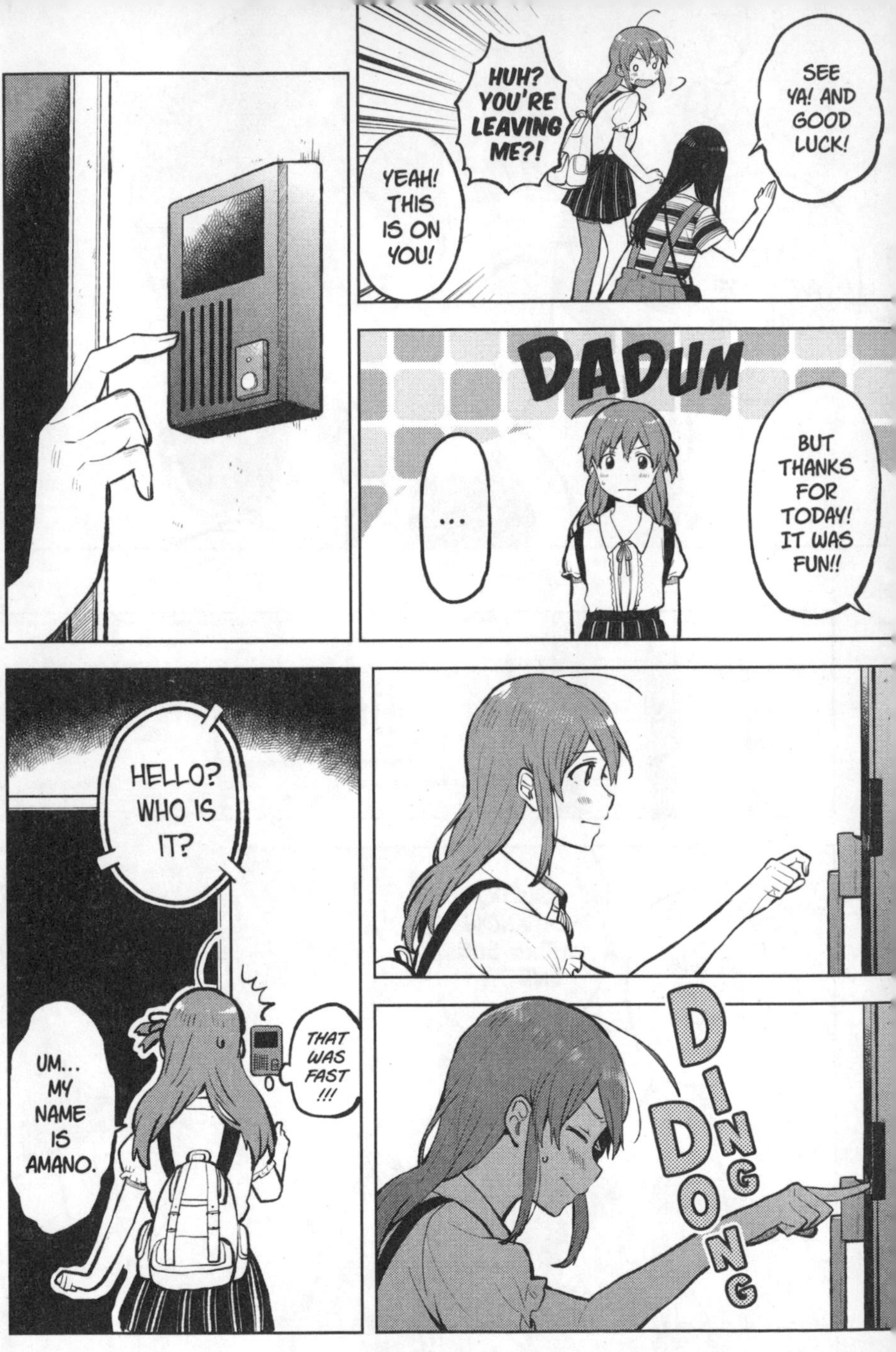
SEE YA! AND GOOD LUCK!
HUH? YOU'RE LEAVING ME?!
YEAH! THIS IS ON YOU!
DADUM
BUT THANKS FOR TODAY! IT WAS FUN!!
...
DING DONG
HELLO? WHO IS IT?
THAT WAS FAST!!!
UM... MY NAME IS AMANO.

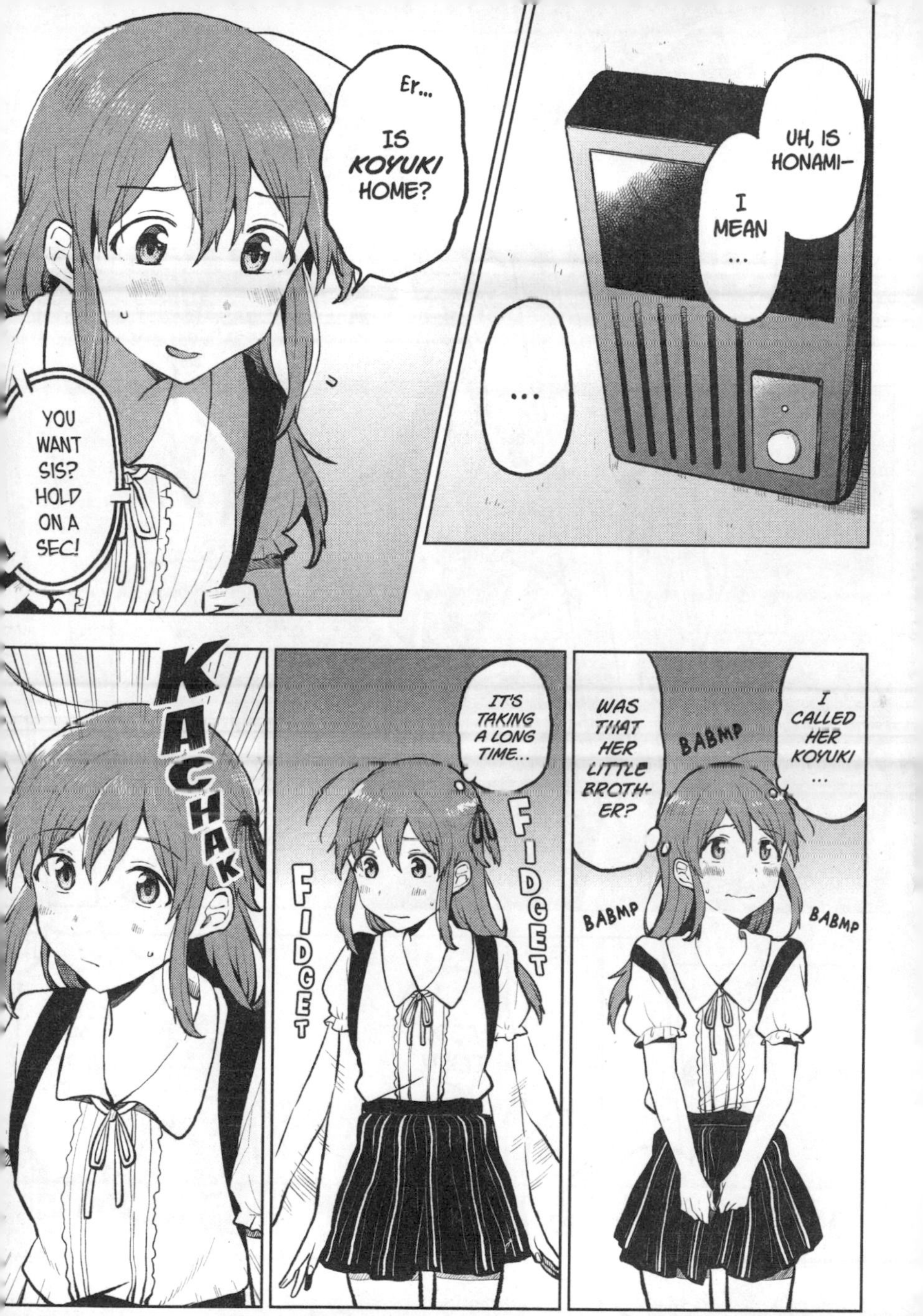
UH, IS HONAMI—
I MEAN ...
...
Er...
IS KOYUKI HOME?
YOU WANT SIS? HOLD ON A SEC!
I CALLED HER KOYUKI ...
BABMP
WAS THAT HER LITTLE BROTHER?
BABMP
BABMP
IT'S TAKING A LONG TIME...
FIDGET
FIDGET
KACHAK

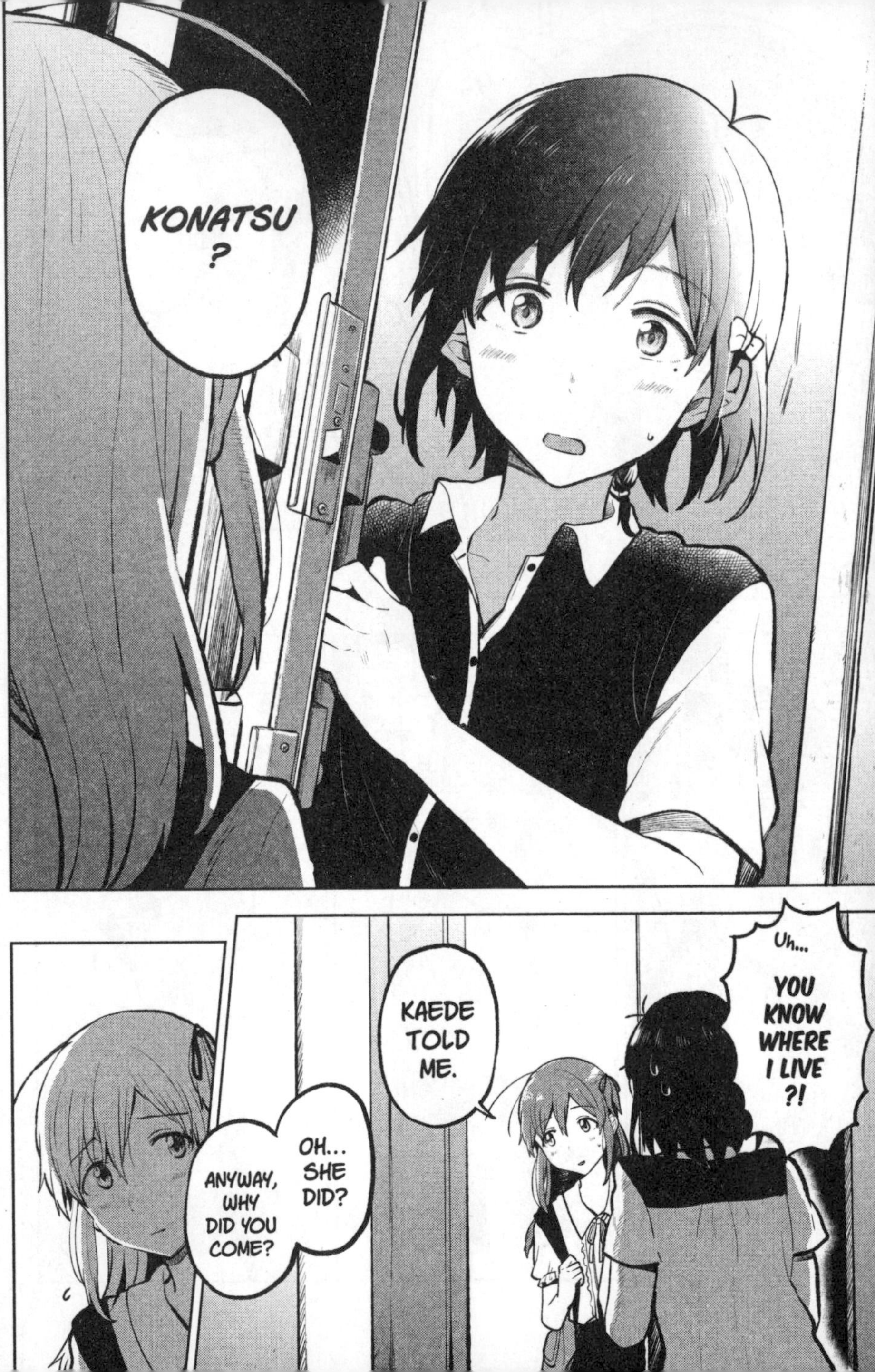
KONATSU ?
Uh... YOU KNOW WHERE I LIVE ?!
KAEDE TOLD ME.
OH... SHE DID?
ANYWAY, WHY DID YOU COME?

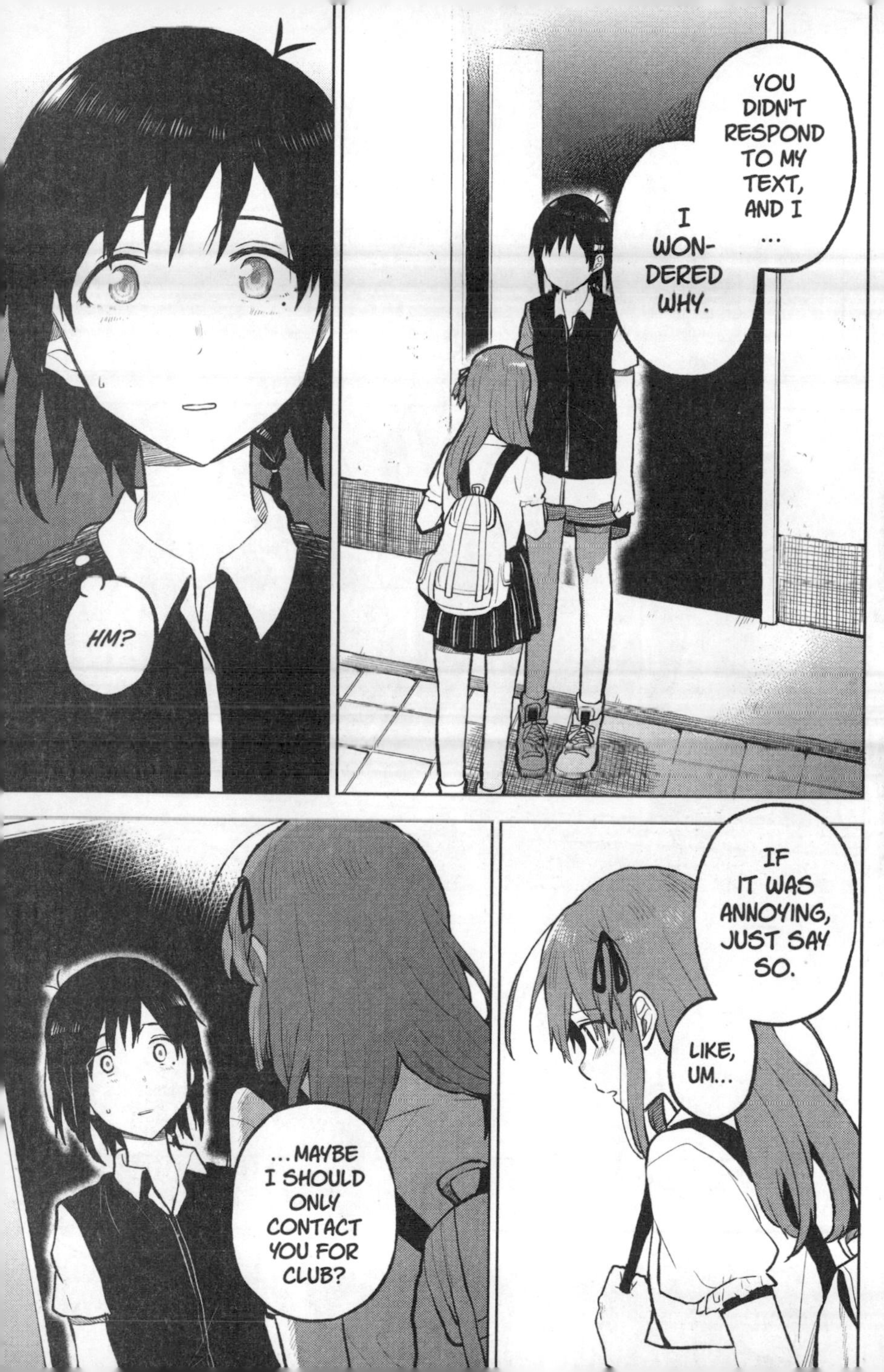
YOU DIDN'T RESPOND TO MY TEXT, AND I ...
I WONDERED WHY.
HM?
IF IT WAS ANNOYING, JUST SAY SO.
LIKE, UM...
...MAYBE I SHOULD ONLY CONTACT YOU FOR CLUB?

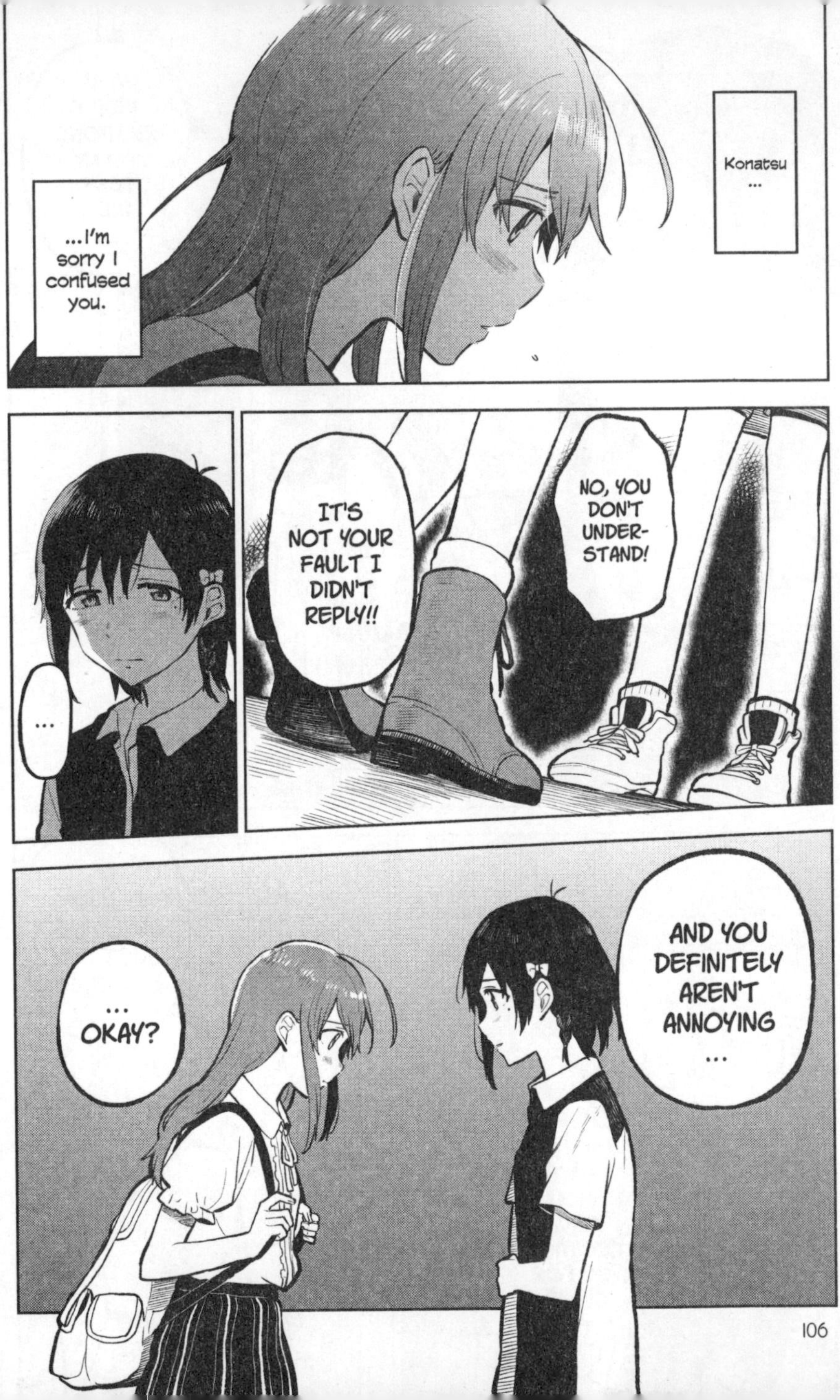
Konatsu ...
...I'm sorry I confused you.
NO, YOU DON'T UNDER-STAND!
IT'S NOT YOUR FAULT I DIDN'T REPLY!!
...
AND YOU DEFINITELY AREN'T ANNOYING ...
... OKAY?

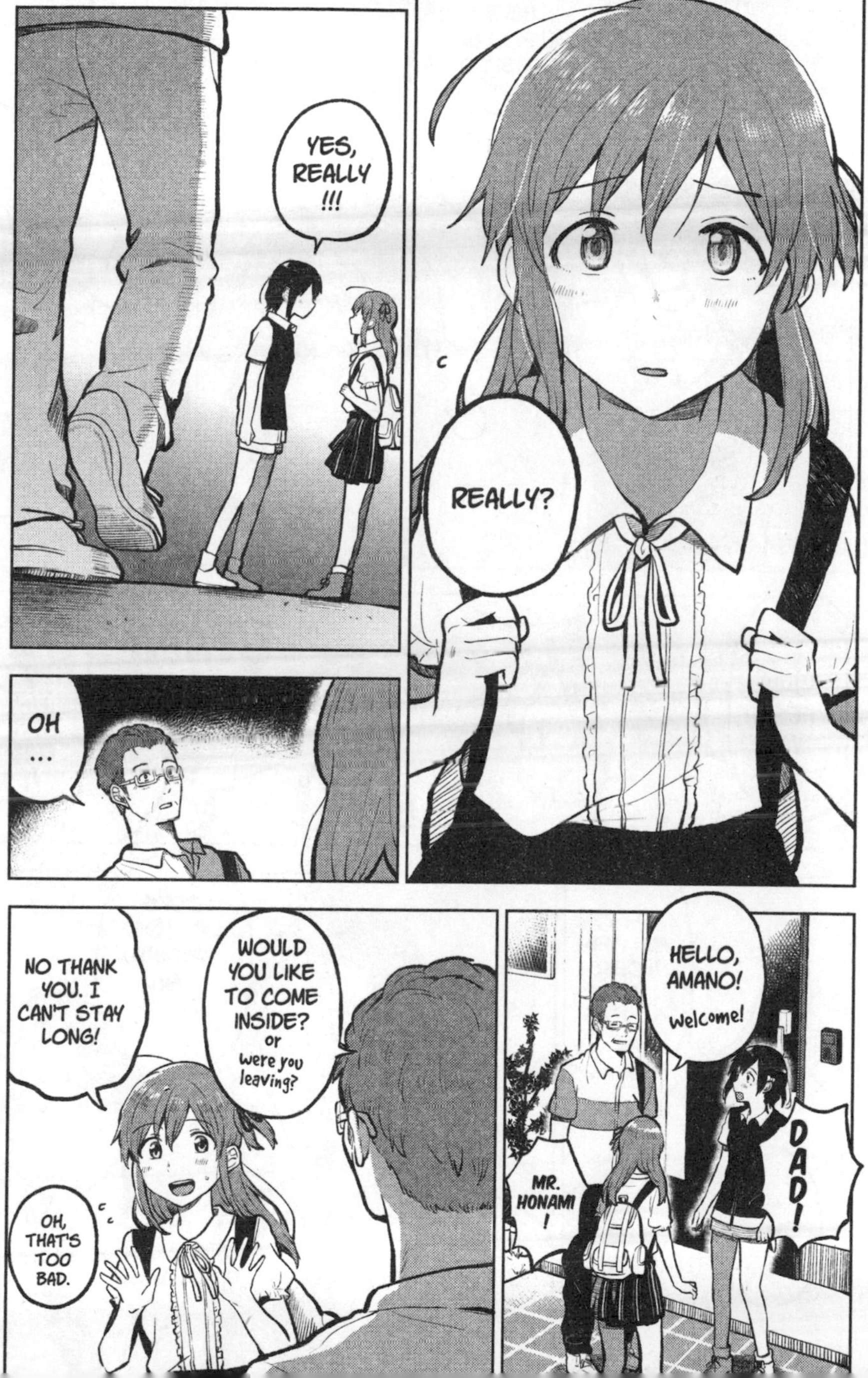
REALLY?
YES, REALLY !!!
OH ...
HELLO, AMANO! welcome!
DAD!
MR. HONAMI!
WOULD YOU LIKE TO COME INSIDE? or were you leaving?
NO THANK YOU. I CAN'T STAY LONG!
OH, THAT'S TOO BAD.

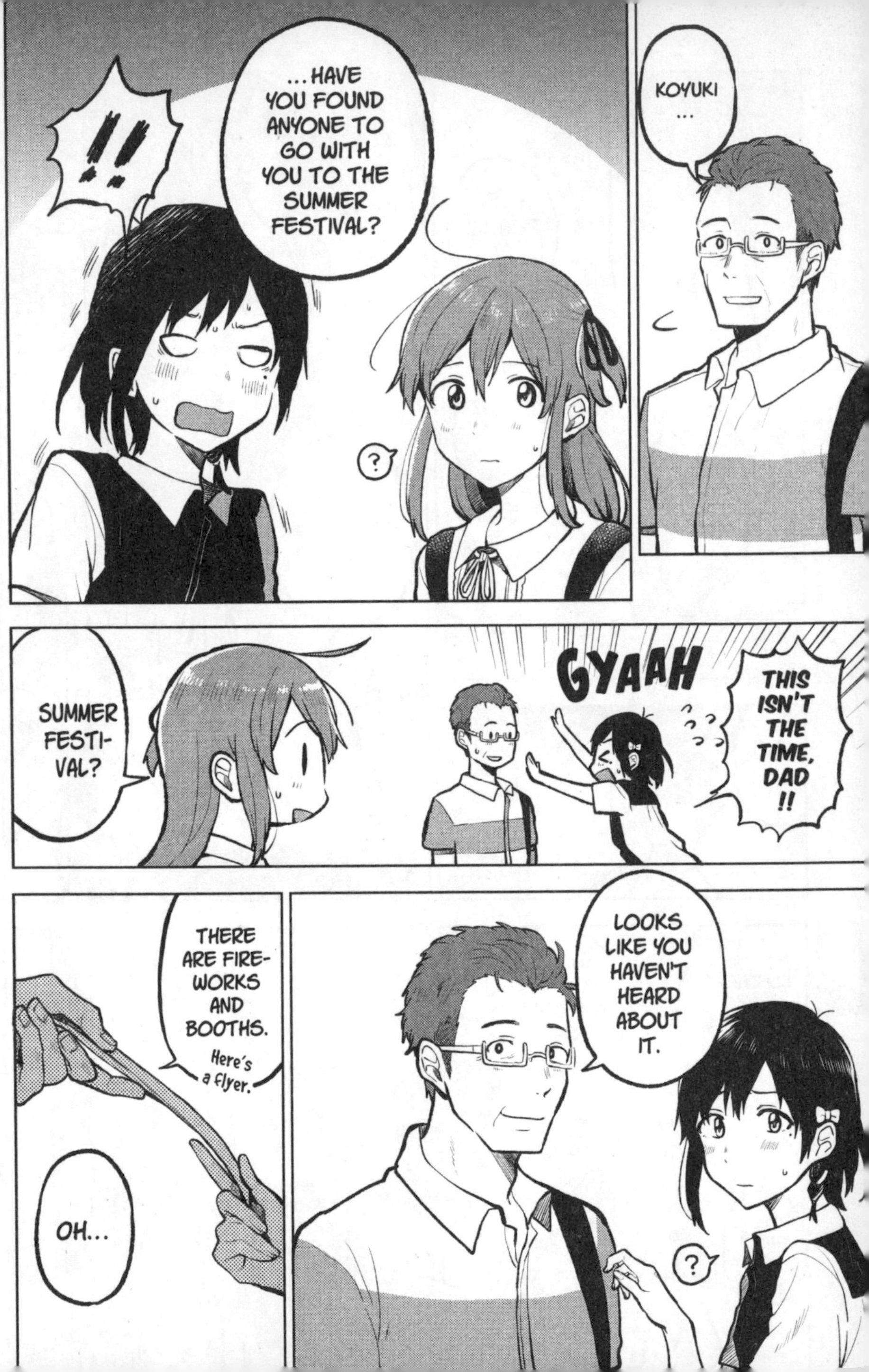
KOYUKI ...
... HAVE YOU FOUND ANYONE TO GO WITH YOU TO THE SUMMER FESTIVAL?
!!
?
GYAAH
THIS ISN'T THE TIME, DAD !!
SUMMER FESTI-VAL?
LOOKS LIKE YOU HAVEN'T HEARD ABOUT IT.
?
THERE ARE FIRE-WORKS AND BOOTHS.
Here's a flyer.
OH...

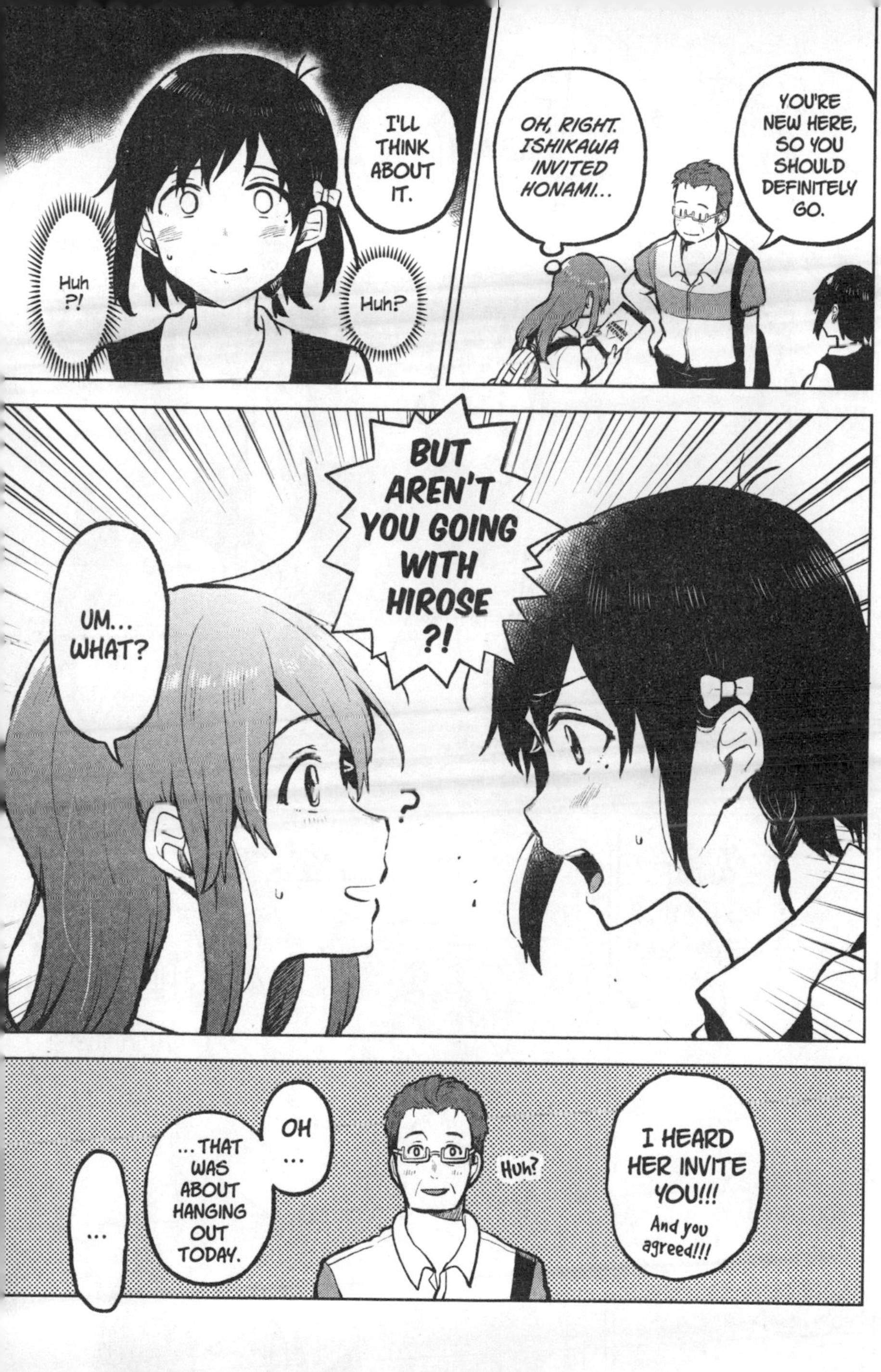
YOU'RE NEW HERE, SO YOU SHOULD DEFINITELY GO.
OH, RIGHT. ISHIKAWA INVITED HONAMI...
I'LL THINK ABOUT IT.
Huh?
Huh ?!
BUT AREN'T YOU GOING WITH HIROSE ?!
UM... WHAT?
I HEARD HER INVITE YOU!!!
And you agreed!!!
Huh?
OH ...
...THAT WAS ABOUT HANGING OUT TODAY.
...

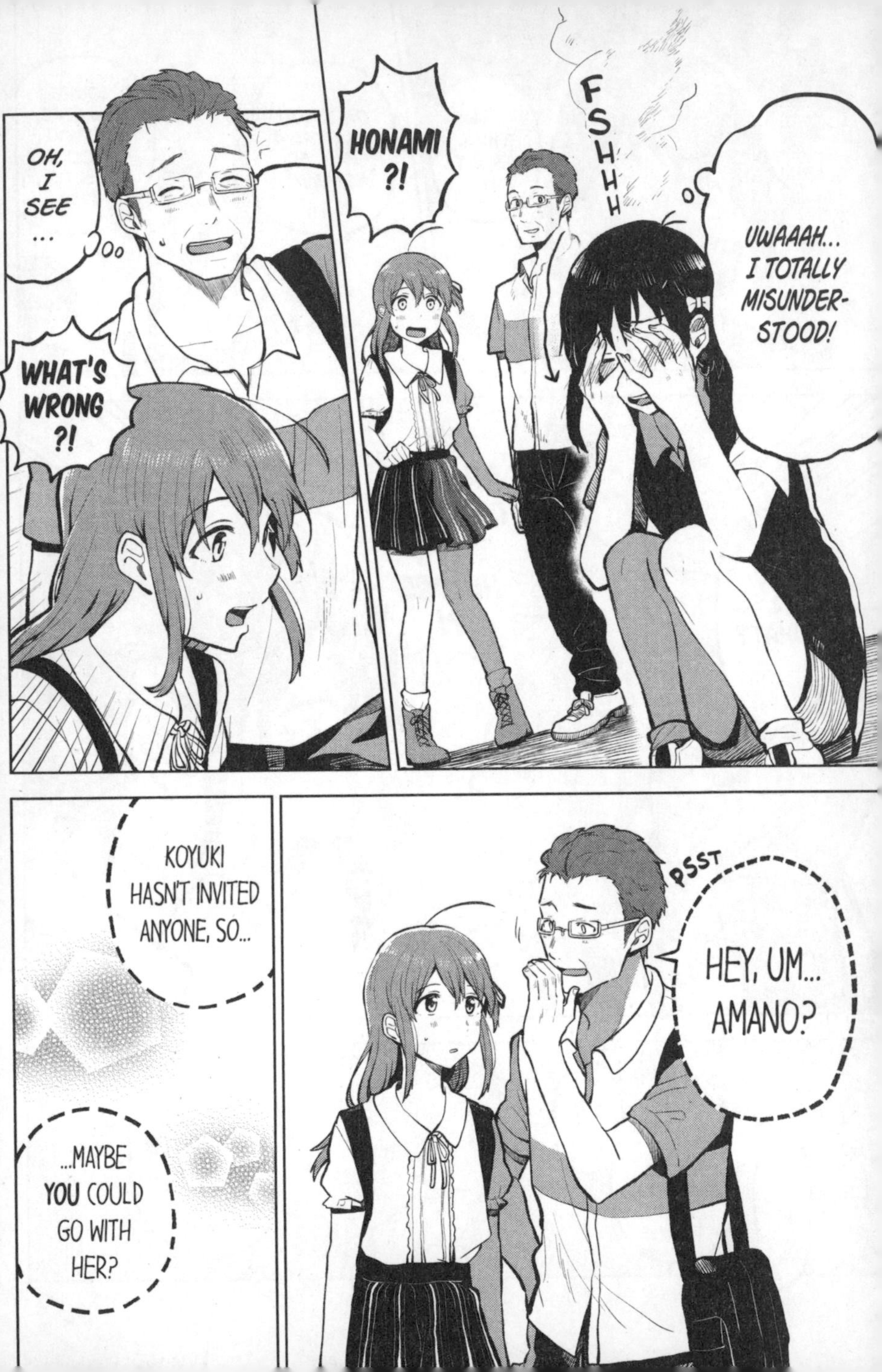
UWAAAH... I TOTALLY MISUNDERSTOOD!
FSHHH
HONAMI?!
OH, I SEE...
WHAT'S WRONG?!
PSST
HEY, UM... AMANO?
KOYUKI HASN'T INVITED ANYONE, SO...
...MAYBE YOU COULD GO WITH HER?

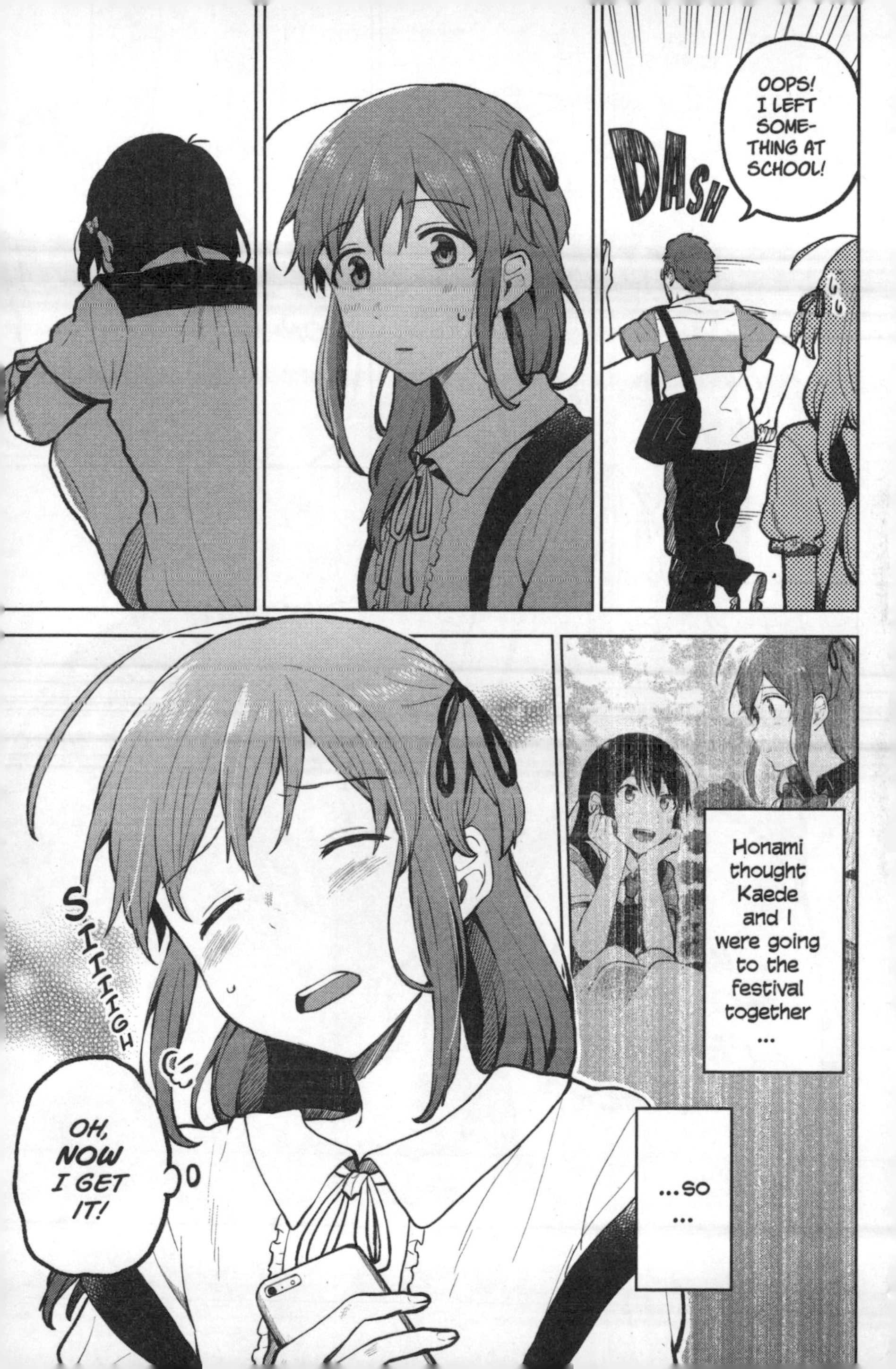
OOPS! I LEFT SOME-THING AT SCHOOL!
DASH
Honami thought Kaede and I were going to the festival together ...
...SO ...
SIIIIIGH
OH, NOW I GET IT!

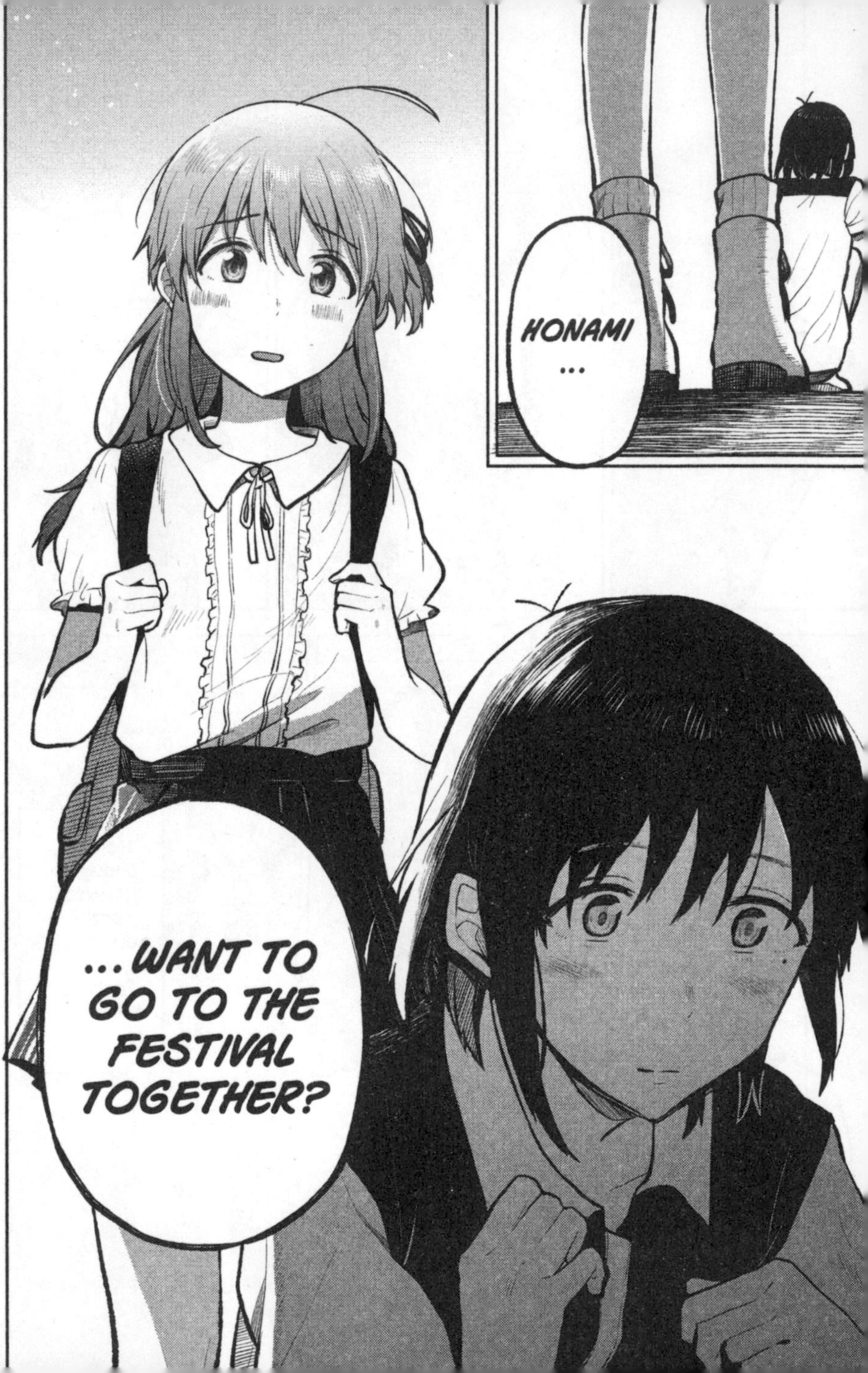
HONAMI ...
...WANT TO GO TO THE FESTIVAL TOGETHER?

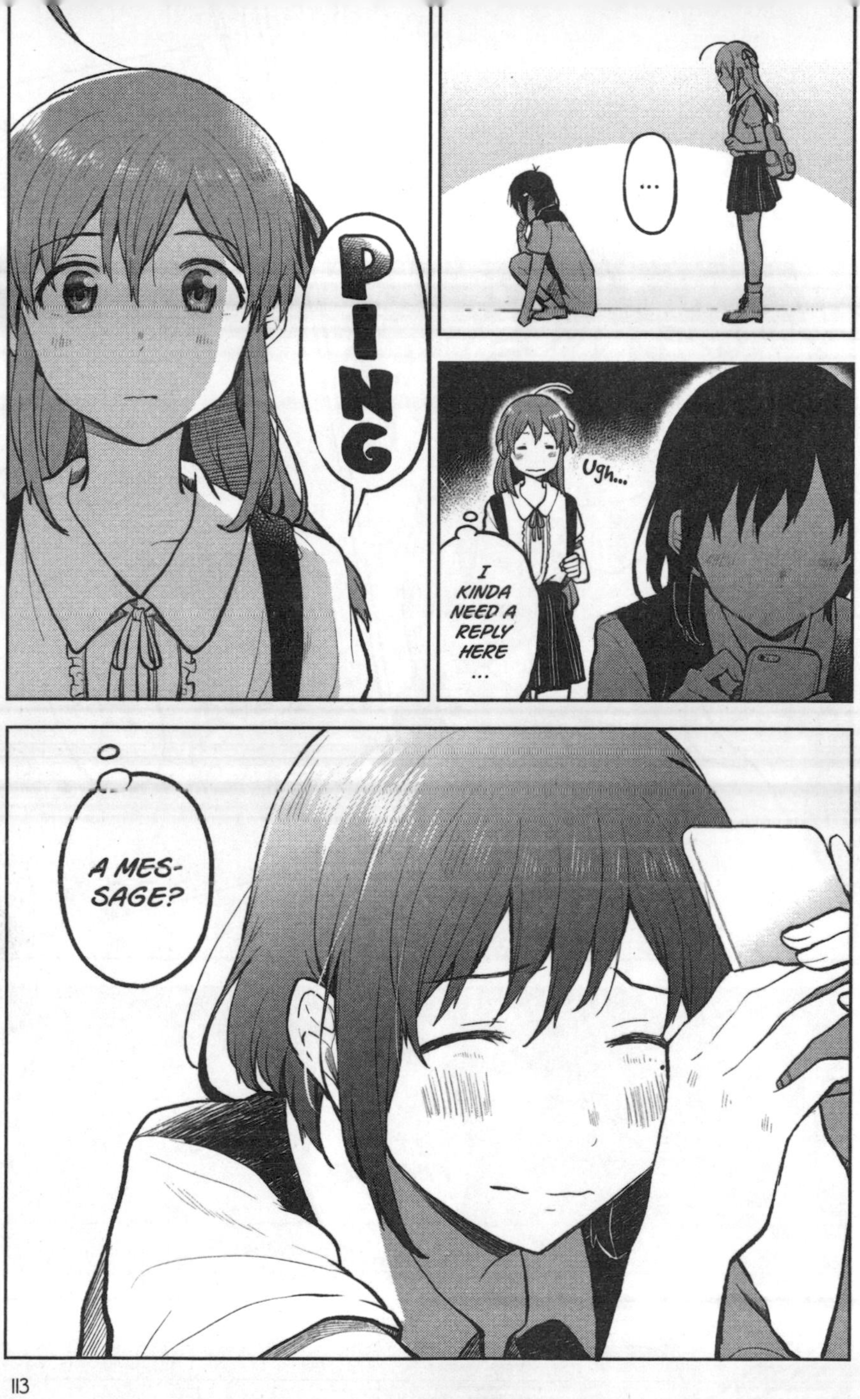
...
Ugh...
I KINDA NEED A REPLY HERE ...
PING
A MES-SAGE?

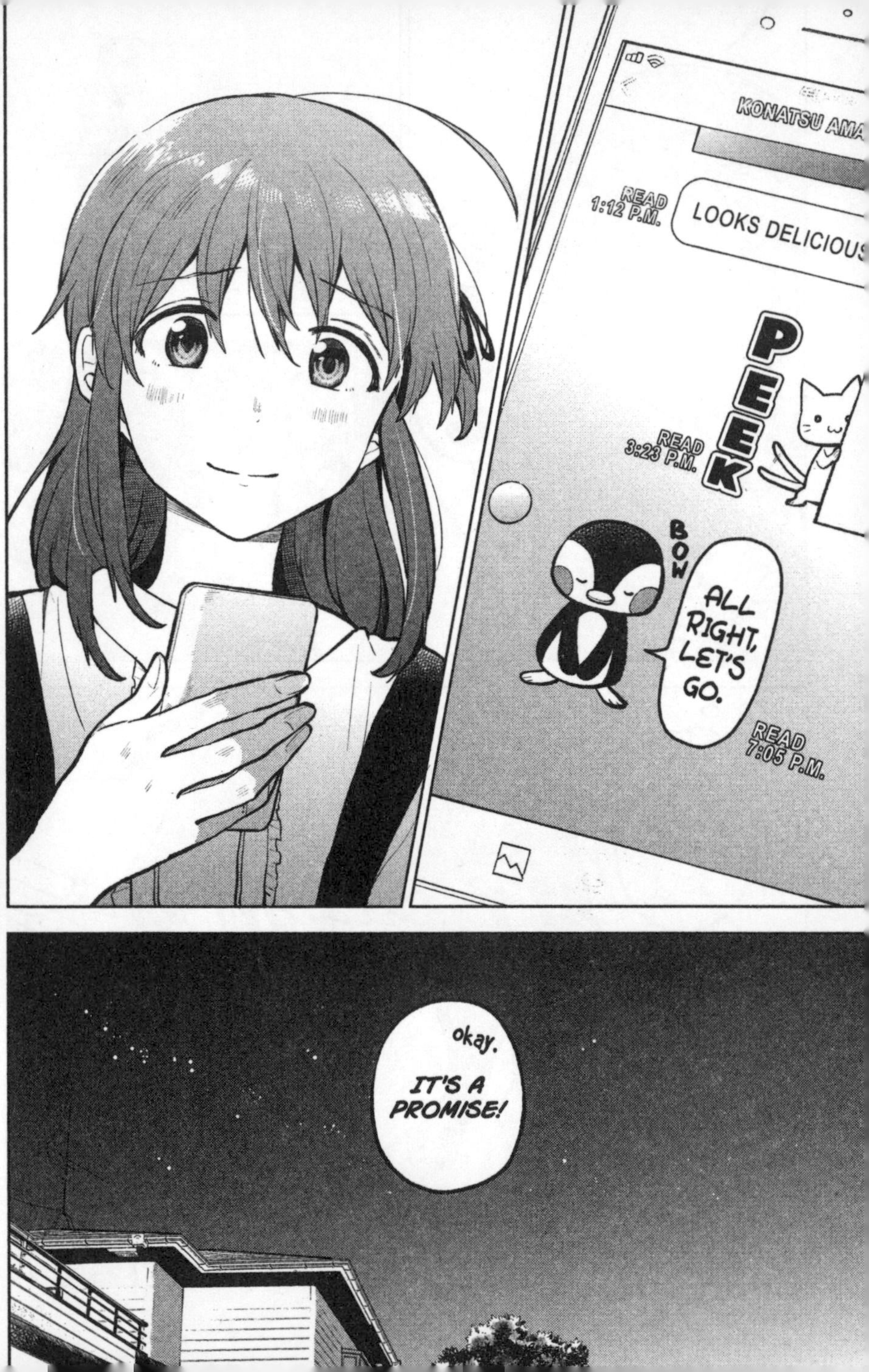
KONATSU AMA
READ 1:12 P.M.
LOOKS DELICIOUS
PEEK
READ 3:23 P.M.
BOW
ALL RIGHT, LET'S GO.
READ 7:05 P.M.
okay.
IT'S A PROMISE!

A Tropical Fish
Yearns for Snow

Tank 8

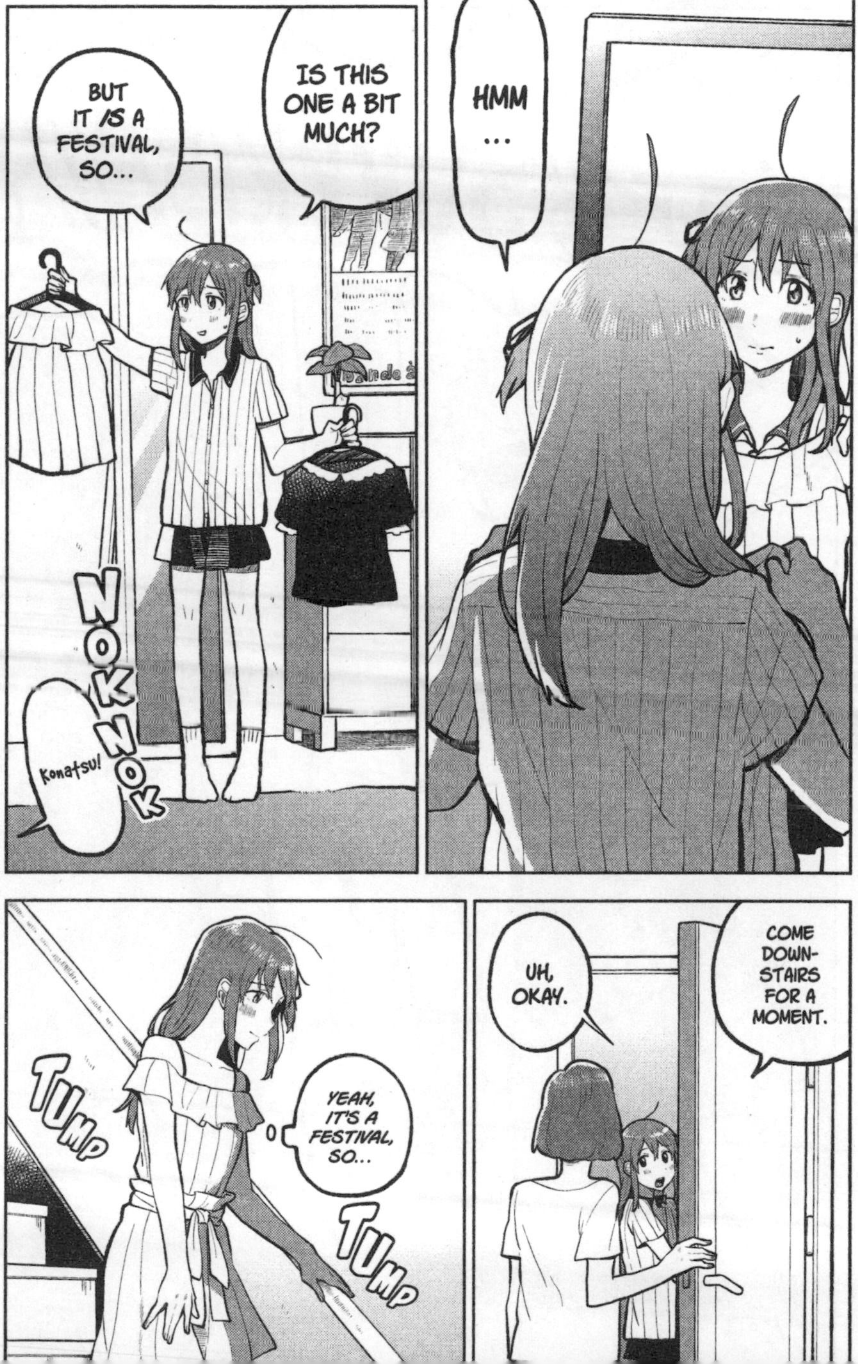
HMM...
IS THIS ONE A BIT MUCH?
BUT IT IS A FESTIVAL, SO...
NOK NOK
Konatsu!
COME DOWN-STAIRS FOR A MOMENT.
UH, OKAY.
TUMP
YEAH, IT'S A FESTIVAL, SO...
TUMP

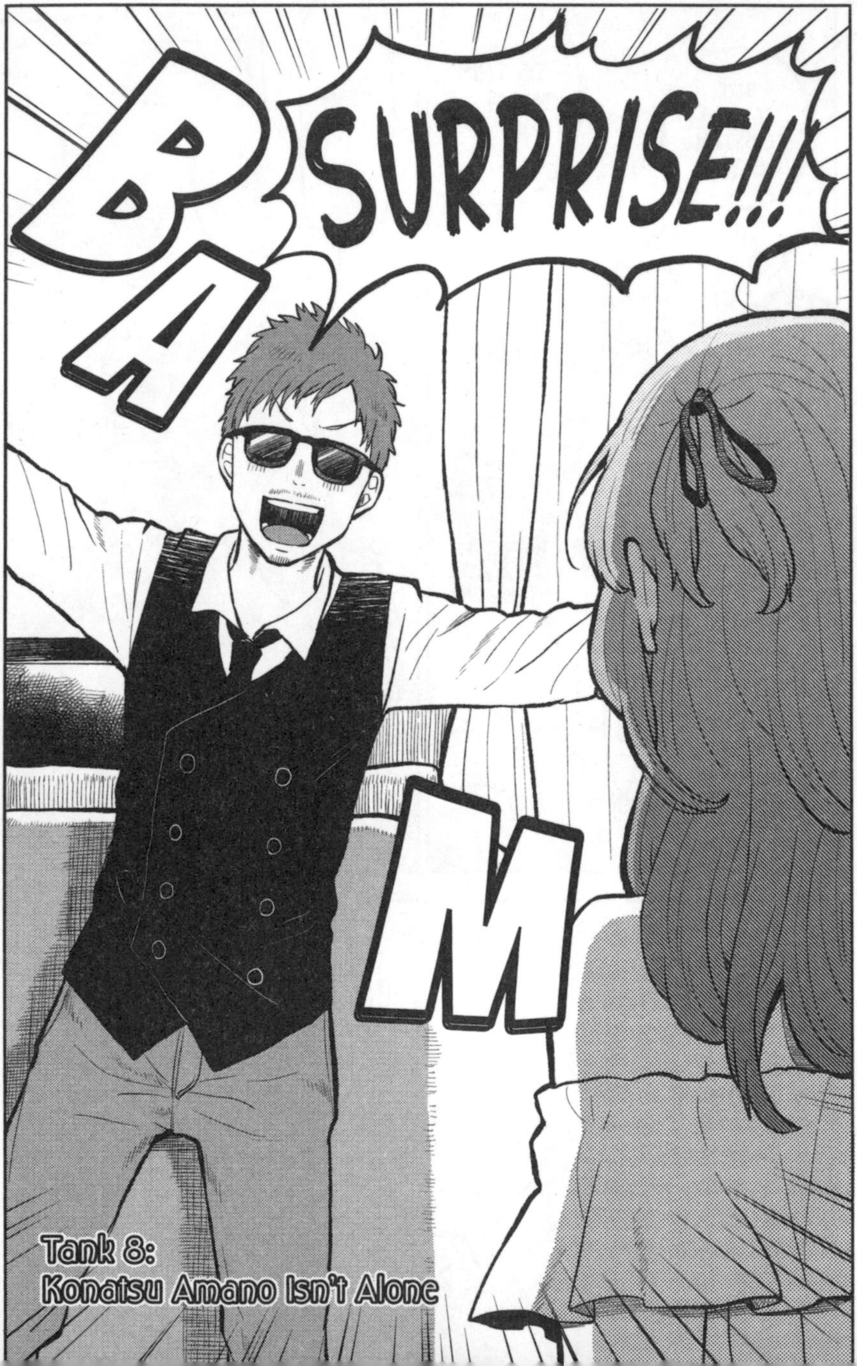
SURPRISE!!!
BAM
Tank 8:
Konatsu Amano Isn't Alone

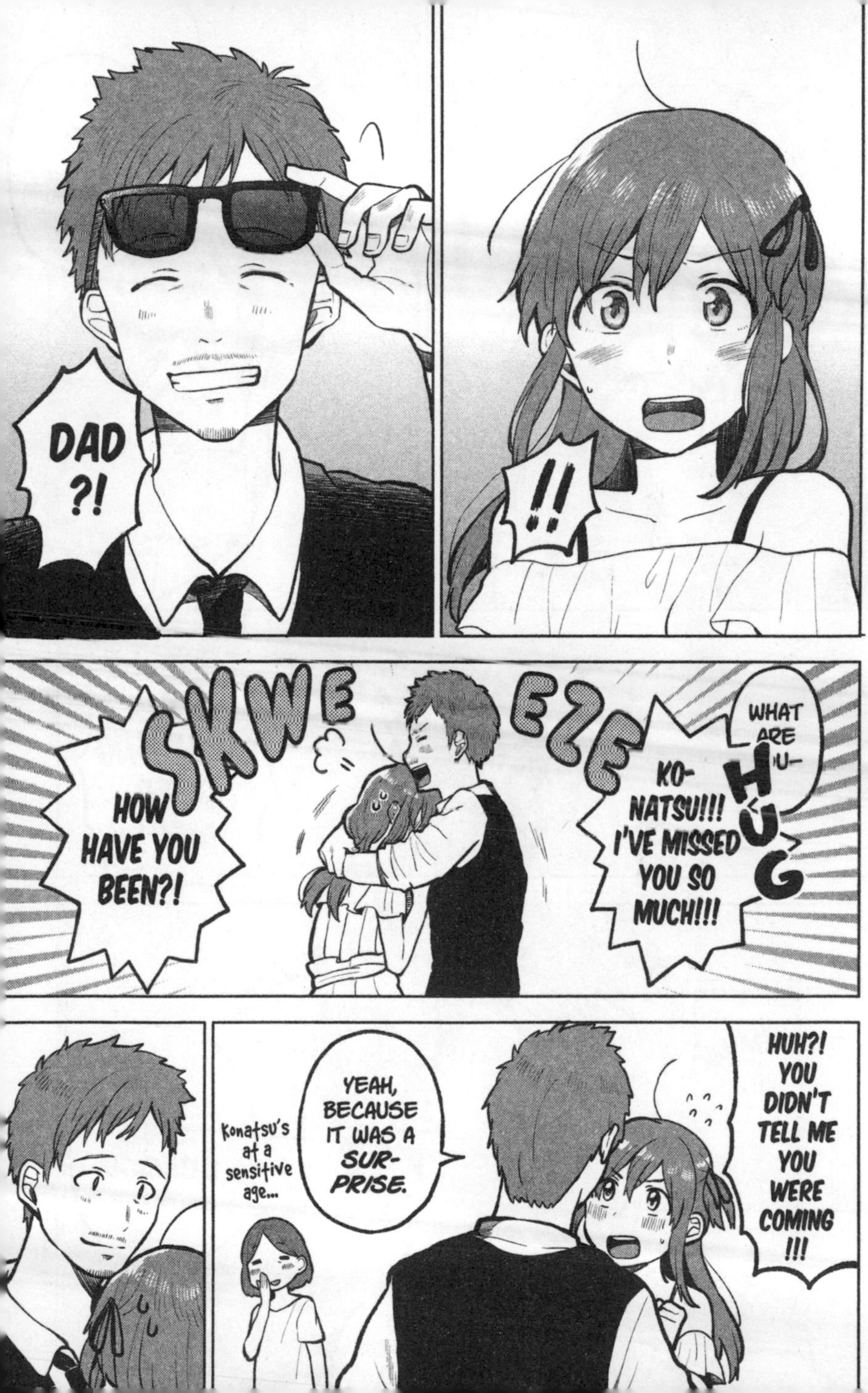
!!
DAD ?!
WHAT ARE U–
KO-NATSU!!! I'VE MISSED YOU SO MUCH!!!
HUG
SKWEEZE
HOW HAVE YOU BEEN?!
HUH?! YOU DIDN'T TELL ME YOU WERE COMING !!!
YEAH, BECAUSE IT WAS A SURPRISE.
Konatsu's at a sensitive age...

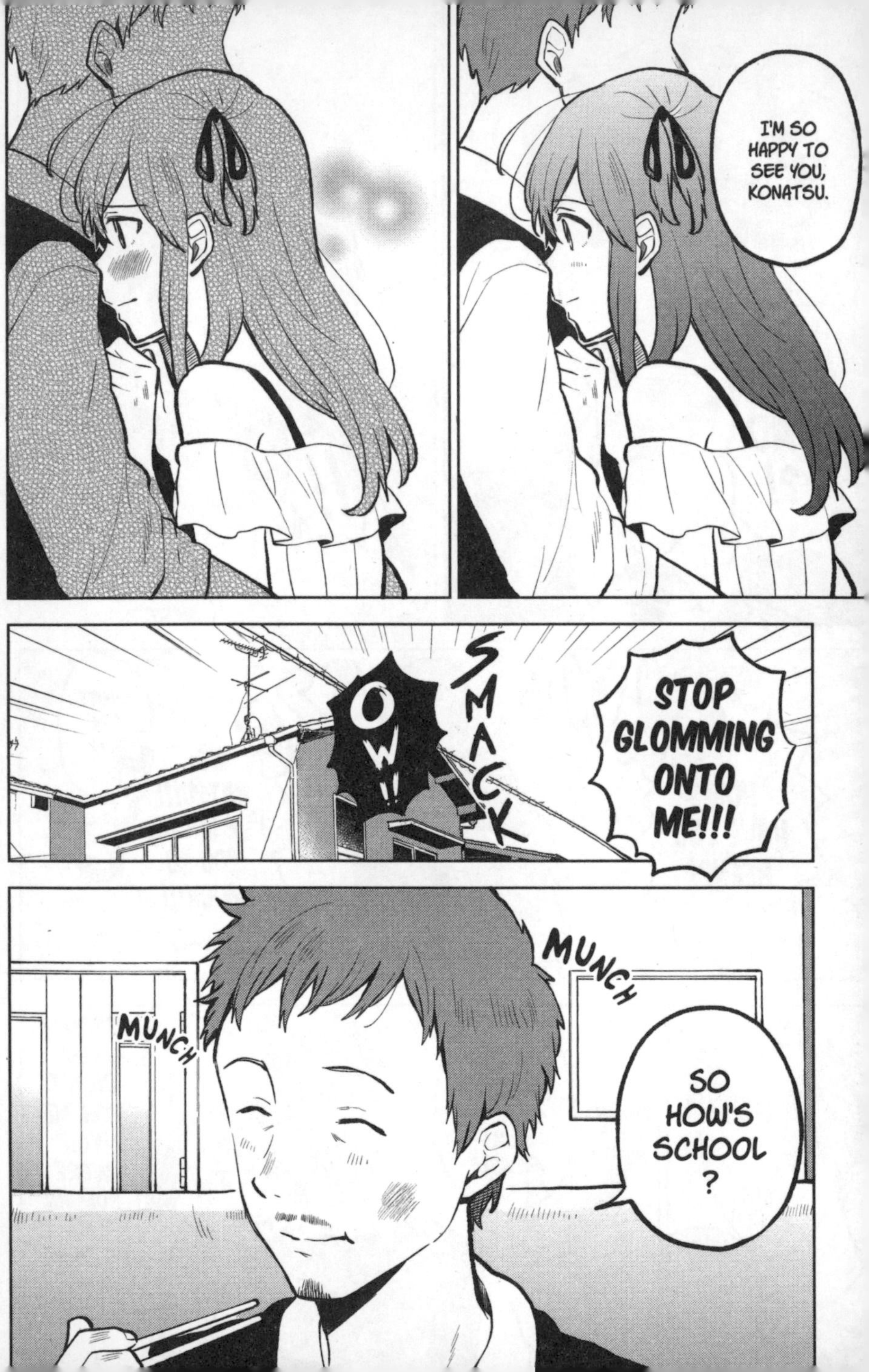
I'M SO HAPPY TO SEE YOU, KONATSU.
STOP GLOMMING ONTO ME!!!
SMACK
OW!!
MUNCH
SO HOW'S SCHOOL?
MUNCH

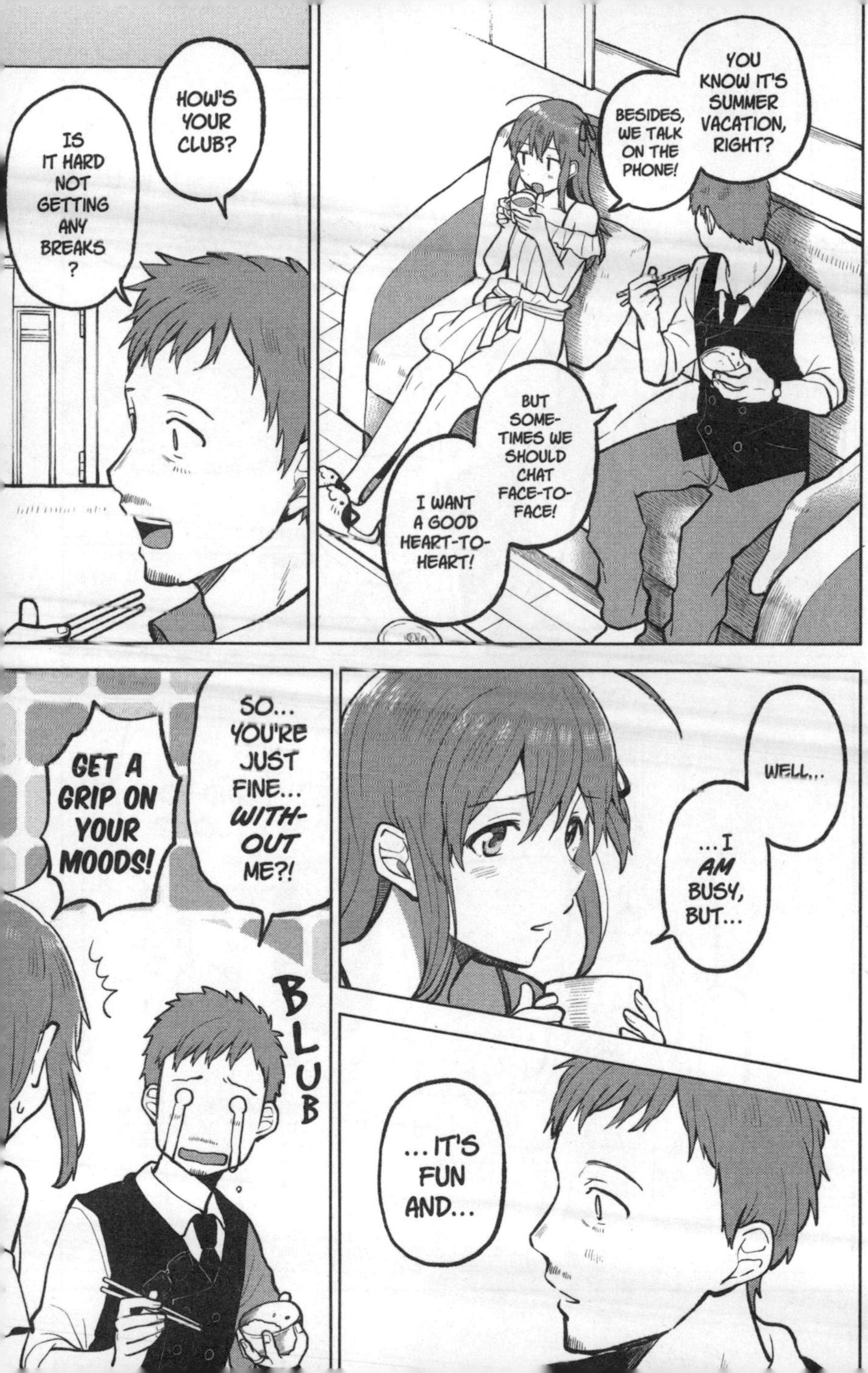
YOU KNOW IT'S SUMMER VACATION, RIGHT?
BESIDES, WE TALK ON THE PHONE!
BUT SOME-TIMES WE SHOULD CHAT FACE-TO-FACE!
I WANT A GOOD HEART-TO-HEART!
HOW'S YOUR CLUB?
IS IT HARD NOT GETTING ANY BREAKS?
WELL...
...I AM BUSY, BUT...
...IT'S FUN AND...
SO... YOU'RE JUST FINE... WITH-OUT ME?!
GET A GRIP ON YOUR MOODS!
BLUB

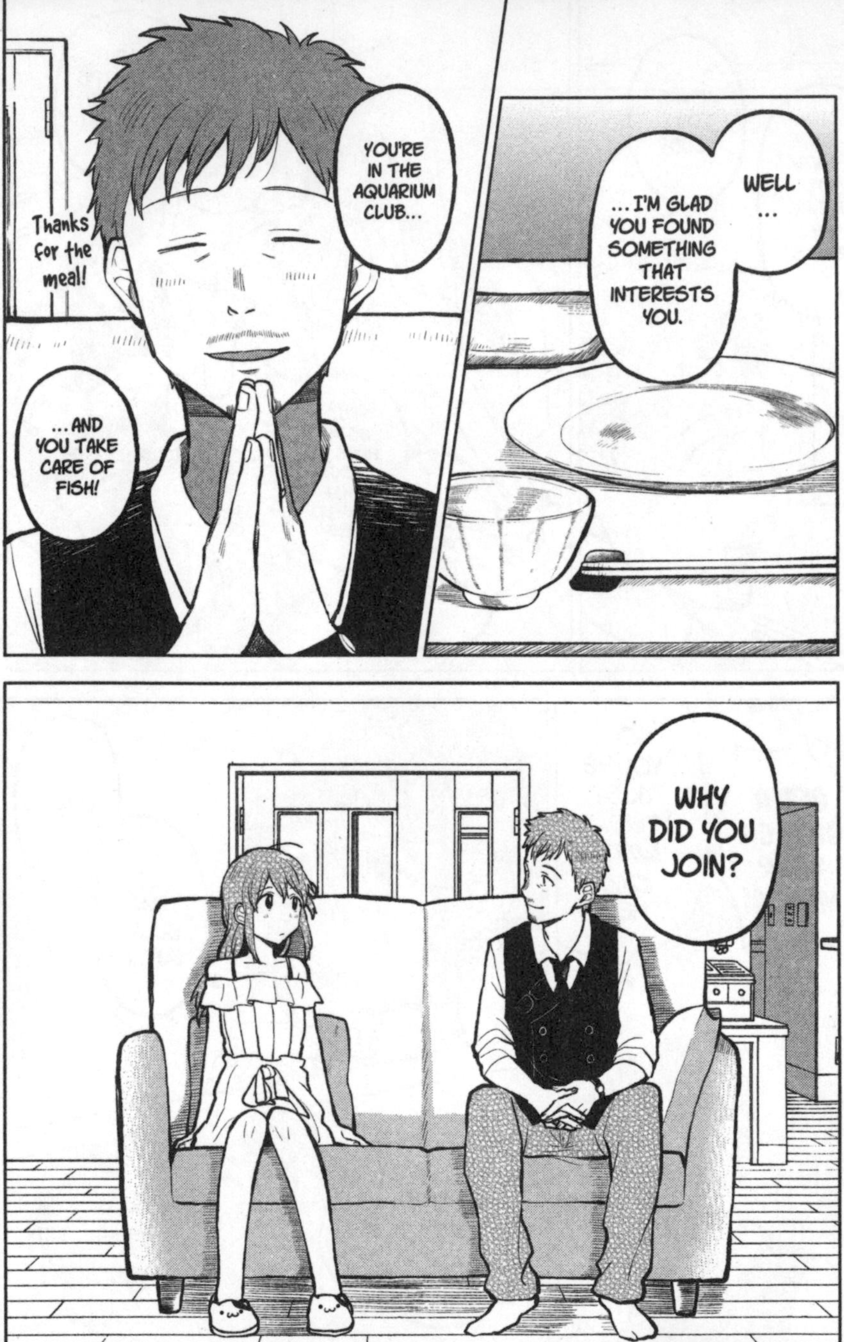
WELL ...
... I'M GLAD YOU FOUND SOMETHING THAT INTERESTS YOU.
YOU'RE IN THE AQUARIUM CLUB...
Thanks for the meal!
... AND YOU TAKE CARE OF FISH!
WHY DID YOU JOIN?

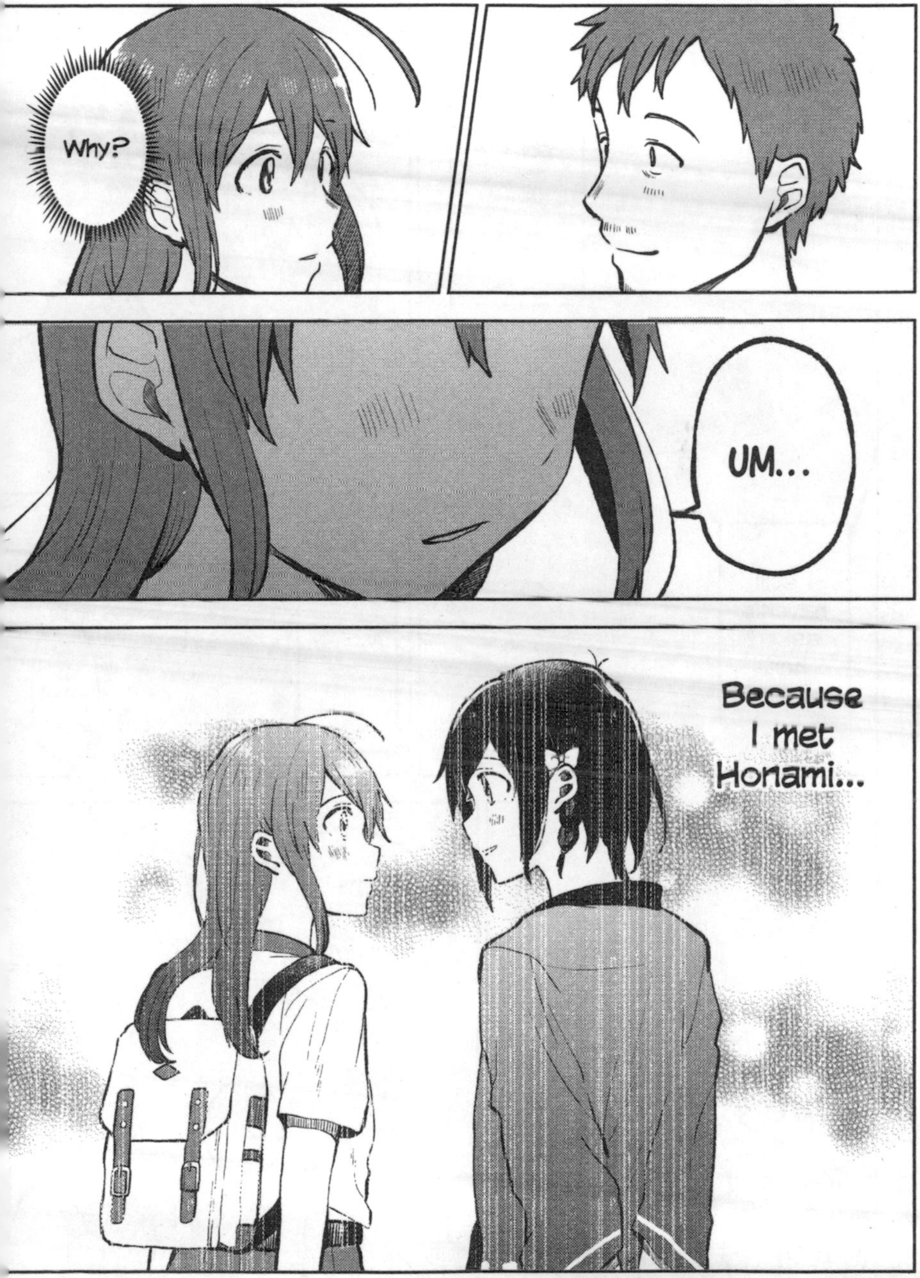
Why?
UM...
Because I met Honami...

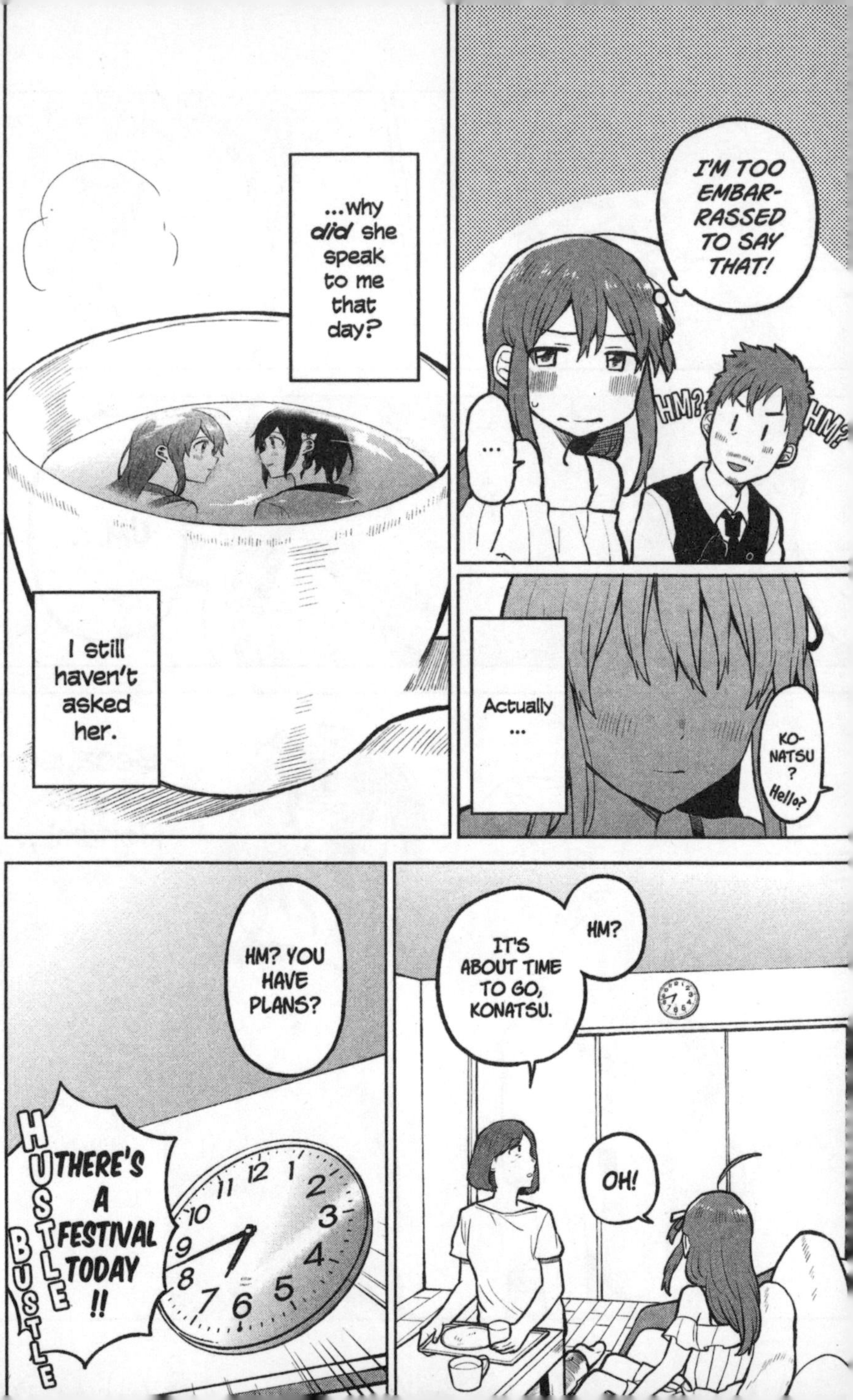
I'M TOO EMBARRASSED TO SAY THAT!
HM?
HM?
...
KO-NATSU? Hello?
Actually...
...why *did* she speak to me that day?
I still haven't asked her.
HM?
IT'S ABOUT TIME TO GO, KONATSU.
OH!
HM? YOU HAVE PLANS?
THERE'S A FESTIVAL TODAY!!
HUSTLE
BUSTLE

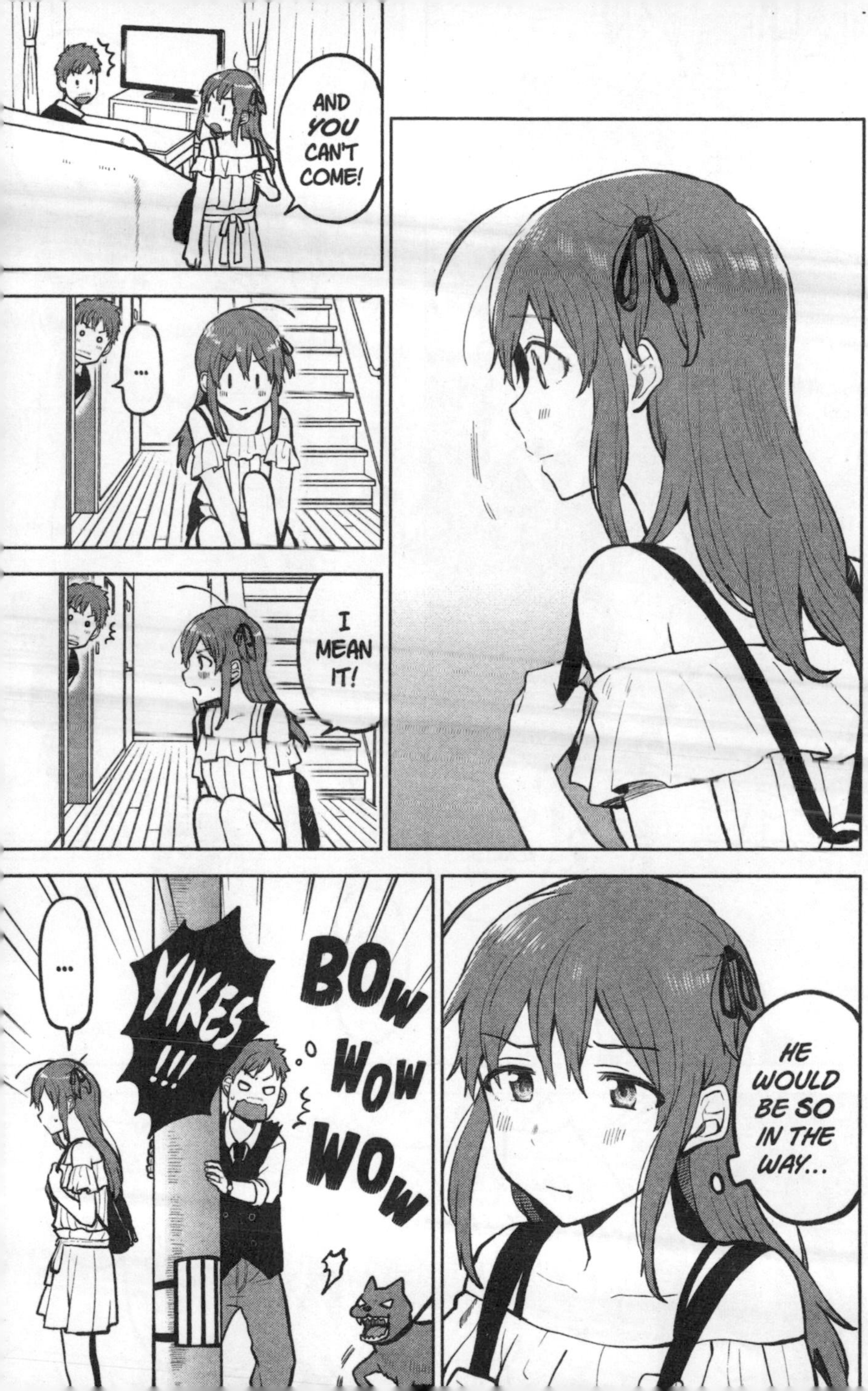
AND YOU CAN'T COME!
...
I MEAN IT!
HE WOULD BE SO IN THE WAY...
...
YIKES!!!
BOW WOW WOW

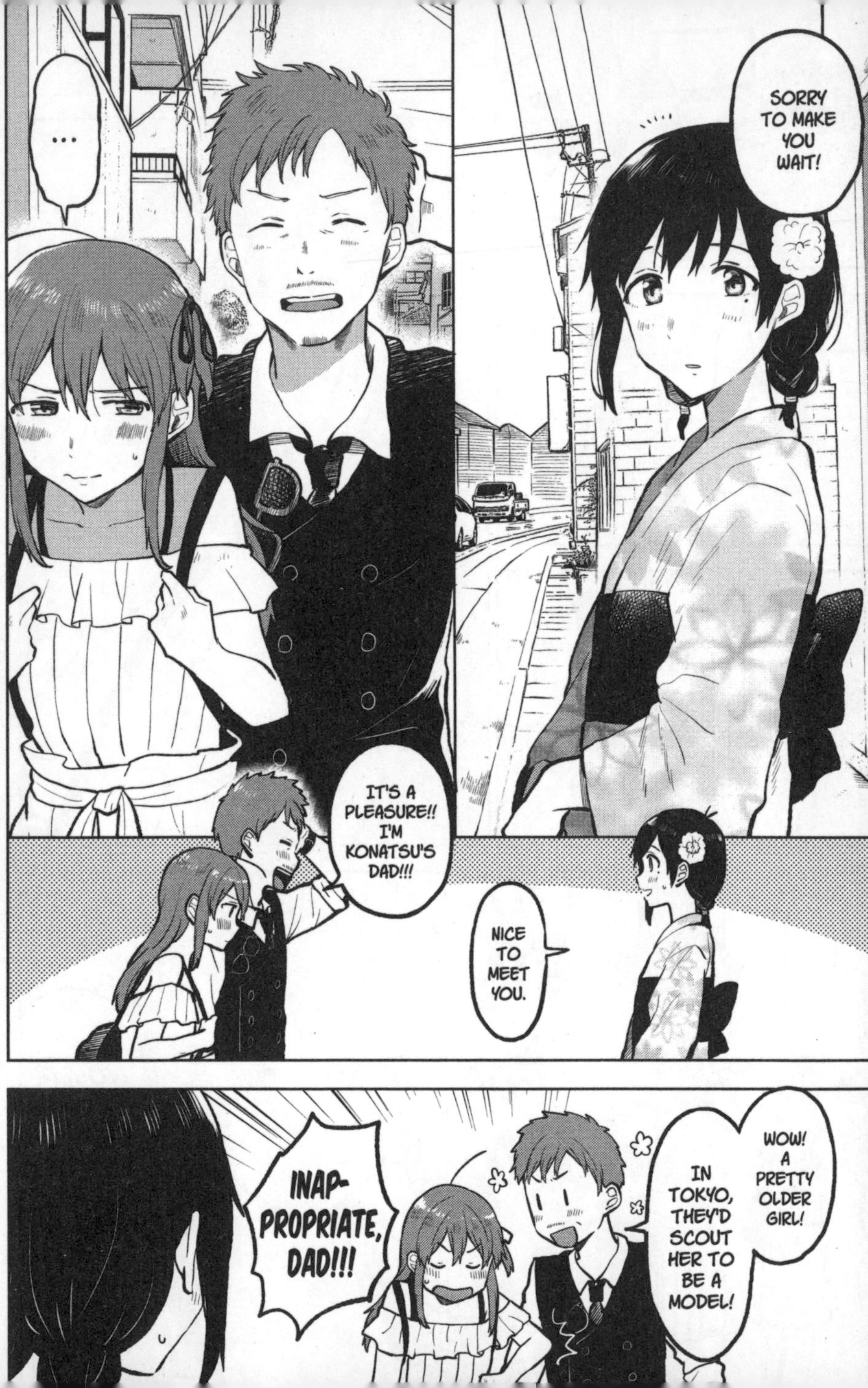
SORRY TO MAKE YOU WAIT!
...
NICE TO MEET YOU.
IT'S A PLEASURE!! I'M KONATSU'S DAD!!!
WOW! A PRETTY OLDER GIRL!
IN TOKYO, THEY'D SCOUT HER TO BE A MODEL!
INAP-PROPRIATE, DAD!!!

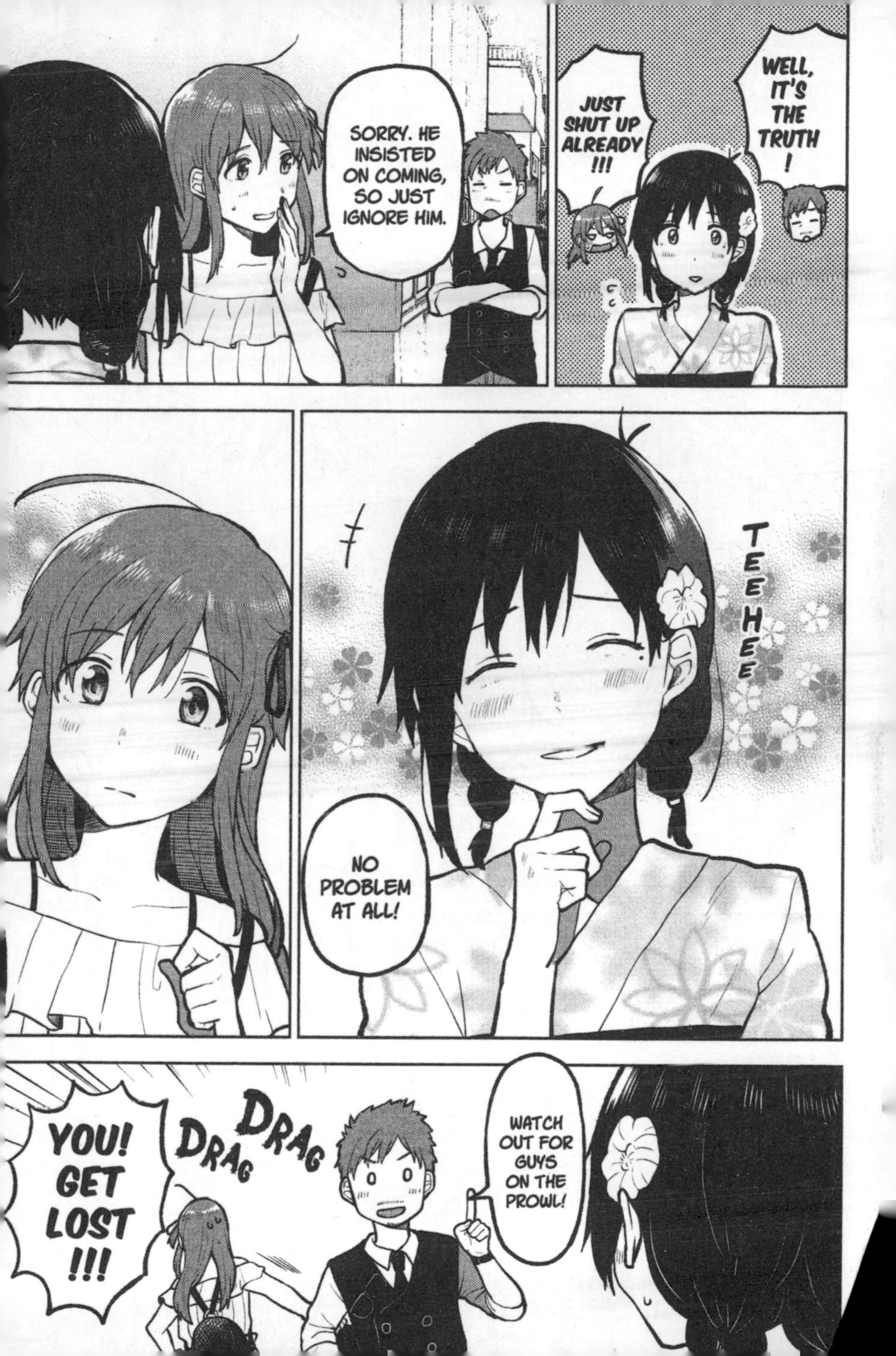
WELL, IT'S THE TRUTH!
JUST SHUT UP ALREADY!!!
SORRY. HE INSISTED ON COMING, SO JUST IGNORE HIM.
TEEHEE
NO PROBLEM AT ALL!
WATCH OUT FOR GUYS ON THE PROWL!
DRAG
DRAG
YOU! GET LOST!!!

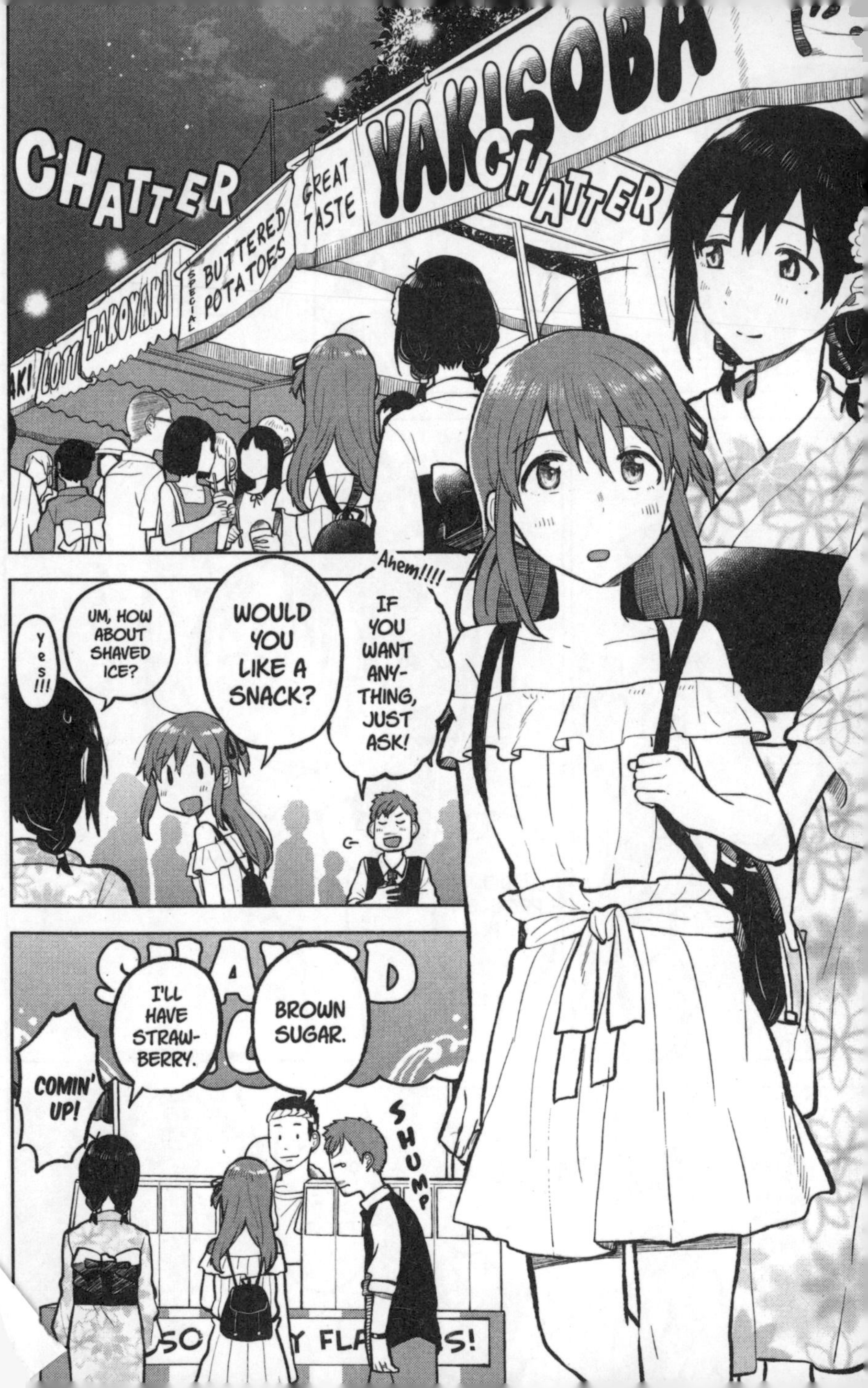
YAKISOBA
CHATTER
GREAT TASTE
SPECIAL
BUTTERED POTATOES
TAKOYAKI
CHATTER
Ahem!!!!
IF YOU WANT ANY-THING, JUST ASK!
WOULD YOU LIKE A SNACK?
UM, HOW ABOUT SHAVED ICE?
Yes!!!
BROWN SUGAR.
I'LL HAVE STRAW-BERRY.
COMIN' UP!
SHUMP

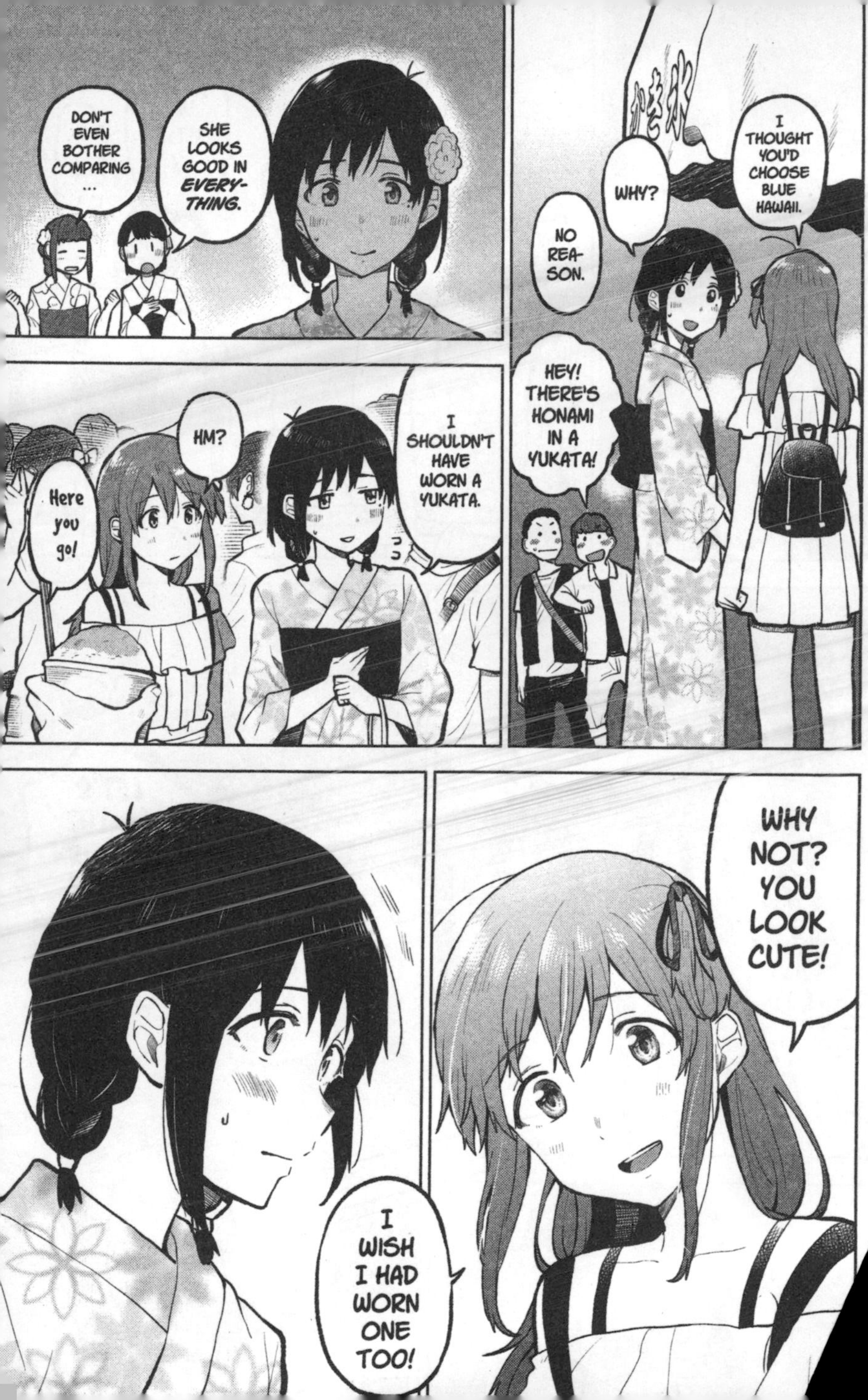

かき氷
I THOUGHT YOU'D CHOOSE BLUE HAWAII.
WHY?
NO REA-SON.
HEY! THERE'S HONAMI IN A YUKATA!
SHE LOOKS GOOD IN EVERY-THING.
DON'T EVEN BOTHER COMPARING ...
I SHOULDN'T HAVE WORN A YUKATA.
HM?
Here you go!
WHY NOT? YOU LOOK CUTE!
I WISH I HAD WORN ONE TOO!

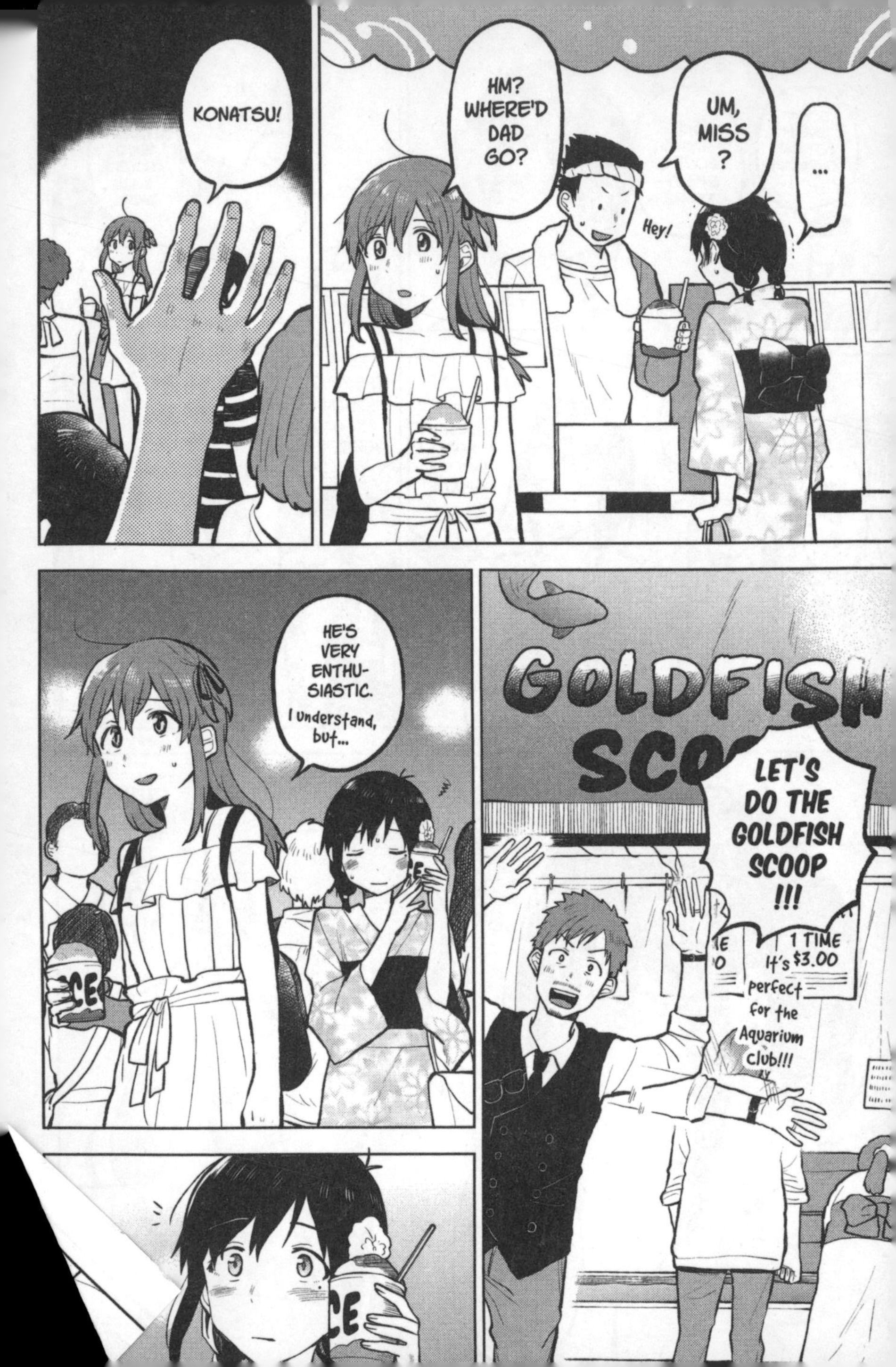
...
UM, MISS ?
Hey!
HM? WHERE'D DAD GO?
KONATSU!
GOLDFISH SCOO
LET'S DO THE GOLDFISH SCOOP !!!
1 TIME $3.00
It's perfect for the Aquarium club!!!
HE'S VERY ENTHU-SIASTIC.
I understand, but...

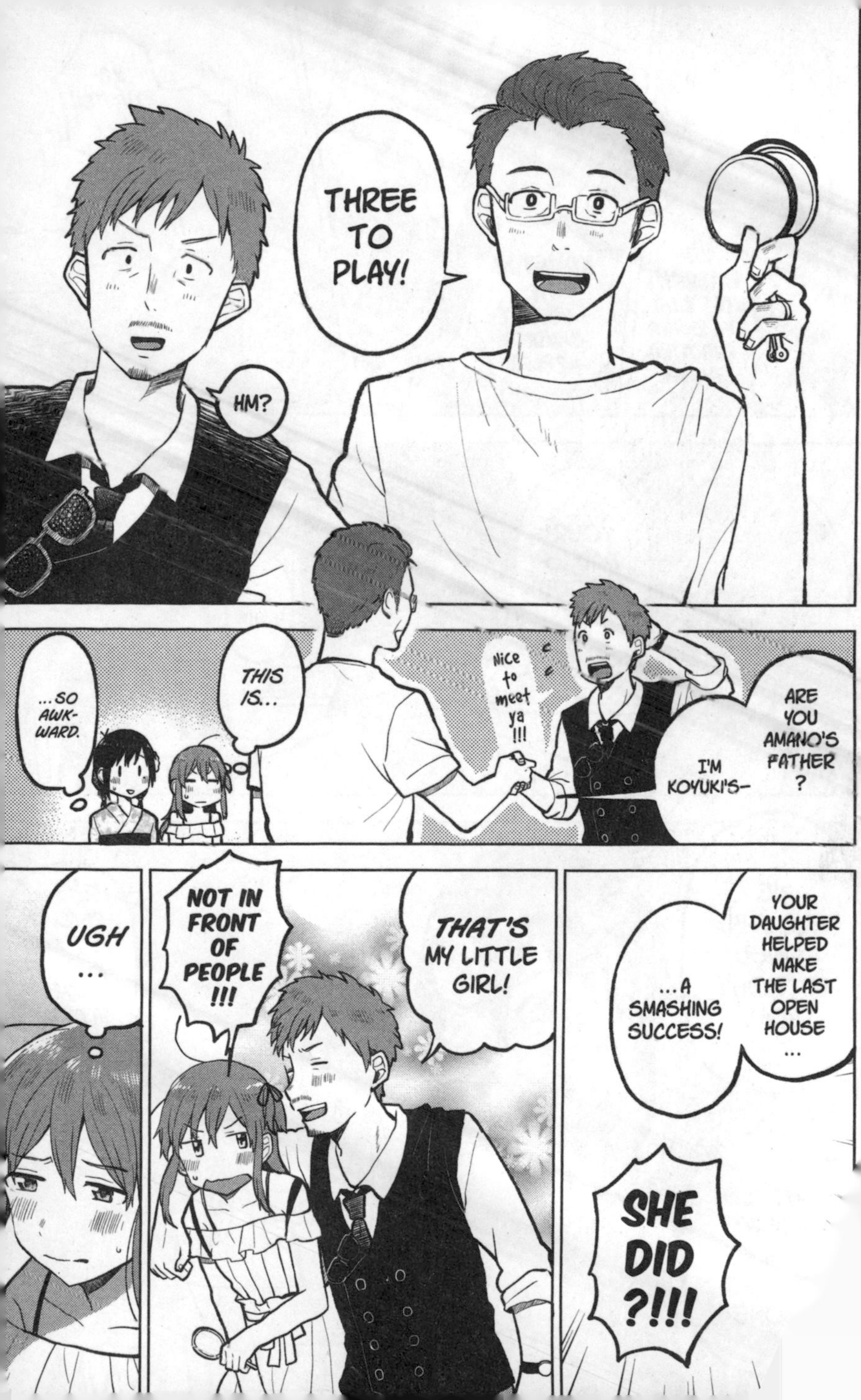
THREE TO PLAY!
HM?
ARE YOU AMANO'S FATHER?
I'M KOYUKI'S—
Nice to meet ya!!!
THIS IS...
...SO AWKWARD.
YOUR DAUGHTER HELPED MAKE THE LAST OPEN HOUSE...
...A SMASHING SUCCESS!
SHE DID?!!!
THAT'S MY LITTLE GIRL!
NOT IN FRONT OF PEOPLE!!!
UGH...

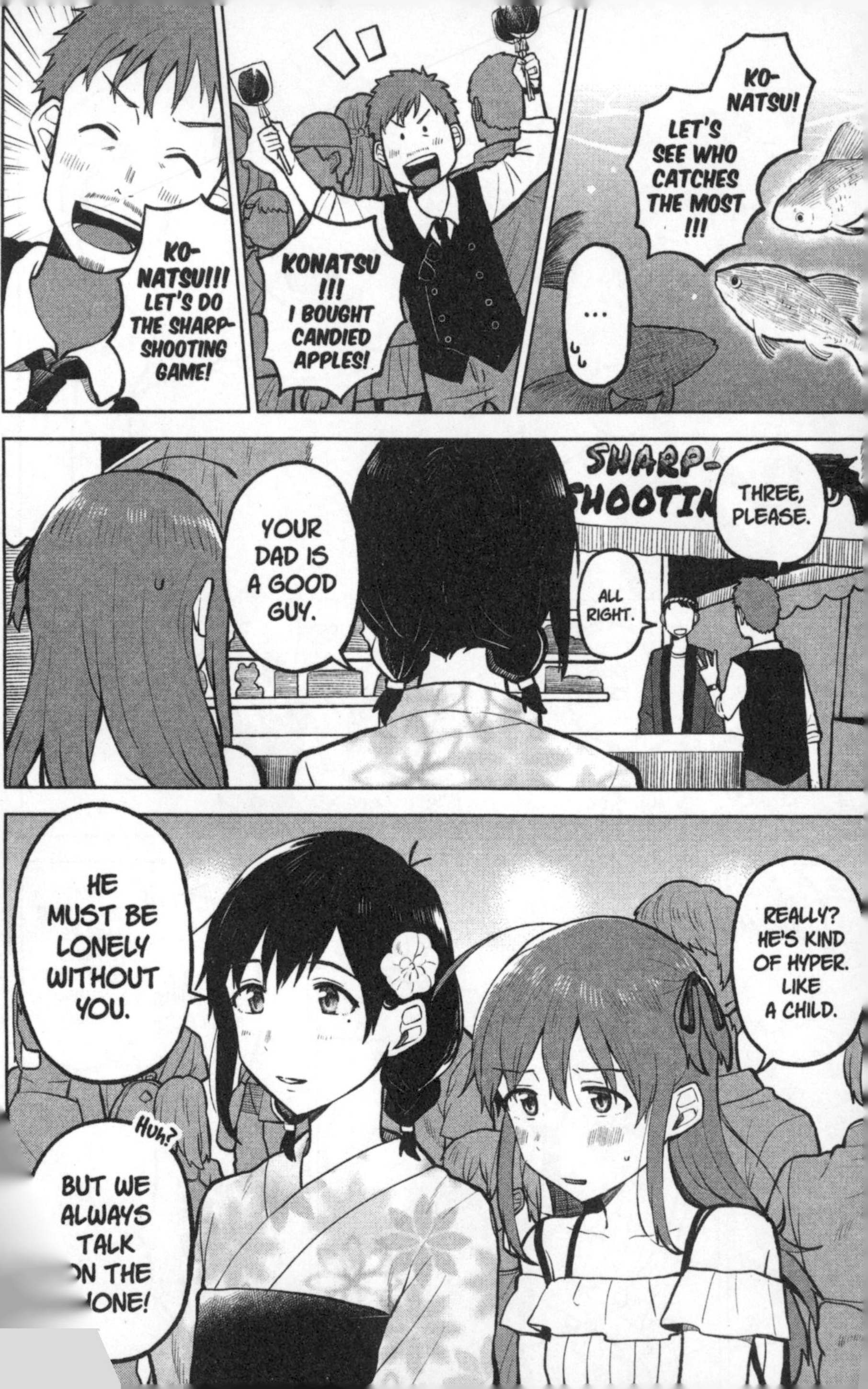
KO-NATSU! LET'S SEE WHO CATCHES THE MOST!!!
...
KONATSU!!! I BOUGHT CANDIED APPLES!
KO-NATSU!!! LET'S DO THE SHARP-SHOOTING GAME!
THREE, PLEASE.
SHARP-SHOOTIN
ALL RIGHT.
YOUR DAD IS A GOOD GUY.
REALLY? HE'S KIND OF HYPER. LIKE A CHILD.
HE MUST BE LONELY WITHOUT YOU.
Huh?
BUT WE ALWAYS TALK ON THE PHONE!

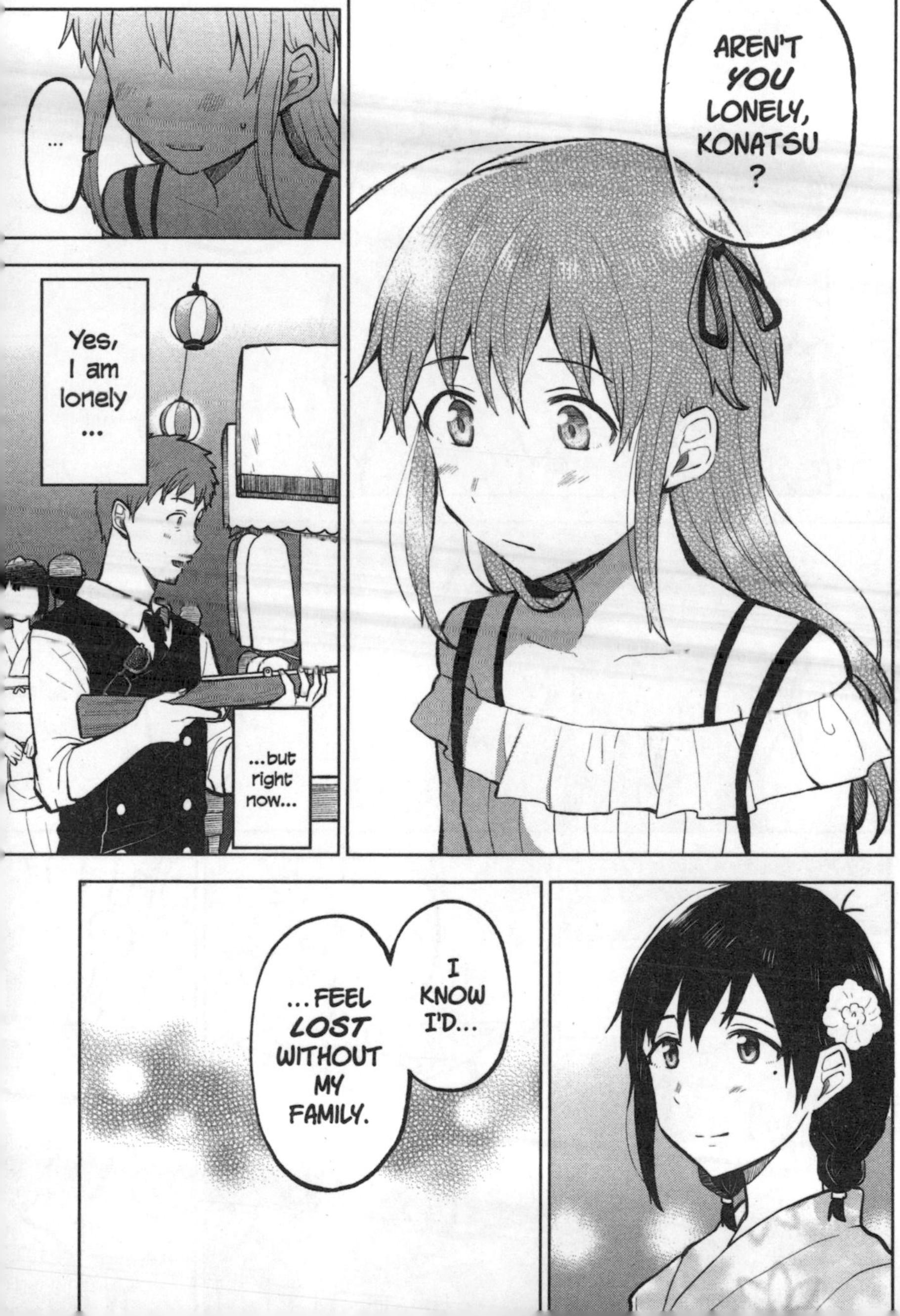
AREN'T *YOU* LONELY, KONATSU?
...
Yes, I am lonely...
...but right now...
I KNOW I'D...
...FEEL *LOST* WITHOUT MY FAMILY.

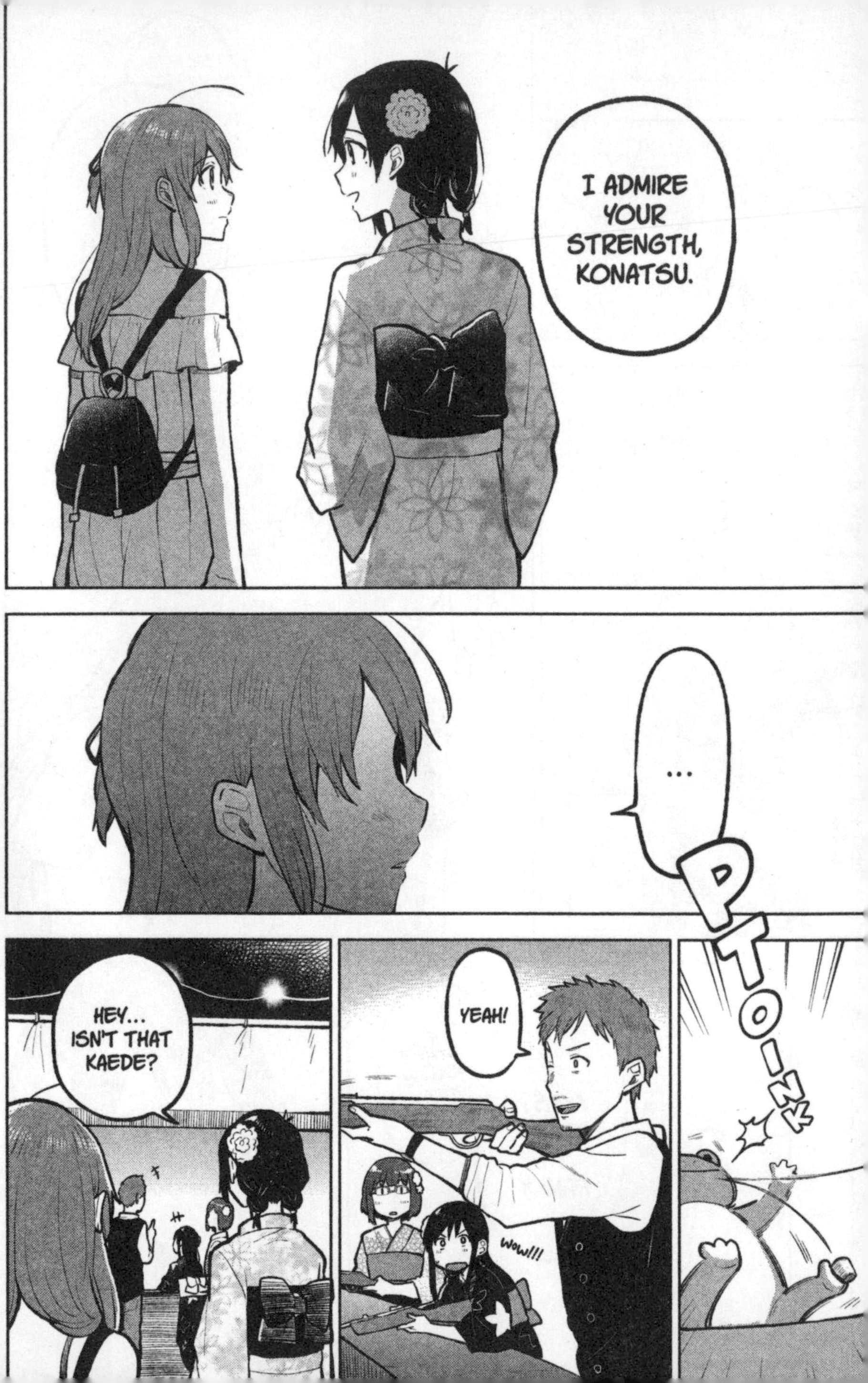
I ADMIRE YOUR STRENGTH, KONATSU.
...
PTOINK
YEAH!
WOW!!!
HEY... ISN'T THAT KAEDE?

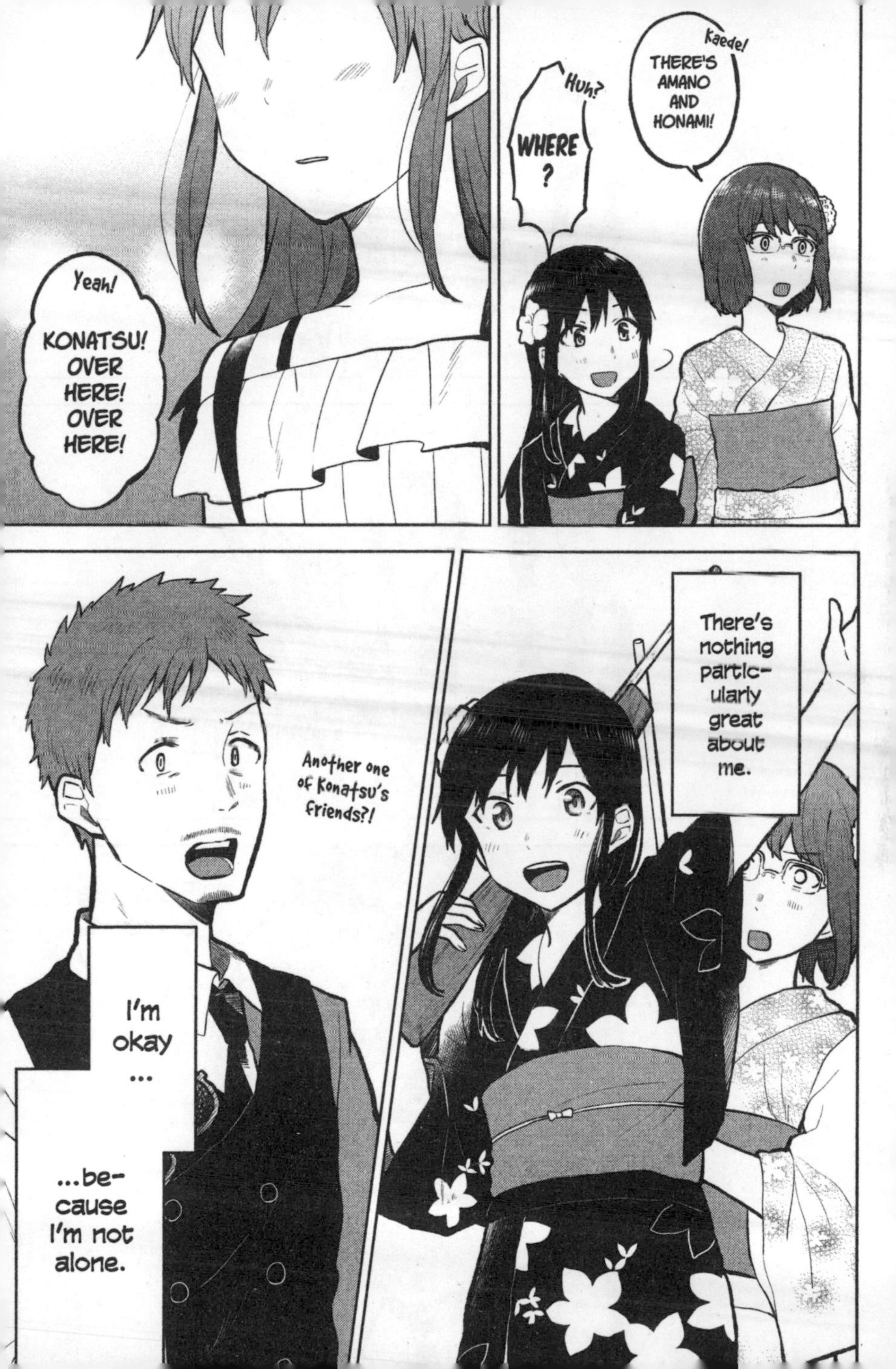
Kaede!
THERE'S AMANO AND HONAMI!
Huh?
WHERE?
Yeah!
KONATSU! OVER HERE! OVER HERE!
There's nothing partic-ularly great about me.
Another one of Konatsu's friends?!
I'm okay...
...be-cause I'm not alone.

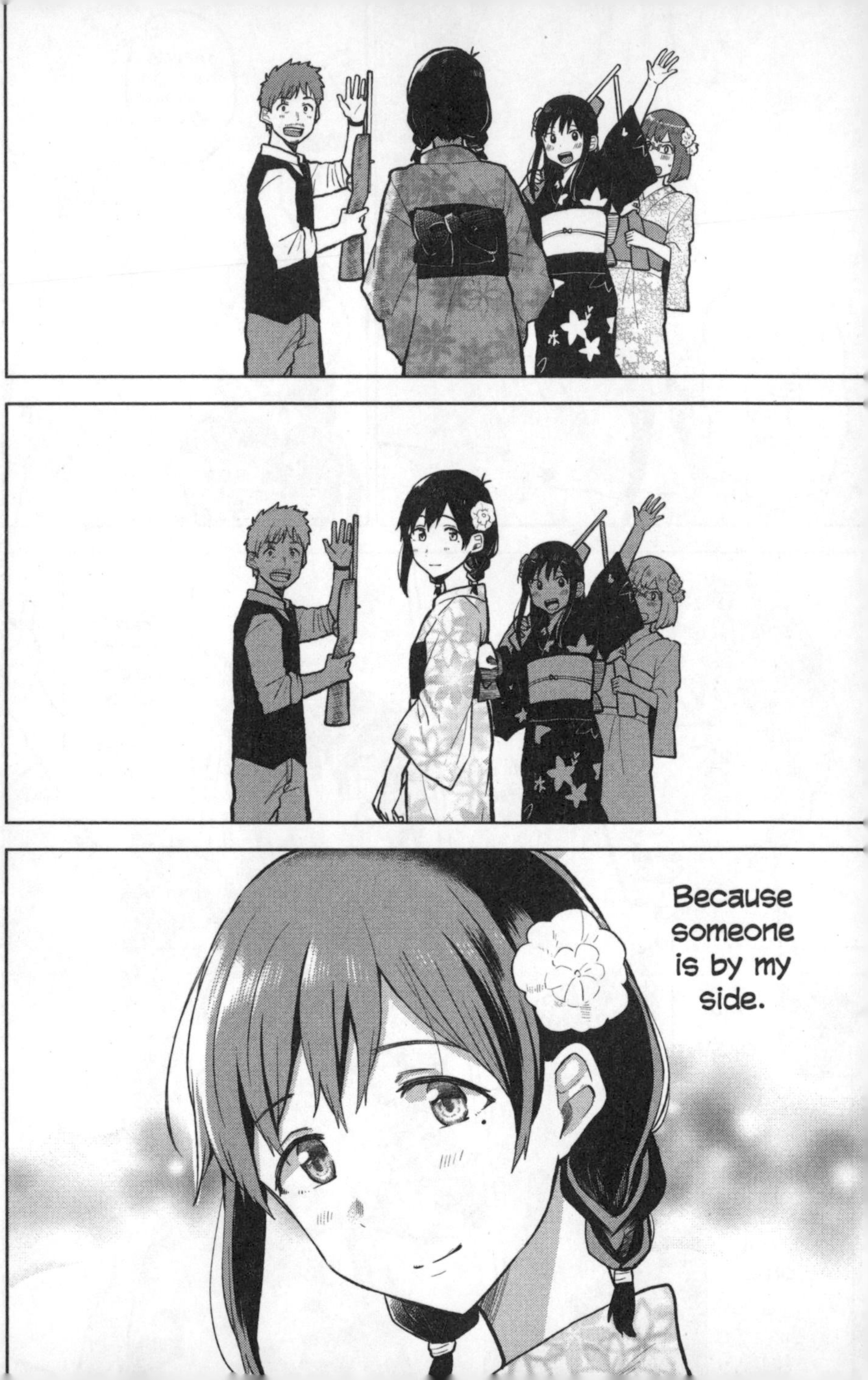
Because someone is by my side.

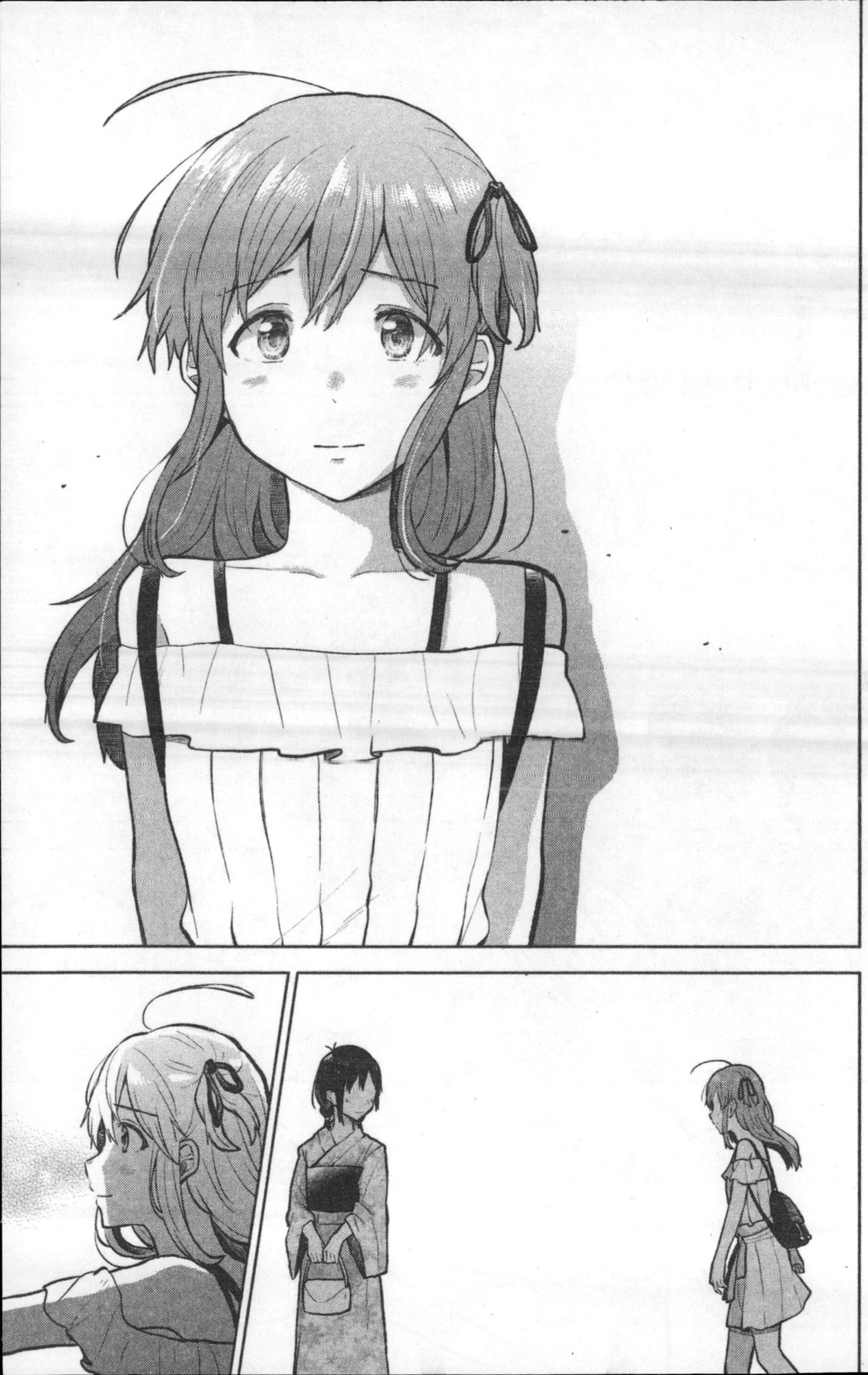

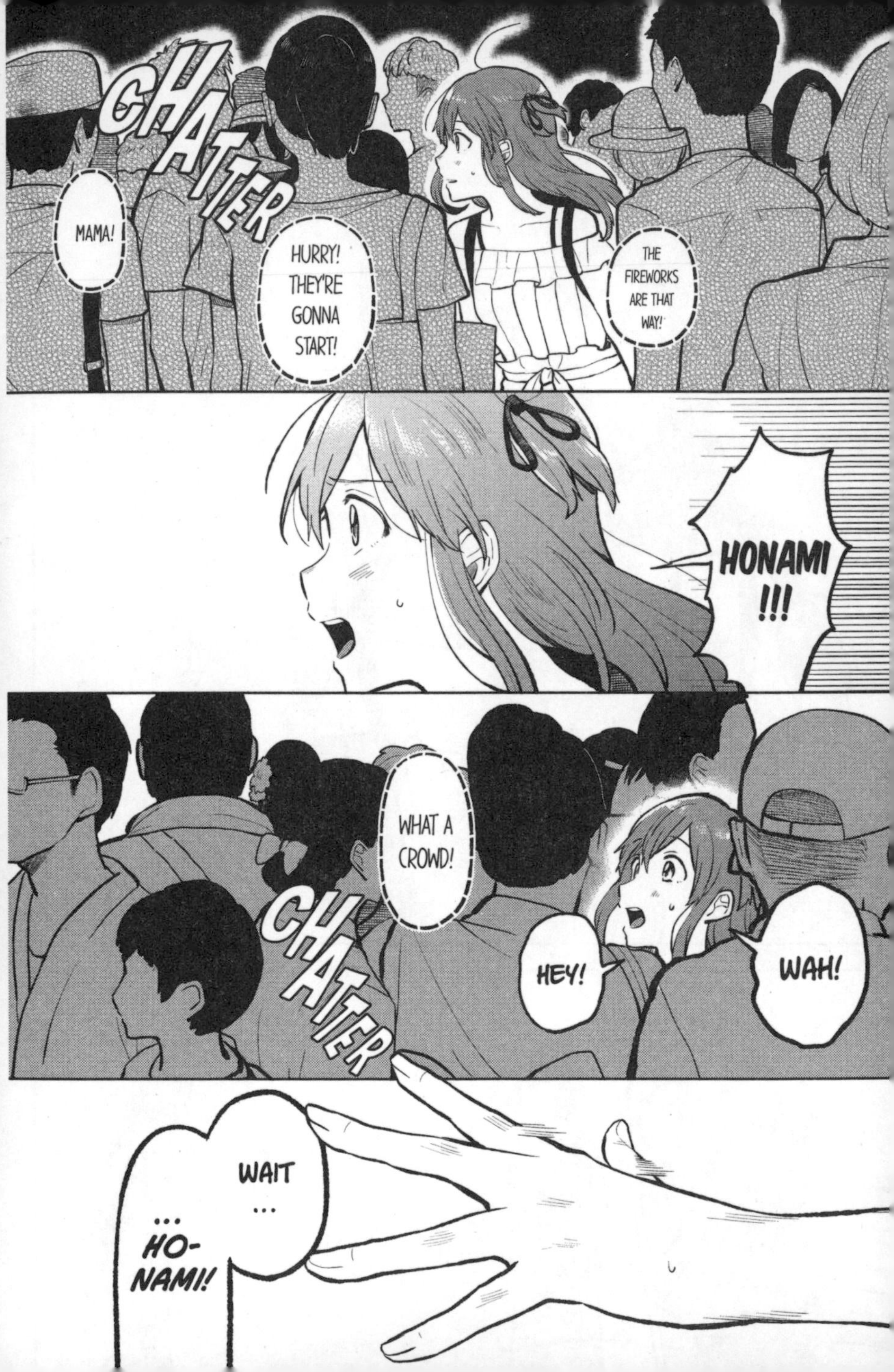
THE FIREWORKS ARE THAT WAY!
HURRY! THEY'RE GONNA START!
CHATTER
MAMA!
HONAMI !!!
WAH!
HEY!
WHAT A CROWD!
CHATTER
WAIT ...
... HO-NAMI!

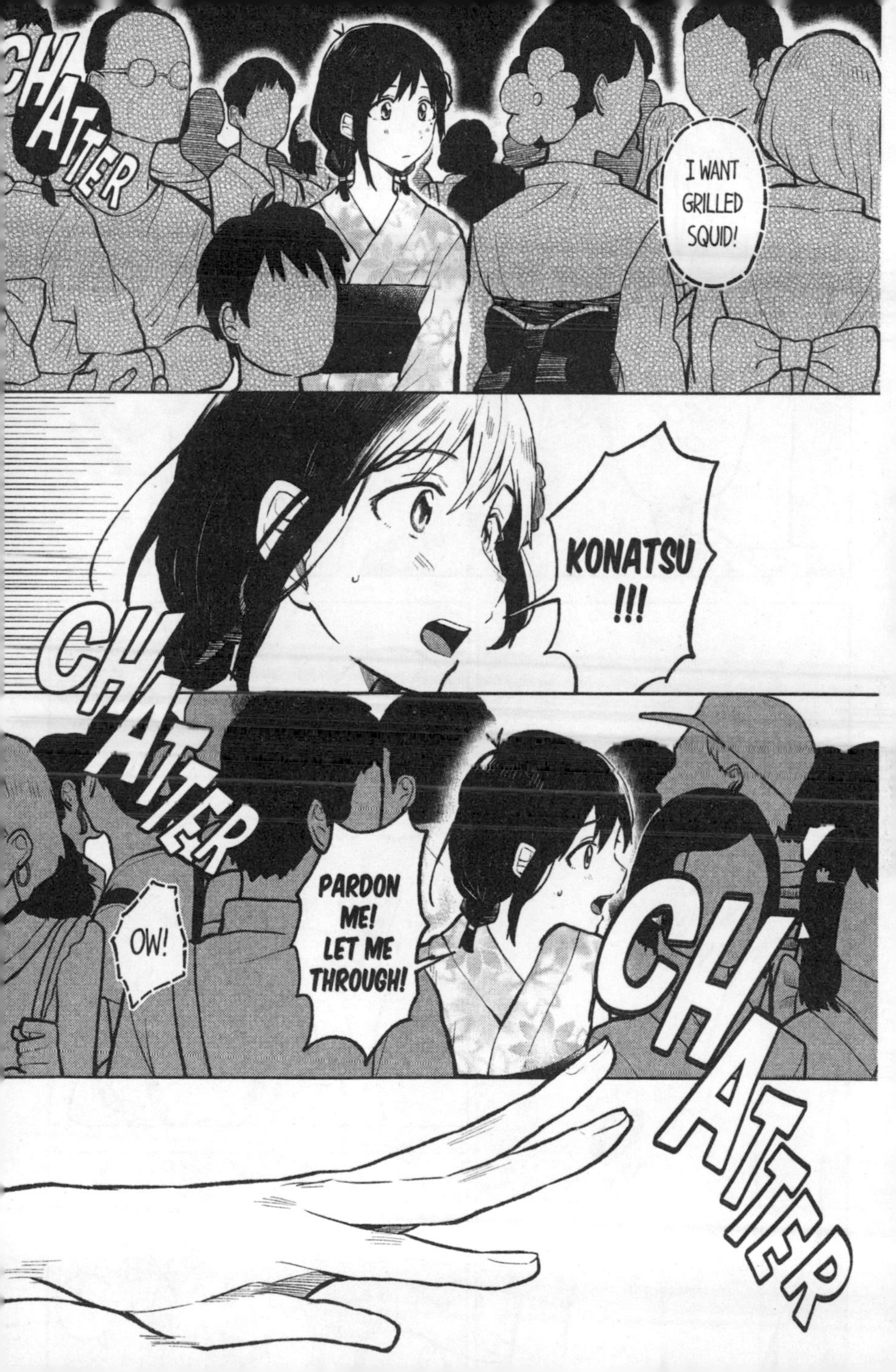
I WANT GRILLED SQUID!
CHATTER
KONATSU!!!
CHATTER
CHATTER
PARDON ME! LET ME THROUGH!
OW!

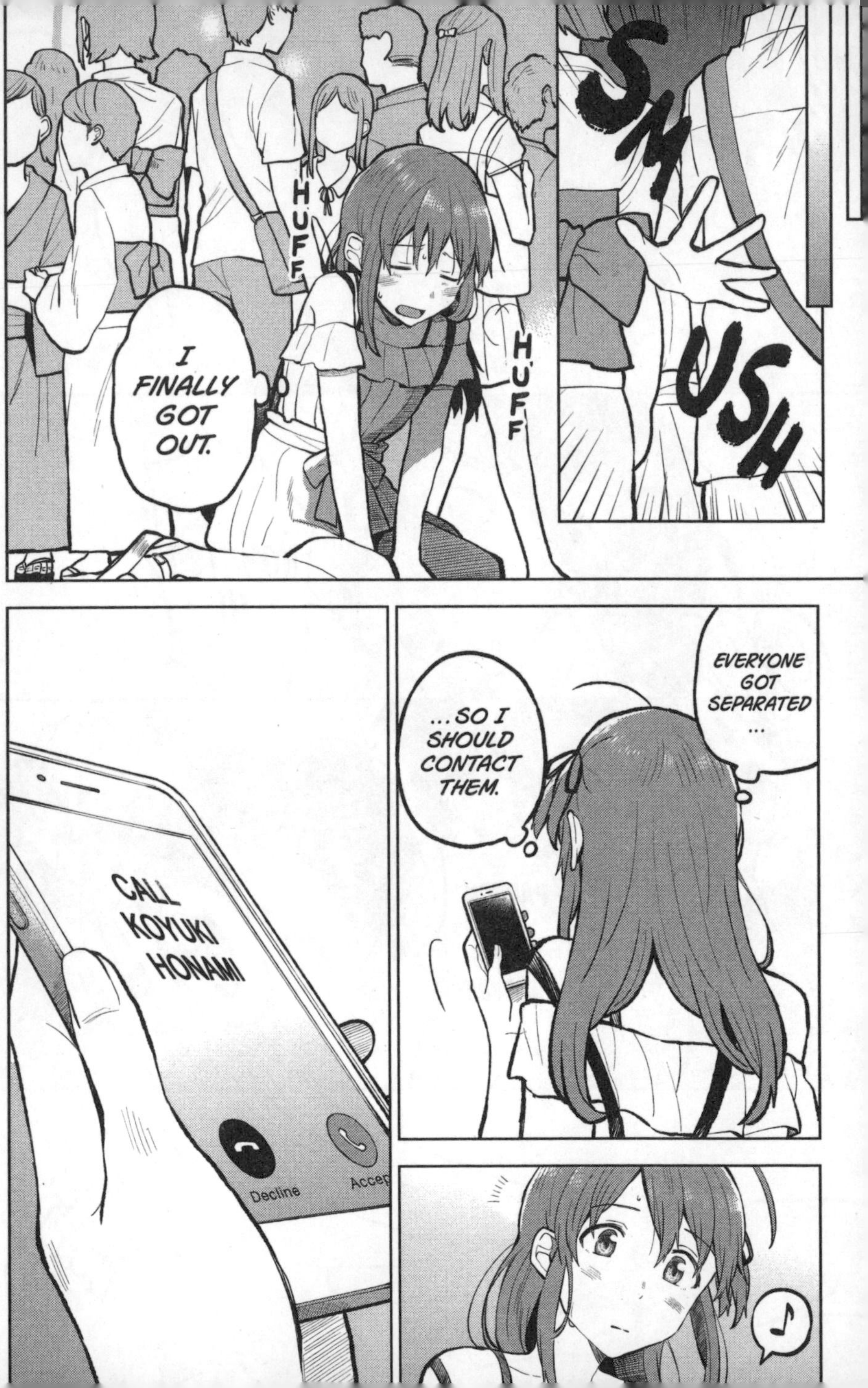
SMUSH
HUFF HUFF
I FINALLY GOT OUT.
EVERYONE GOT SEPARATED ...
...SO I SHOULD CONTACT THEM.
♪
CALL KOYUKI HONAMI
Decline

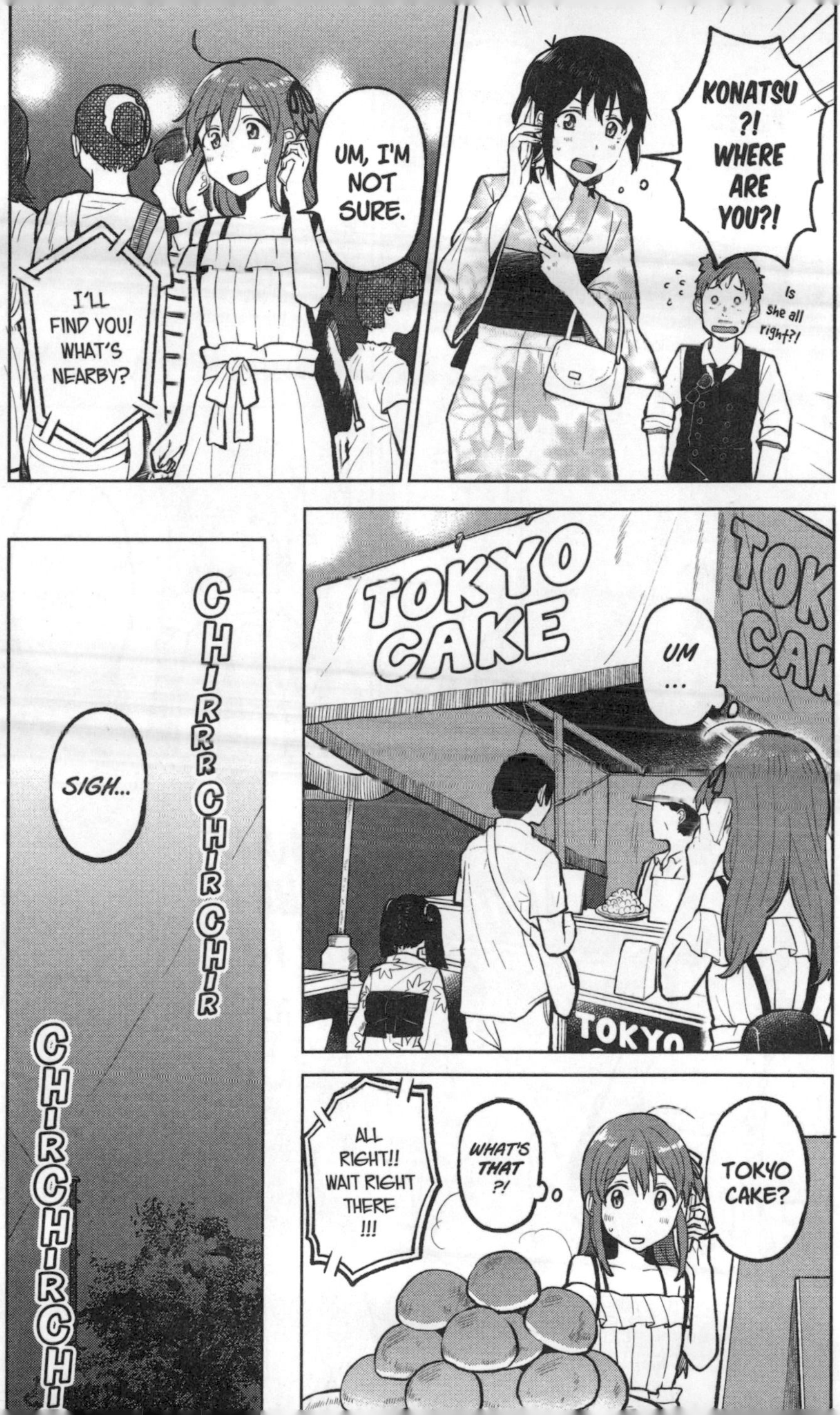
KONATSU ?! WHERE ARE YOU?!
Is she all right?!
UM, I'M NOT SURE.
I'LL FIND YOU! WHAT'S NEARBY?
TOKYO CAKE
UM ...
TOKYO
TOKYO CAKE?
WHAT'S THAT ?!
ALL RIGHT!! WAIT RIGHT THERE !!!
CHIRRR CHIR CHIR
SIGH...
CHIRCHIRCHI

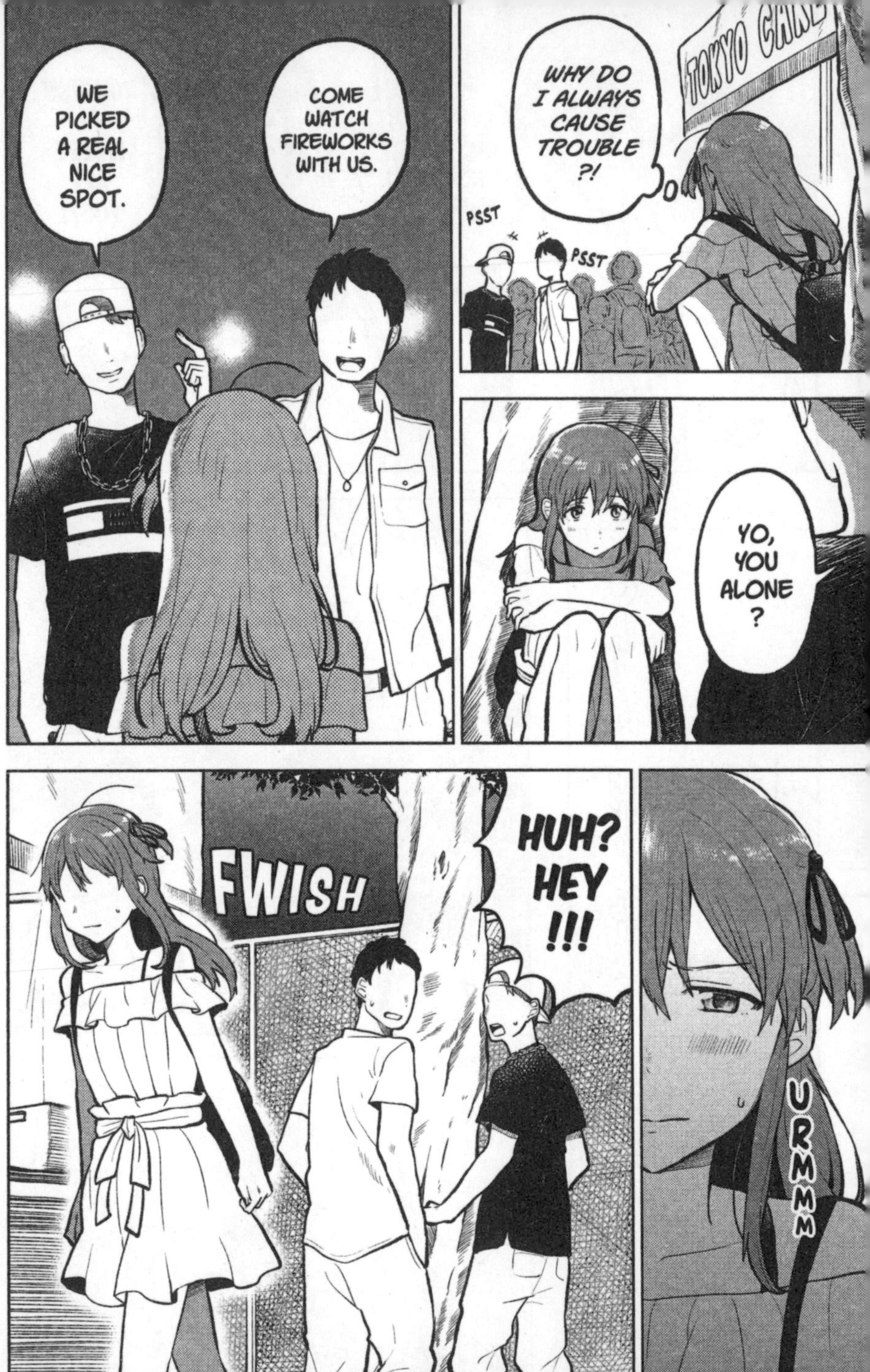
WHY DO I ALWAYS CAUSE TROUBLE ?!
PSST
PSST
YO, YOU ALONE ?
COME WATCH FIREWORKS WITH US.
WE PICKED A REAL NICE SPOT.
URMMM
HUH? HEY !!!
FWISH

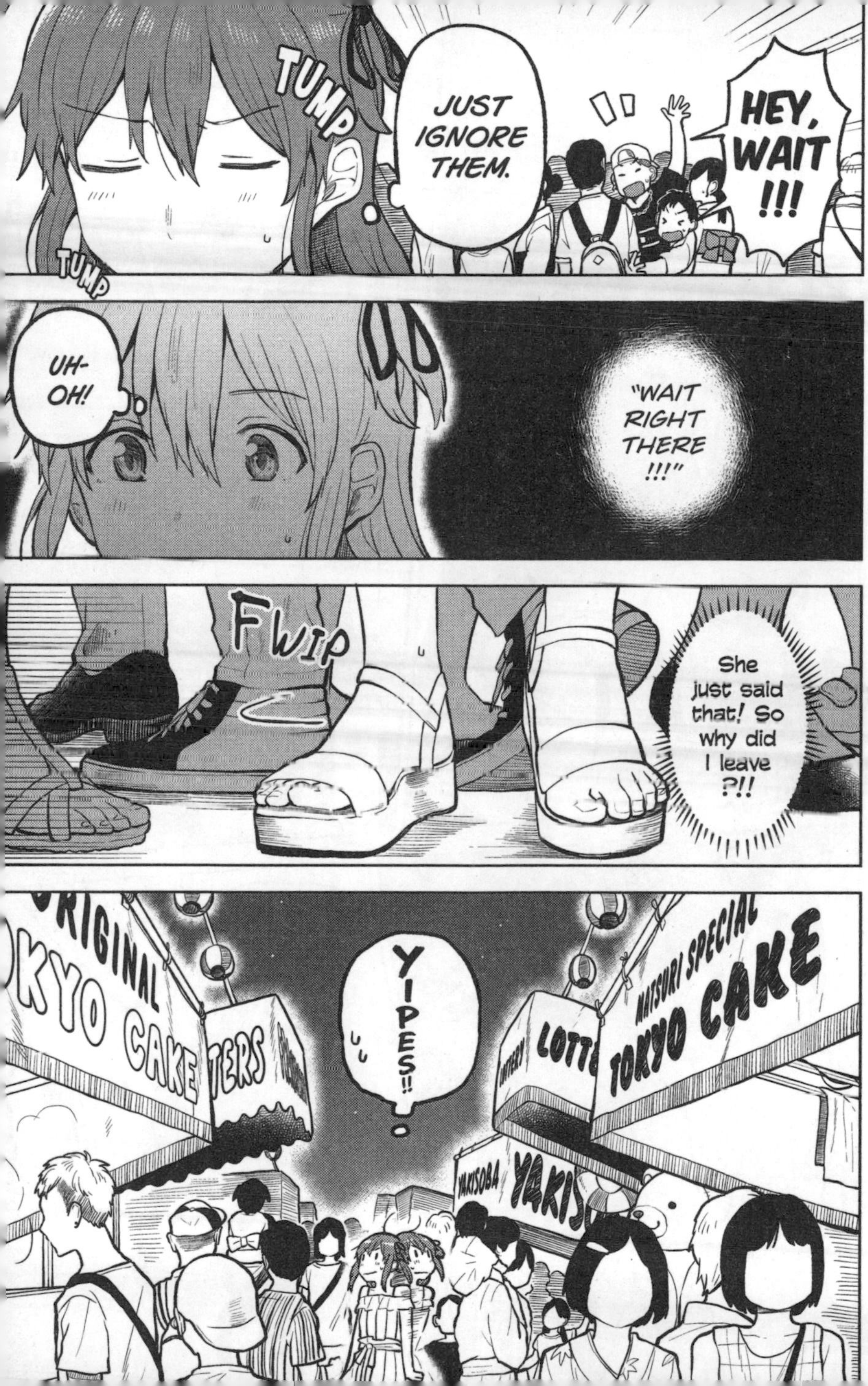
HEY, WAIT!!!
JUST IGNORE THEM.
TUMP
TUMP
"WAIT RIGHT THERE!!!"
UH-OH!
She just said that! So why did I leave?!!
FWIP
MATSURI SPECIAL
TOKYO CAKE
LOTTERY
YIPES!!
ORIGINAL
YAKISOBA

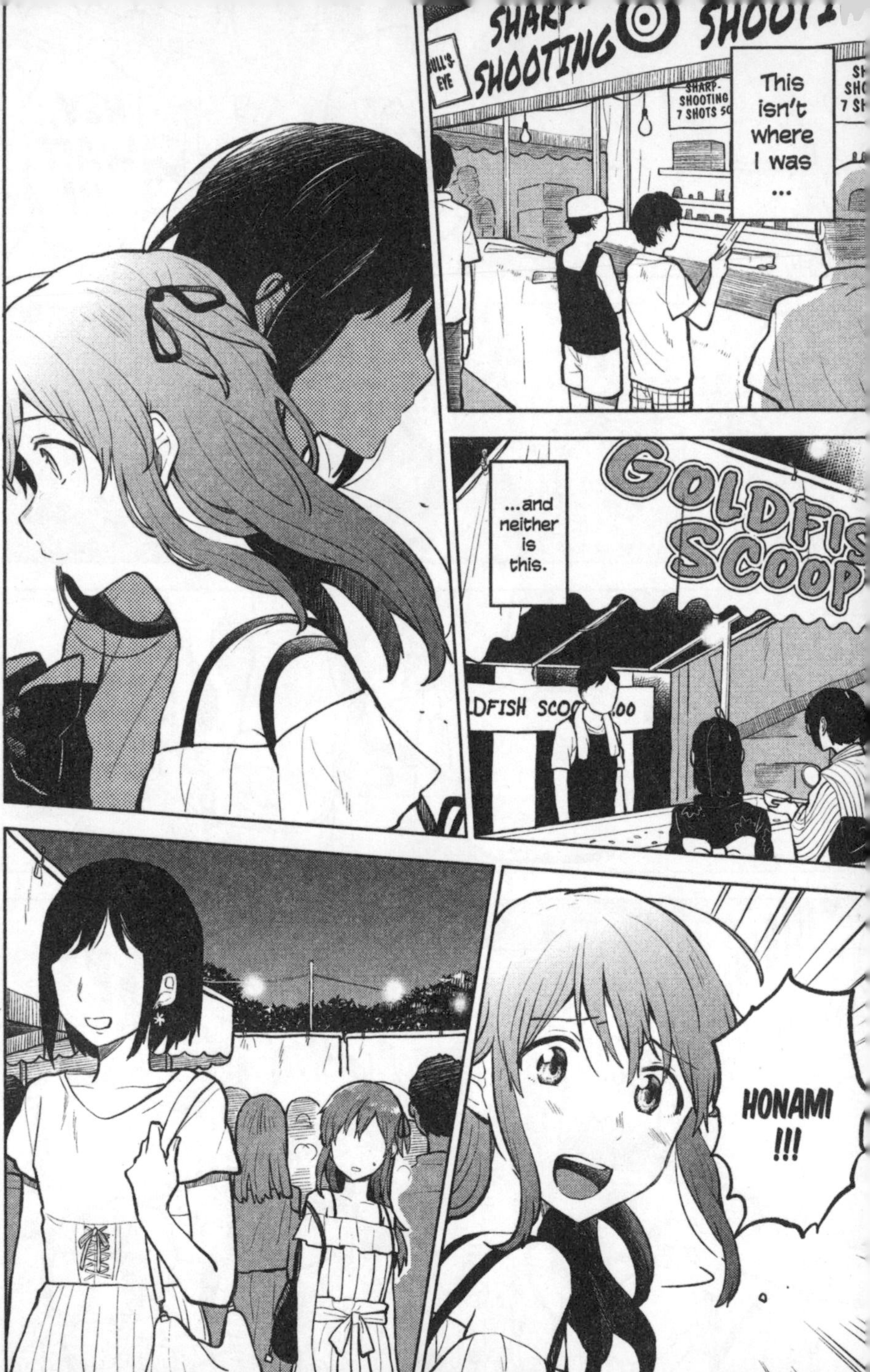
SHOOTING
BULL'S EYE
SHARP-SHOOTING
This isn't where I was ...
...and neither is this.
HONAMI !!!

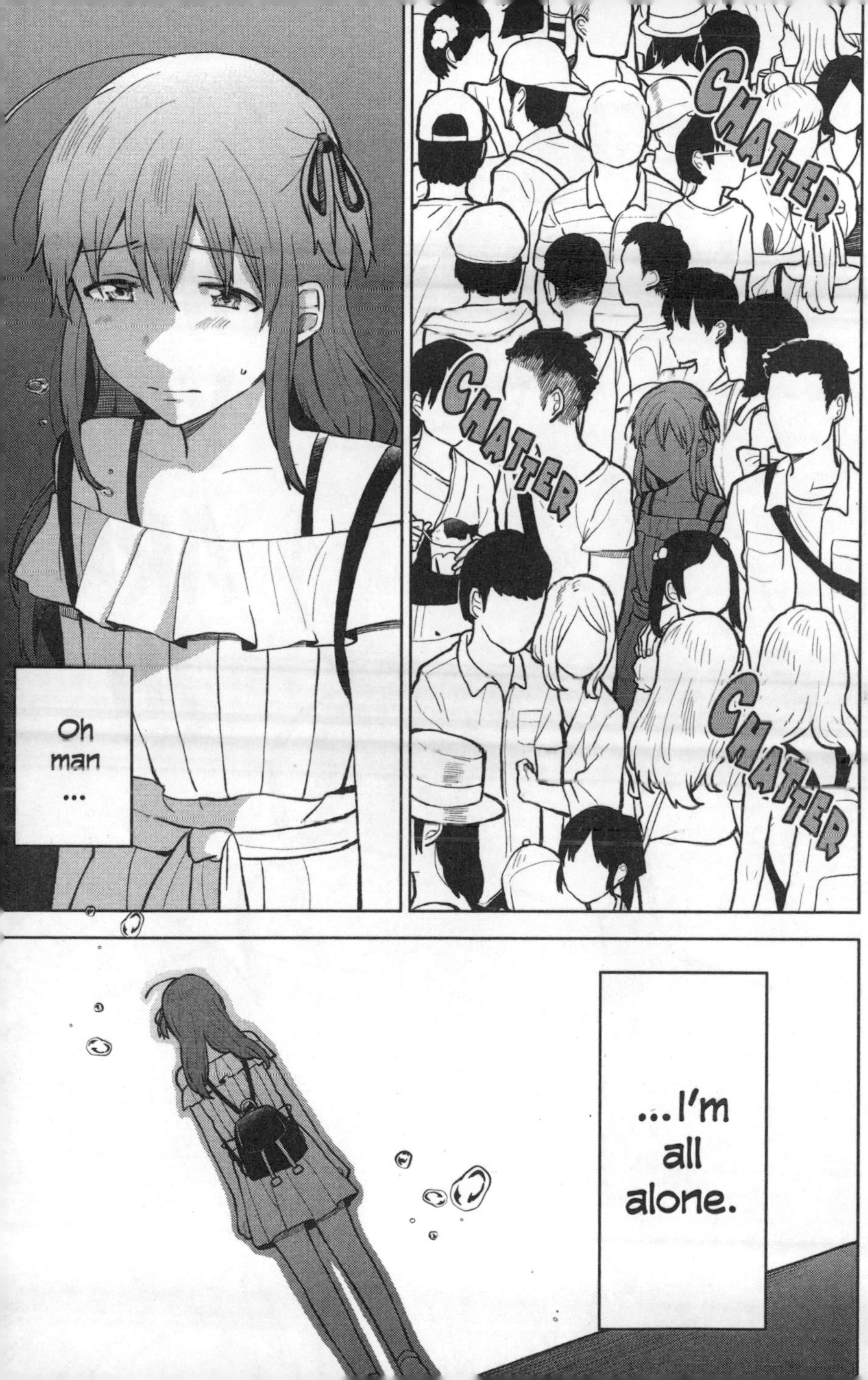
CHATTER
CHATTER
CHATTER
Oh man ...
...I'm all alone.

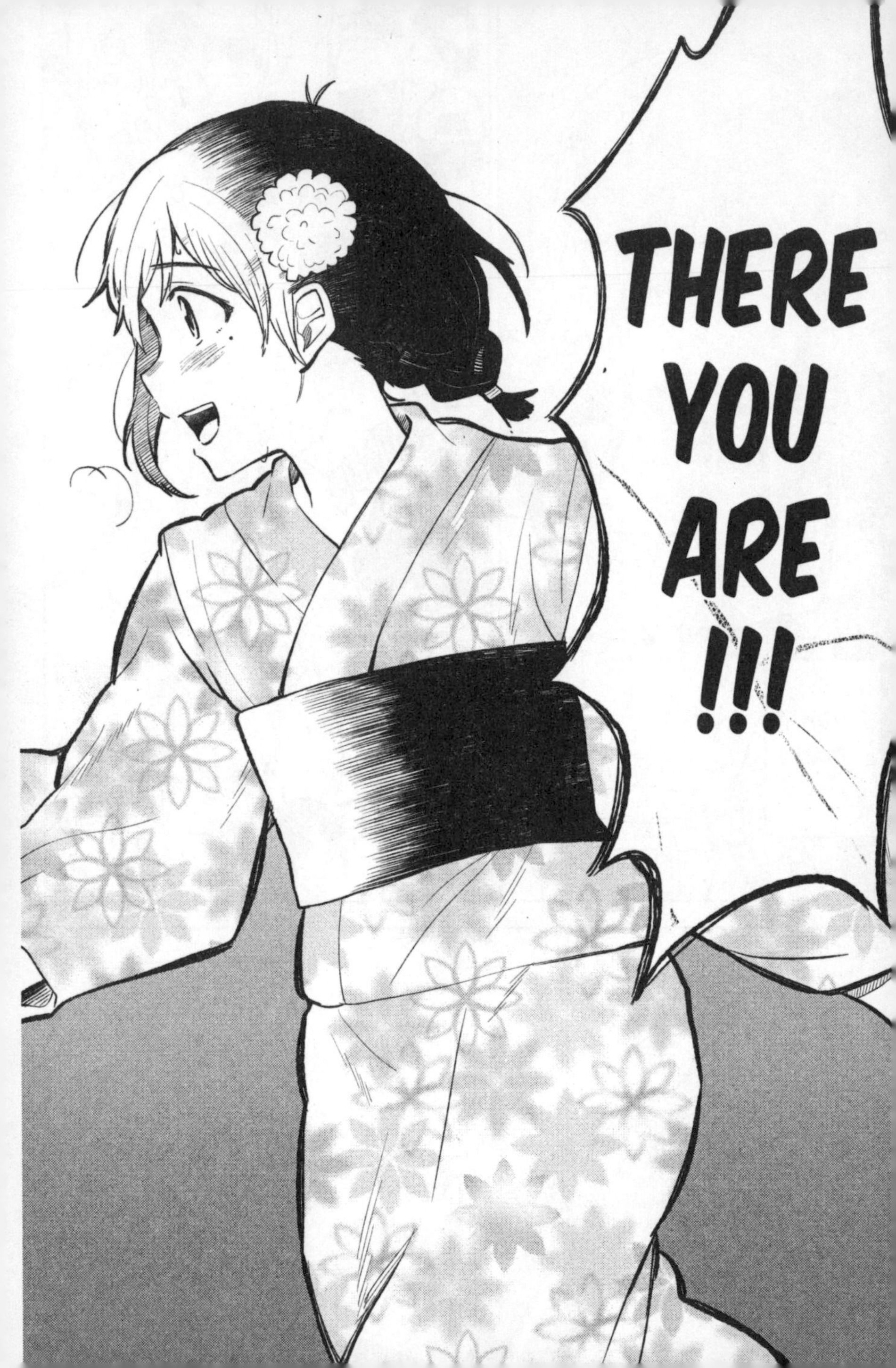
THERE YOU ARE !!!

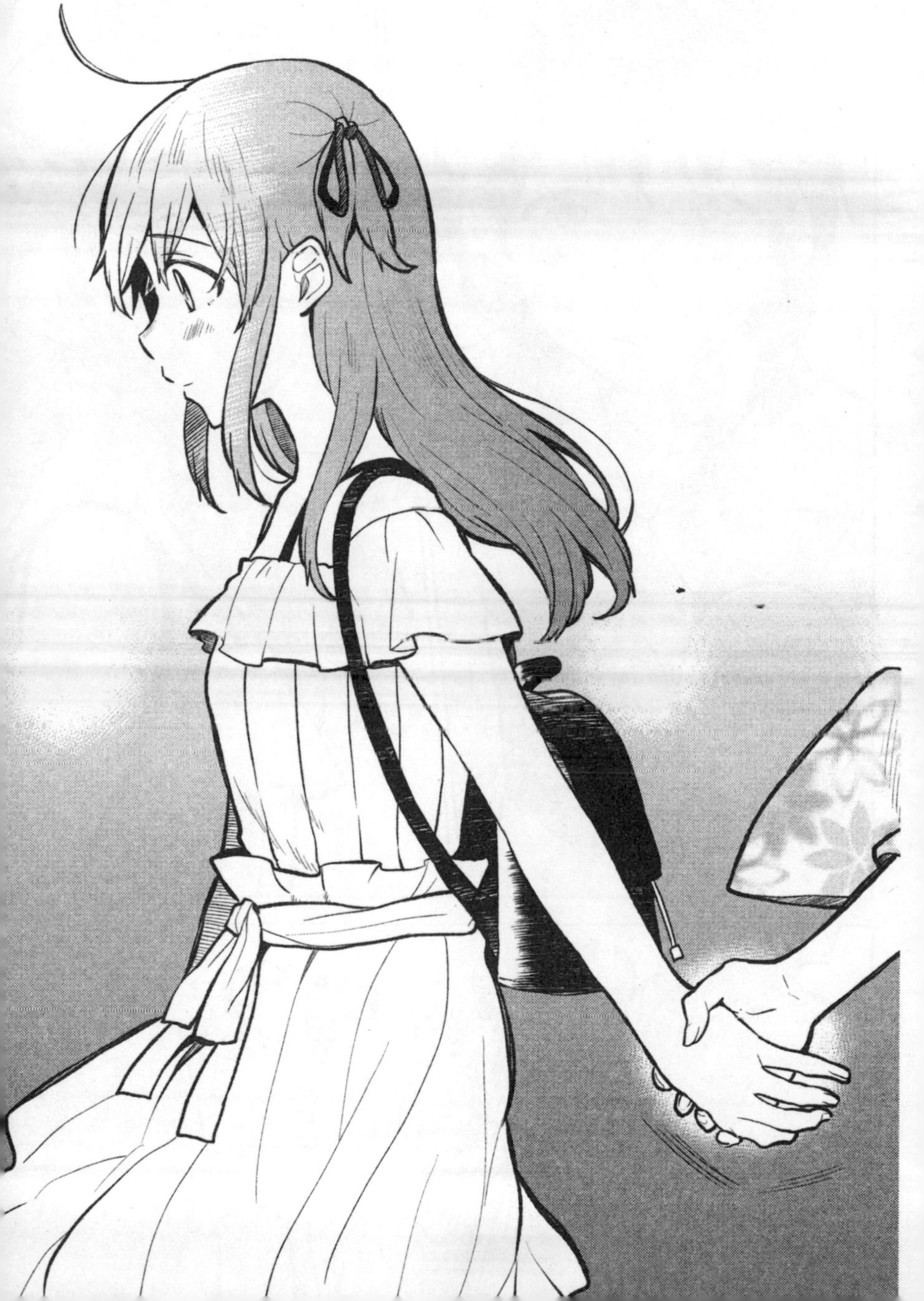

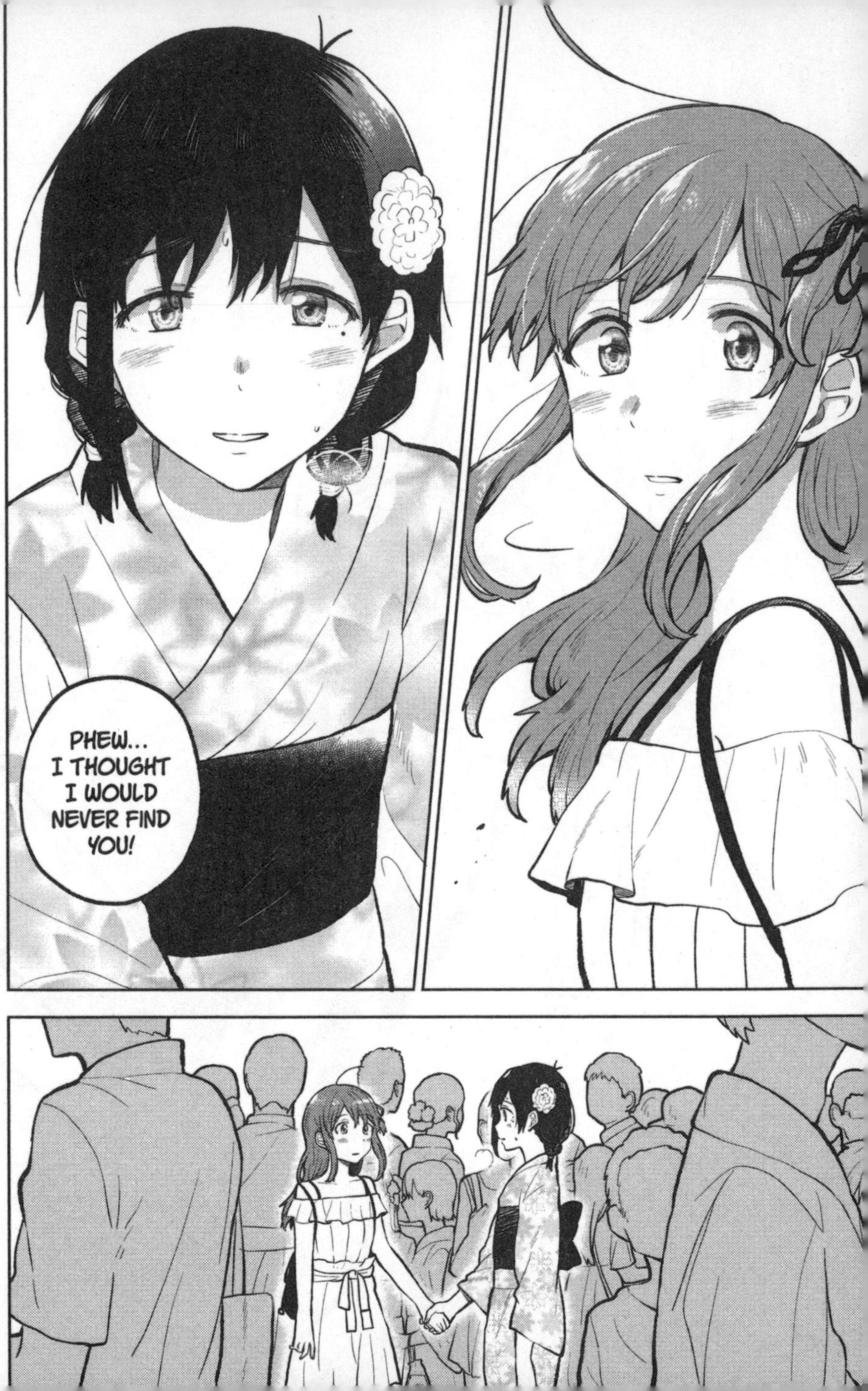
PHEW... I THOUGHT I WOULD NEVER FIND YOU!

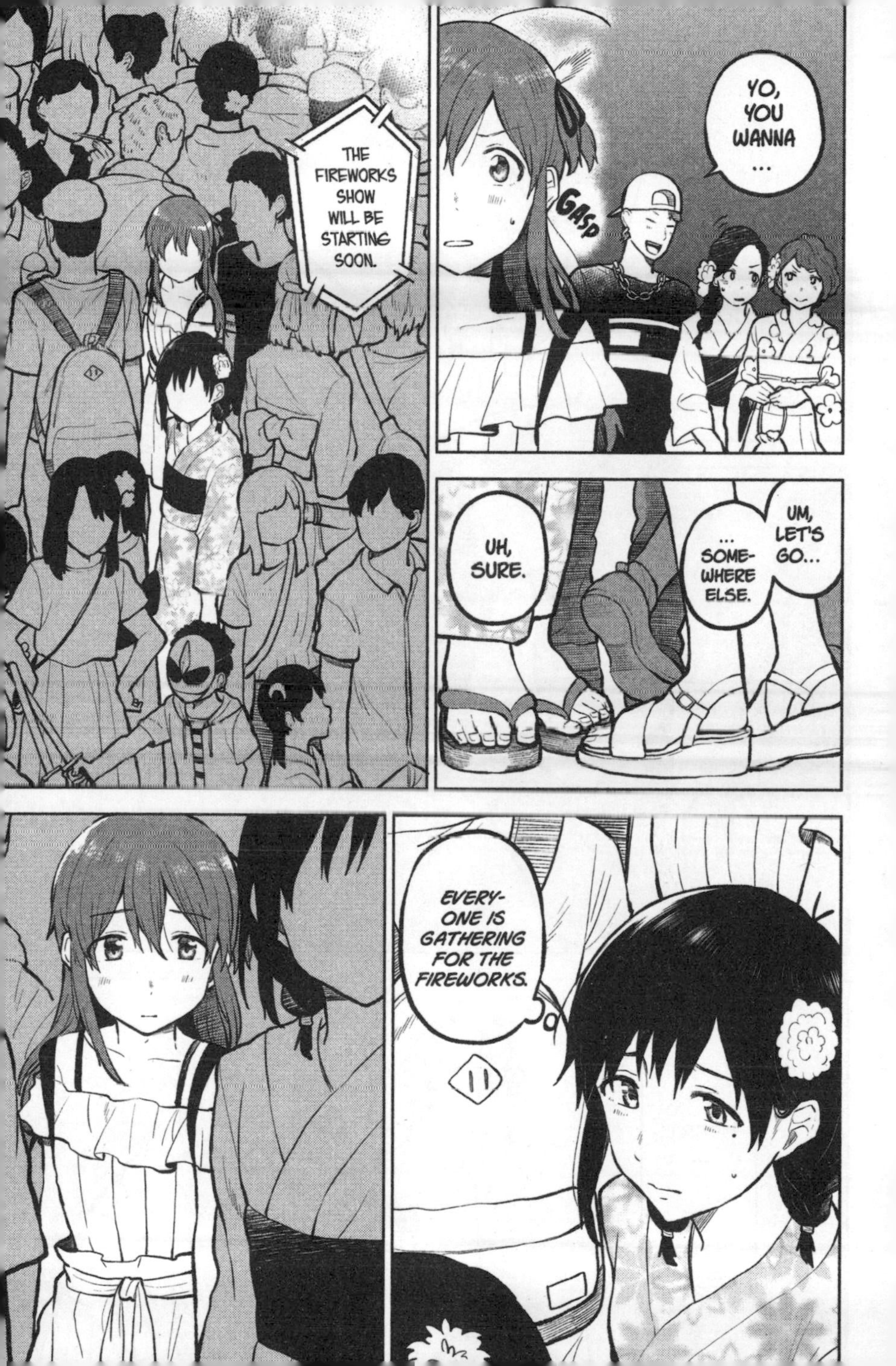
YO, YOU WANNA ...
GASP
UM, LET'S GO...
... SOME-WHERE ELSE.
UH, SURE.
THE FIREWORKS SHOW WILL BE STARTING SOON.
EVERY-ONE IS GATHERING FOR THE FIREWORKS.

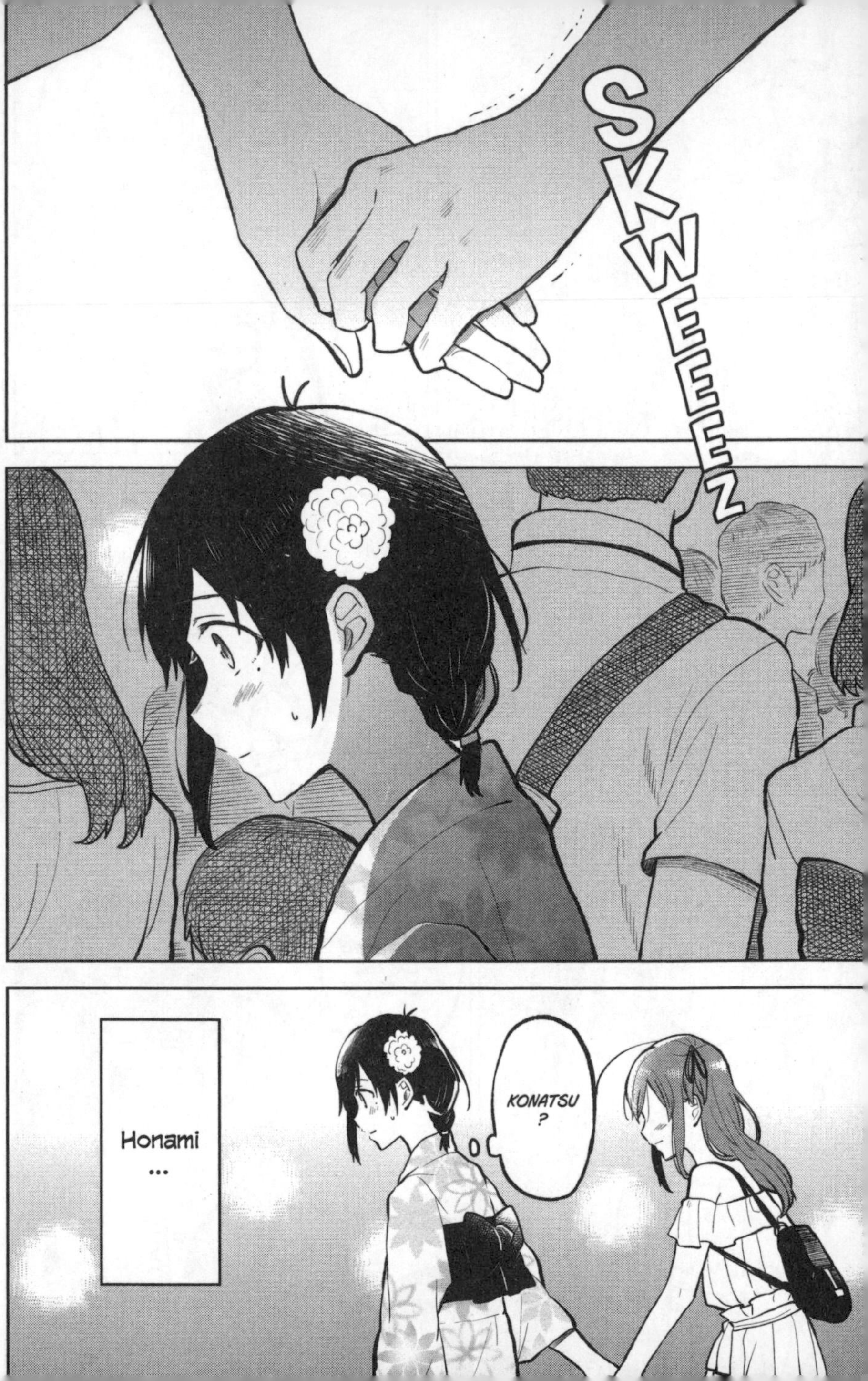
SKWEEZ
KONATSU?
Honami...

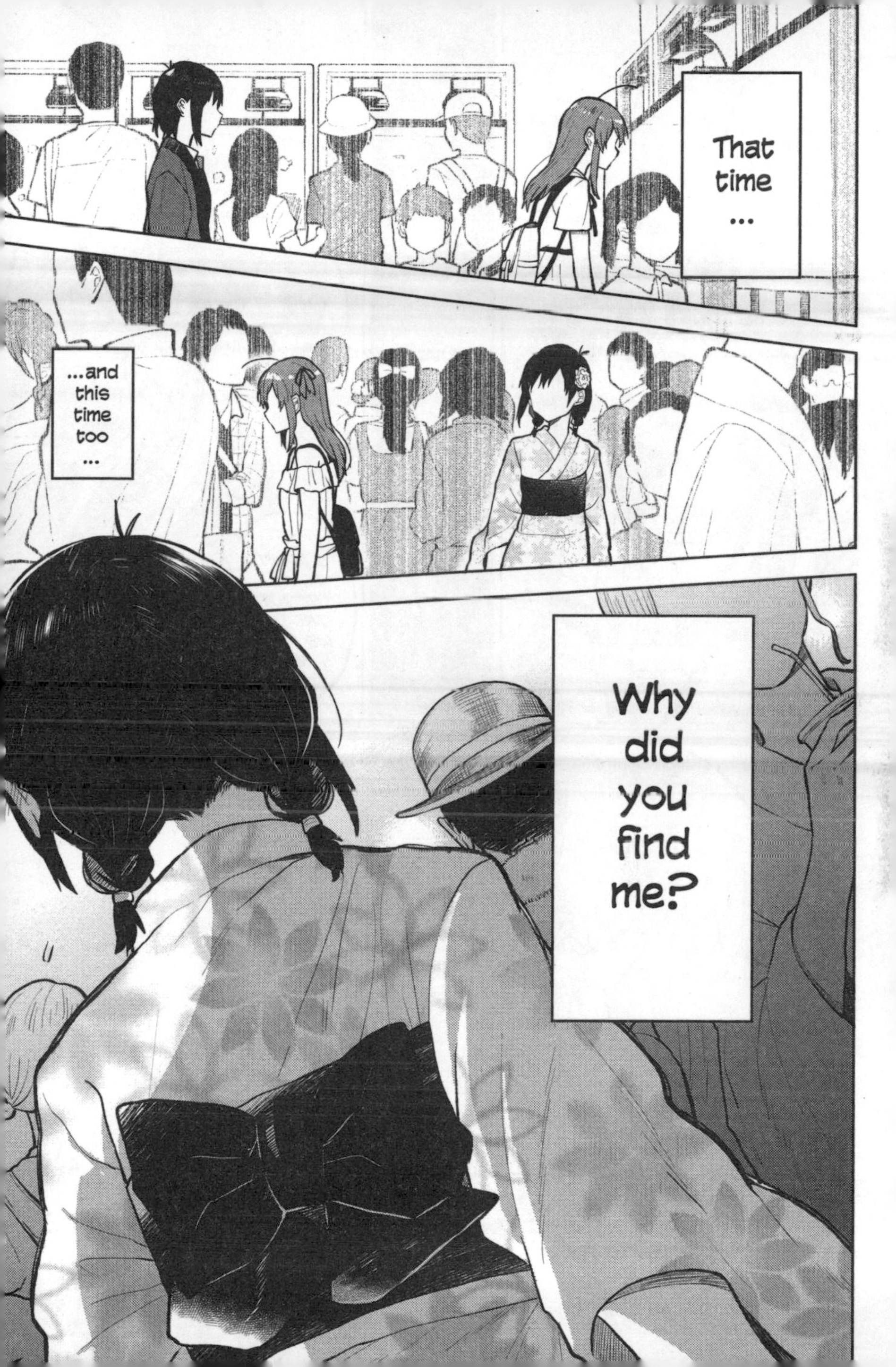
That time ...
...and this time too ...
Why did you find me?

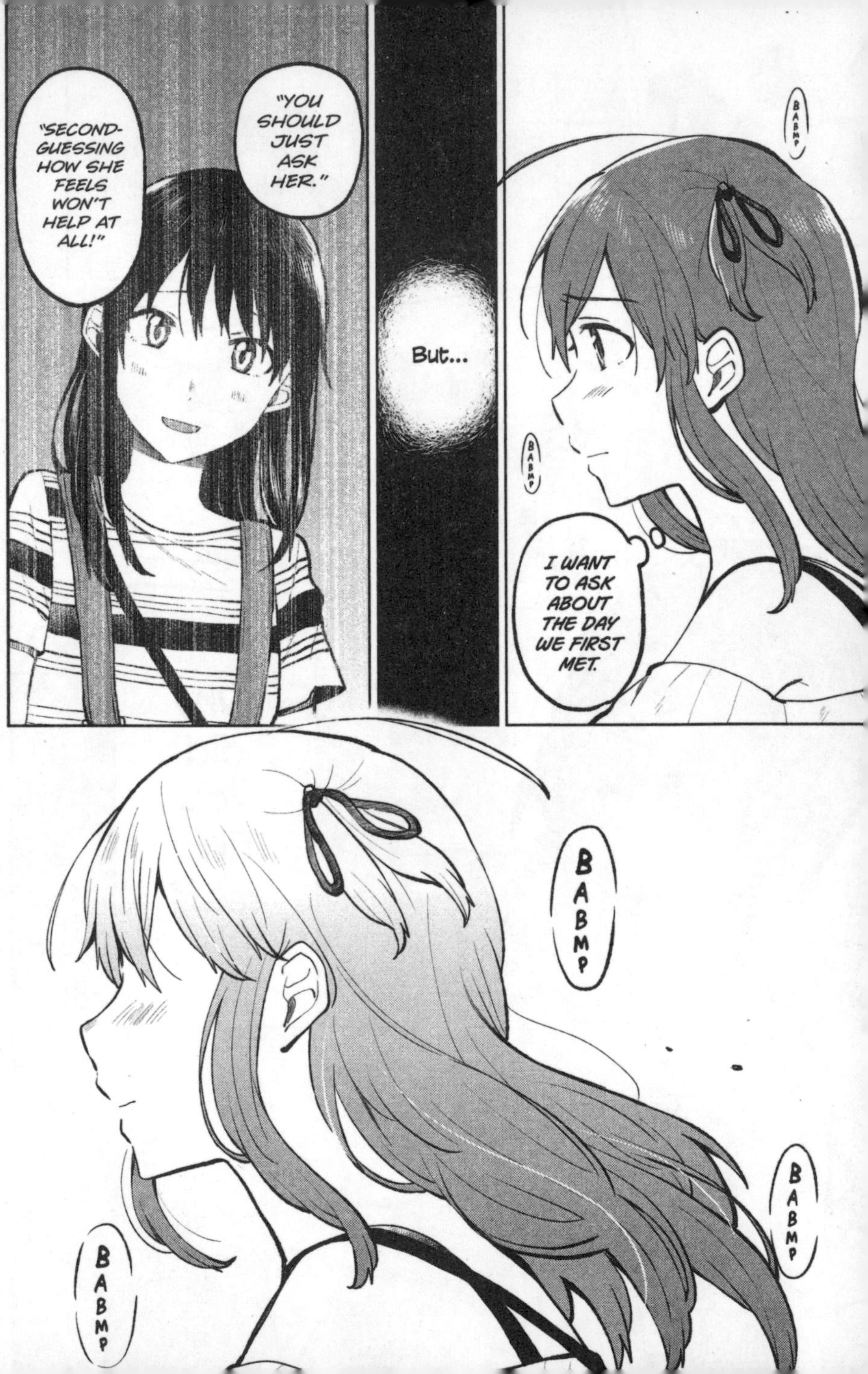
BABMP
BABMP
I WANT TO ASK ABOUT THE DAY WE FIRST MET.
But...
"YOU SHOULD JUST ASK HER."
"SECOND-GUESSING HOW SHE FEELS WON'T HELP AT ALL!"
BABMP
BABMP
BABMP

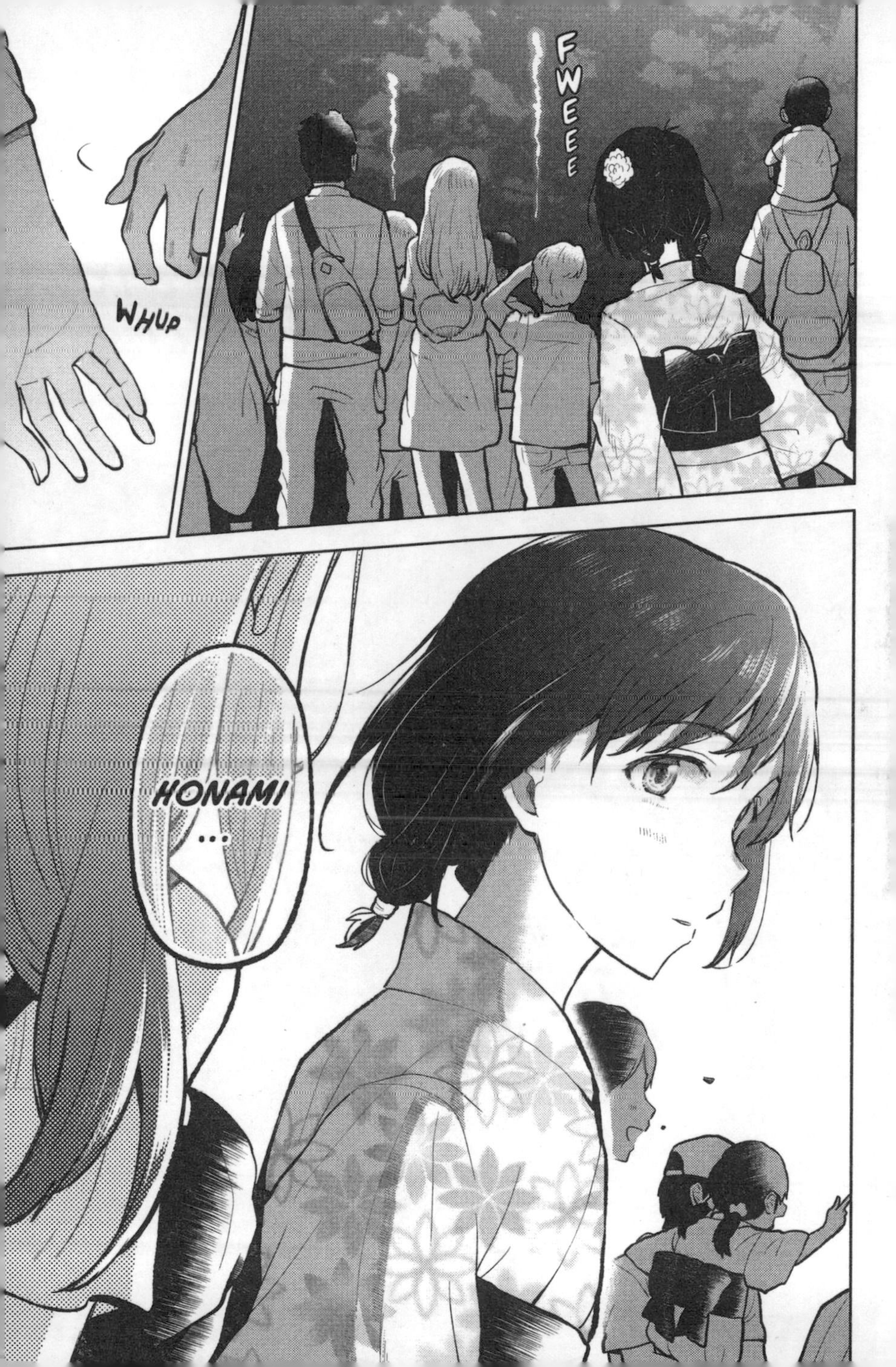
FWEEE
WHUP
HONAMI
...

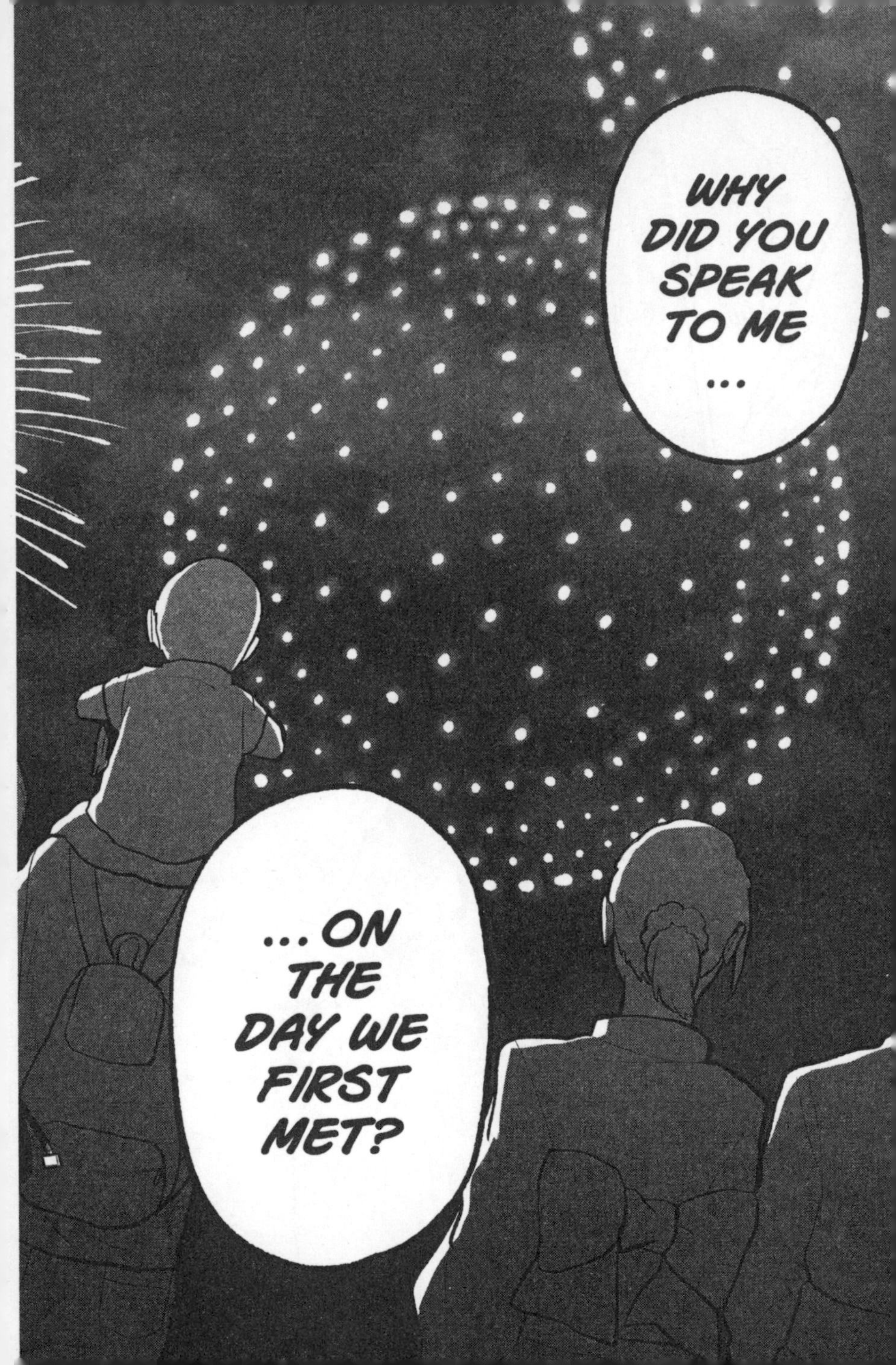
WHY DID YOU SPEAK TO ME ...
... ON THE DAY WE FIRST MET?

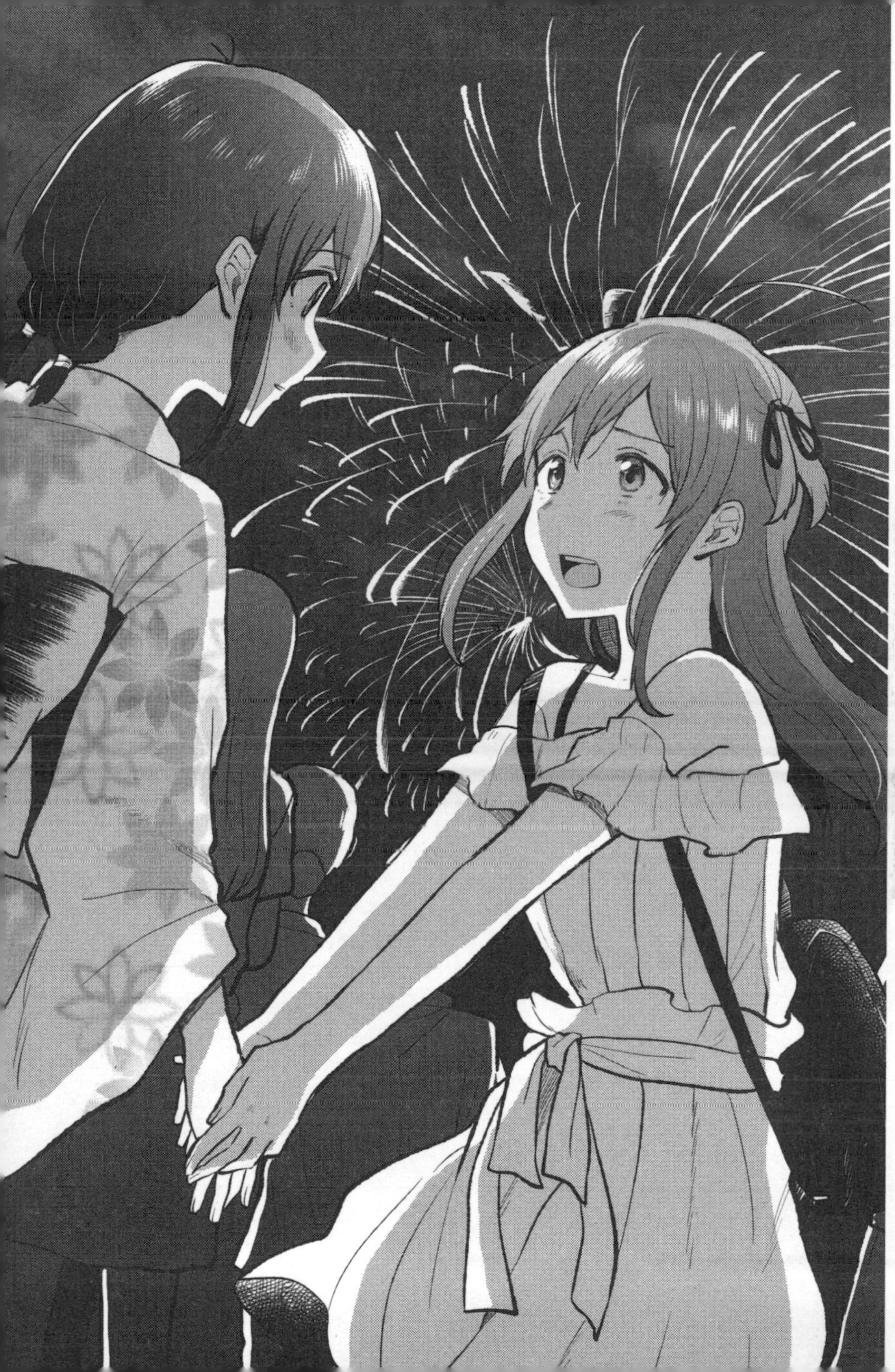

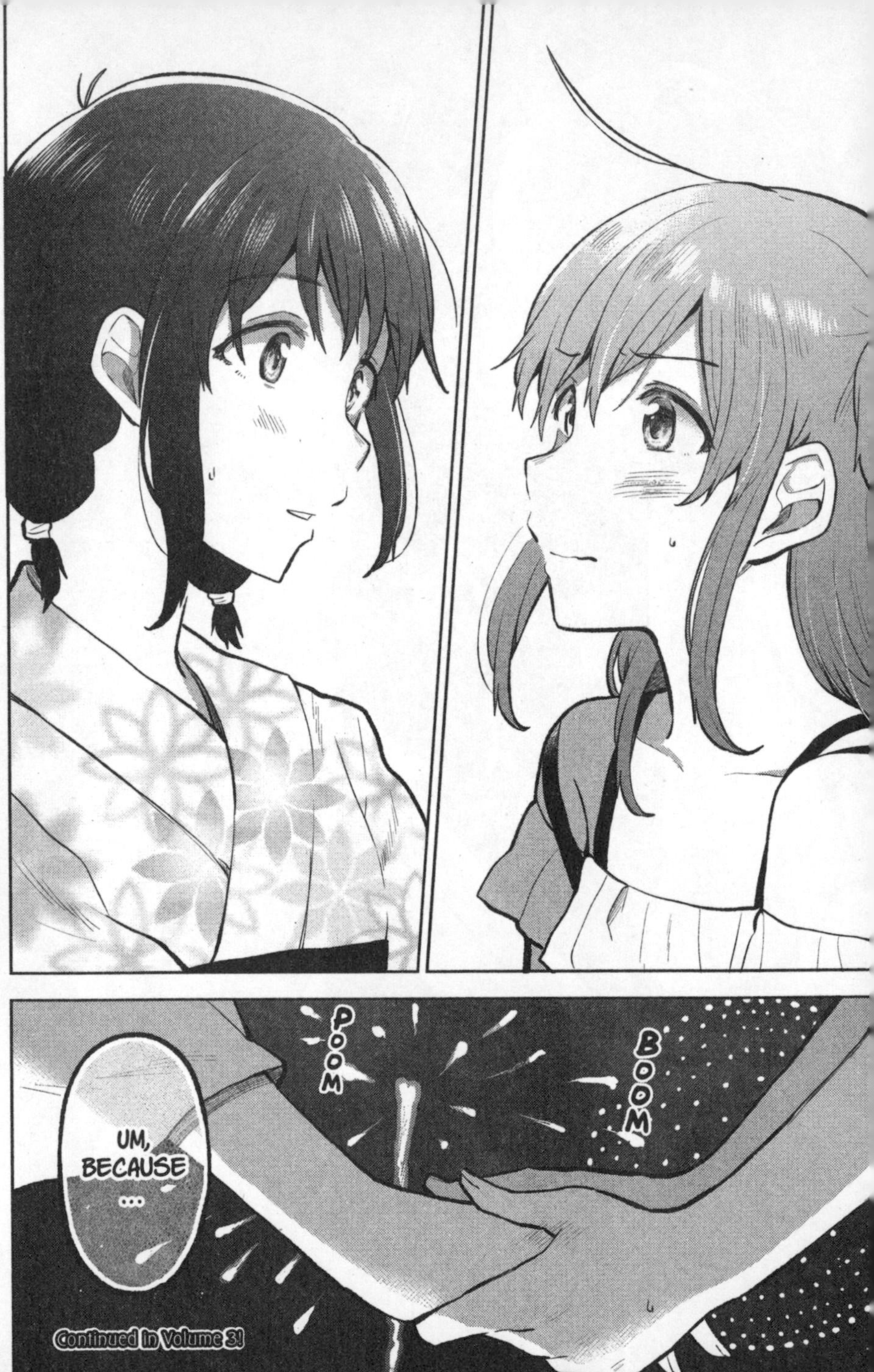
BOOM
POOM
UM, BECAUSE...

Continued in Volume 3!

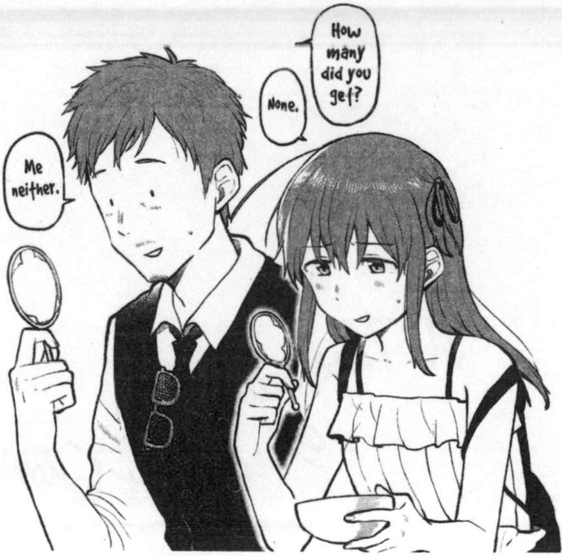
How many did you get?
None.
Me neither.

A Tropical Fish
Yearns for Snow

Afterword

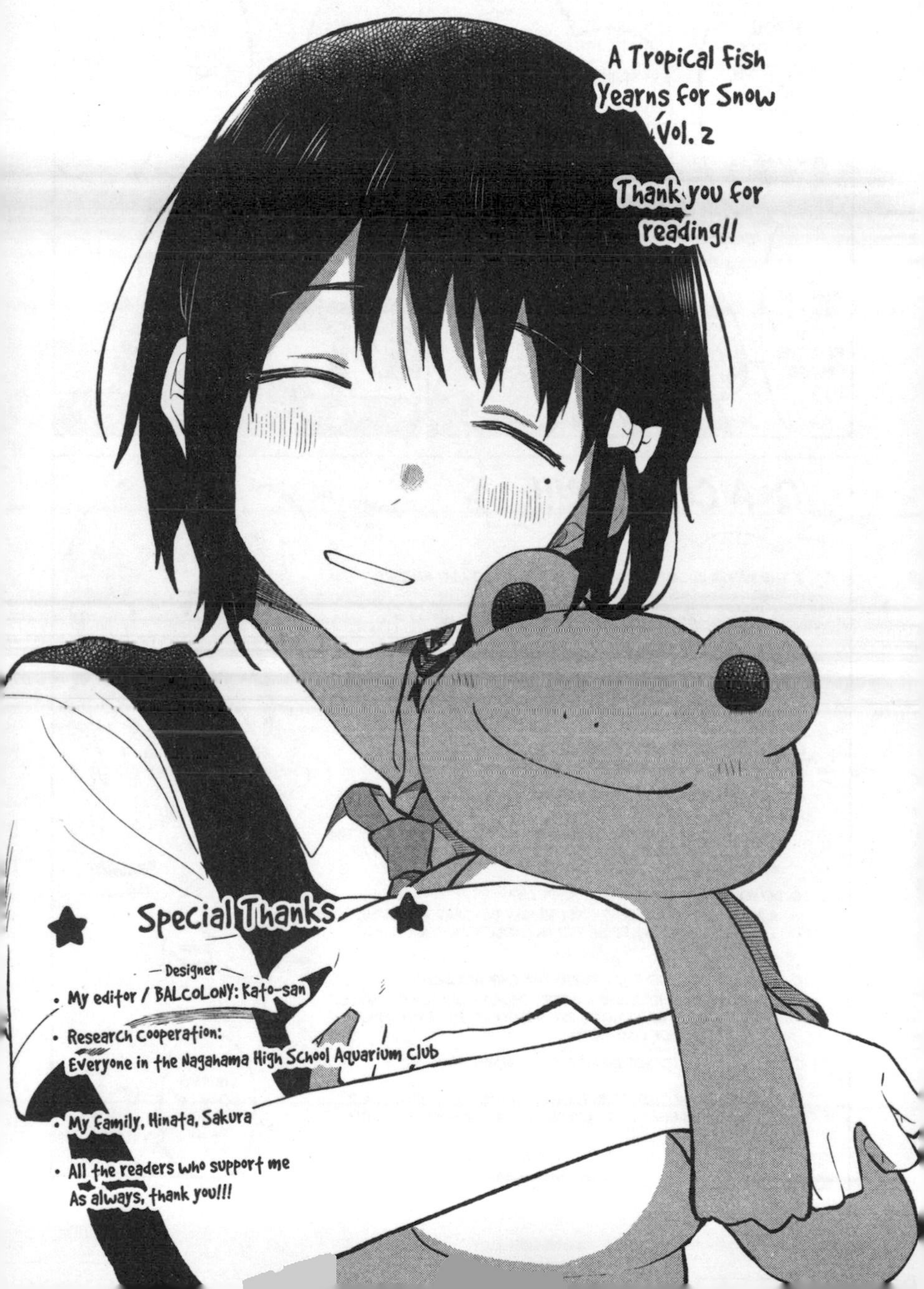
A Tropical Fish Yearns for Snow Vol. 2
Thank you for reading!!
Special Thanks
—Designer—
• My editor / BALCoLoNY: Kato-san
• Research cooperation: Everyone in the Nagahama High School Aquarium Club
• My family, Hinata, Sakura
• All the readers who support me As always, thank you!!!

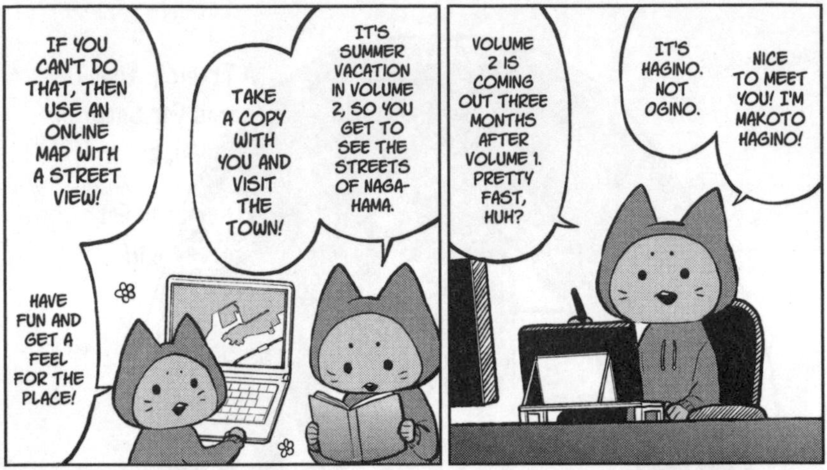
NICE TO MEET YOU! I'M MAKOTO HAGINO!
IT'S HAGINO. NOT OGINO.
VOLUME 2 IS COMING OUT THREE MONTHS AFTER VOLUME 1. PRETTY FAST, HUH?
IT'S SUMMER VACATION IN VOLUME 2, SO YOU GET TO SEE THE STREETS OF NAGA-HAMA.
TAKE A COPY WITH YOU AND VISIT THE TOWN!
IF YOU CAN'T DO THAT, THEN USE AN ONLINE MAP WITH A STREET VIEW!
HAVE FUN AND GET A FEEL FOR THE PLACE!

Q+A CORNER!!!

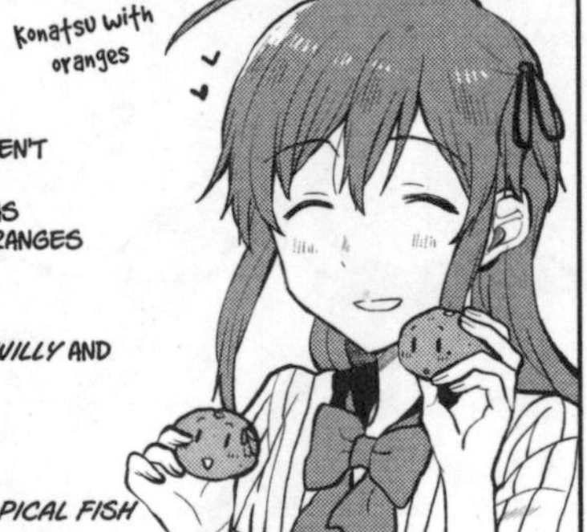
Konatsu with oranges

Q. THE MANGA IS SET IN EHIME PREFECTURE, SO WHY HAVEN'T MANDARIN ORANGES SHOWN UP YET?

A. (LOL) I CHOOSE SPECIFIC LOCATIONS AND ITEMS AS APPROPRIATE FOR THE STORY, AND THE TIME FOR ORANGES SIMPLY HASN'T COME YET.

Q. WHAT ARE YOUR FAVORITE MARINE CREATURES?

A. ORCAS AND DOLPHINS! I LOVE MOVIES LIKE *FREE WILLY* AND *THE BIG BLUE*!

Q. WHAT'S YOUR FAVORITE SNACK?

A. POTATO CHIPS! (SEAWEED FLAVOR)

Q. WHAT MANGA HAS SERVED AS INSPIRATION FOR *A TROPICAL FISH YEARNS FOR SNOW*?

A. NO PARTICULAR WORKS HAVE HAD A DIRECT INFLUENCE ON THIS MANGA, BUT *A SILENT VOICE* BY YOSHITOKI OIMA HAS HAD AN INFLUENCE ON MY GENERAL STYLE.

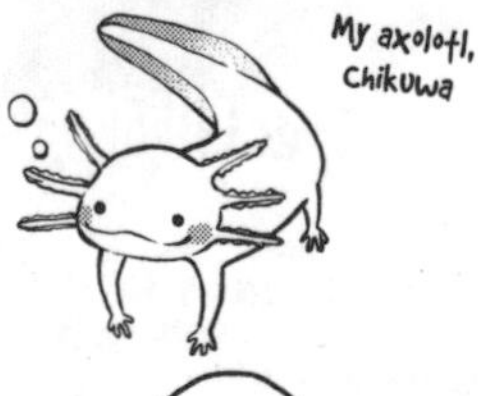
My axolotl, Chikuwa

Q. DO YOU KEEP TROPICAL FISH AS PETS?

A. NO. I HAVE A CAT, SO I CAN'T REALLY DO THAT. HOWEVER, I USED TO HAVE GOLDFISH AND AN AXOLOTL WHEN I LIVED WITH MY PARENTS.

Q. IN WHAT ORDER DID YOU CREATE THE CHARACTERS?

A. THE ORIGINAL IDEA WAS A STORY ABOUT TWO LONELY GIRLS, SO I THOUGHT UP KONATSU AND KOYUKI AT THE SAME TIME. THEY'RE SORT OF LIKE TWINS.

Q. KOYUKI SEEMS TO GET HUNGRY A LOT. DOES SHE HAVE A BIG APPETITE??

A. SOMEONE NOTICED! THE ANSWER IS YES. SO IN CHAPTER 2, SHE REACTS LESS TO ICE CREAM THAN TO ALL-YOU-CAN-EAT!

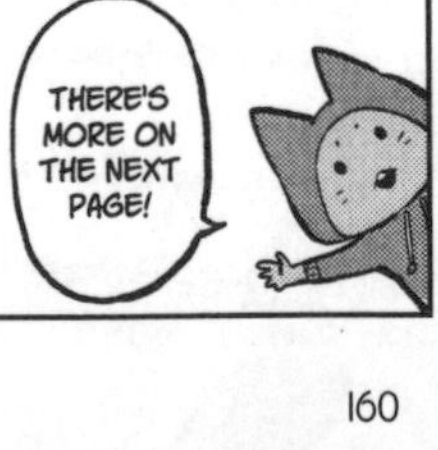
THERE'S MORE ON THE NEXT PAGE!

A Surprise Revelation

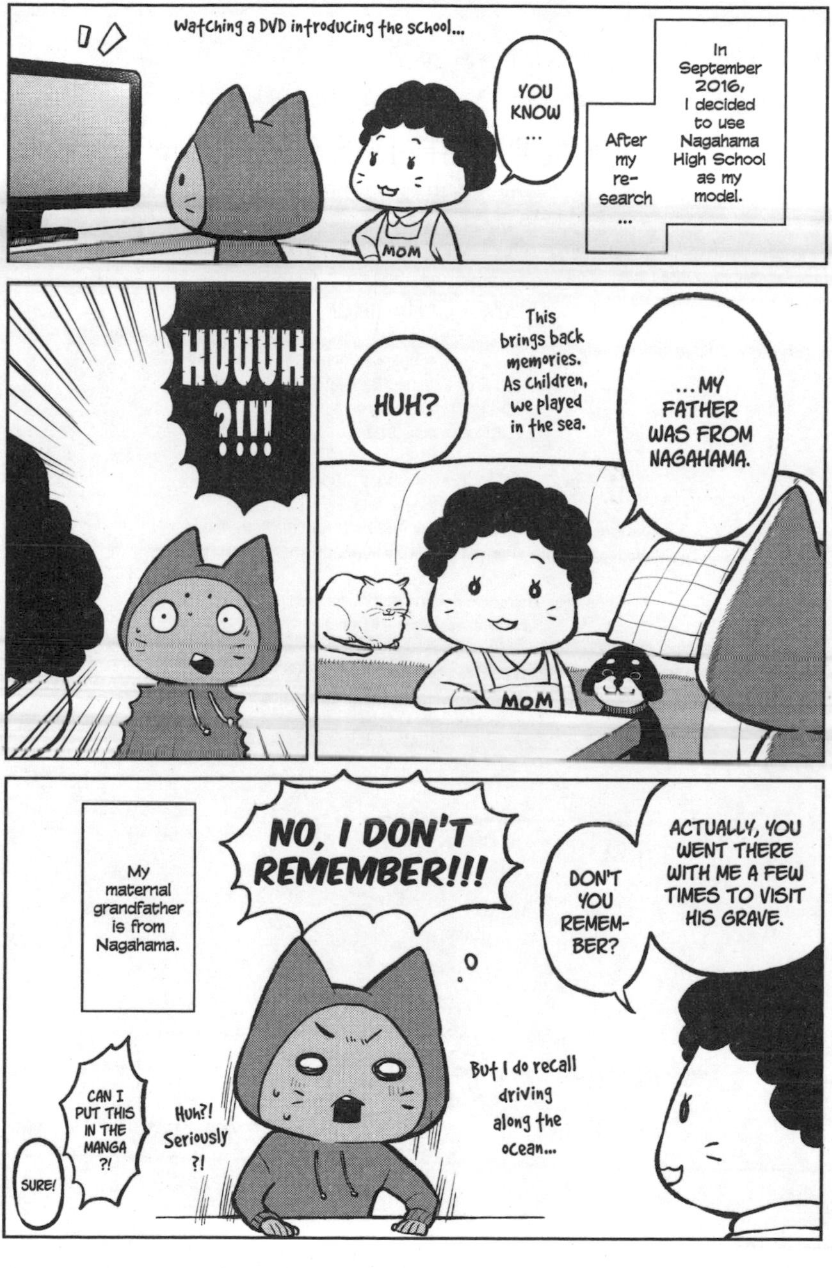

In September 2016, I decided to use Nagahama High School as my model.
After my research...
YOU KNOW ...
Watching a DVD introducing the school...
MOM
... MY FATHER WAS FROM NAGAHAMA.
This brings back memories. As children, we played in the sea.
HUH?
MOM
HUUUH ?!!!!
ACTUALLY, YOU WENT THERE WITH ME A FEW TIMES TO VISIT HIS GRAVE.
DON'T YOU REMEMBER?
NO, I DON'T REMEMBER!!!
My maternal grandfather is from Nagahama.
But I do recall driving along the ocean...
Huh?! Seriously?!
CAN I PUT THIS IN THE MANGA?!
SURE!

A TROPICAL FISH YEARNS FOR SNOW
Vol. 2
VIZ Media Edition

STORY AND ART BY
MAKOTO HAGINO

English Translation & Adaptation/John Werry
Touch-Up Art & Lettering/Eve Grandt
Design/Yukiko Whitley
Editor/Pancha Diaz

NETTAIGYO WA YUKI NI KOGARERU Vol. 2
©Makoto Hagino 2018
First published in Japan in 2018 by KADOKAWA CORPORATION, Tokyo.
English translation rights arranged with KADOKAWA CORPORATION, Tokyo.

The stories, characters and incidents mentioned in this
publication are entirely fictional.

Printed in Italy

Published by VIZ Media, LLC
P.O. Box 77010
San Francisco, CA 94107

10 9 8 7 6 5 4 3 2
First printing, February 2020
Second printing, March 2022

viz.com

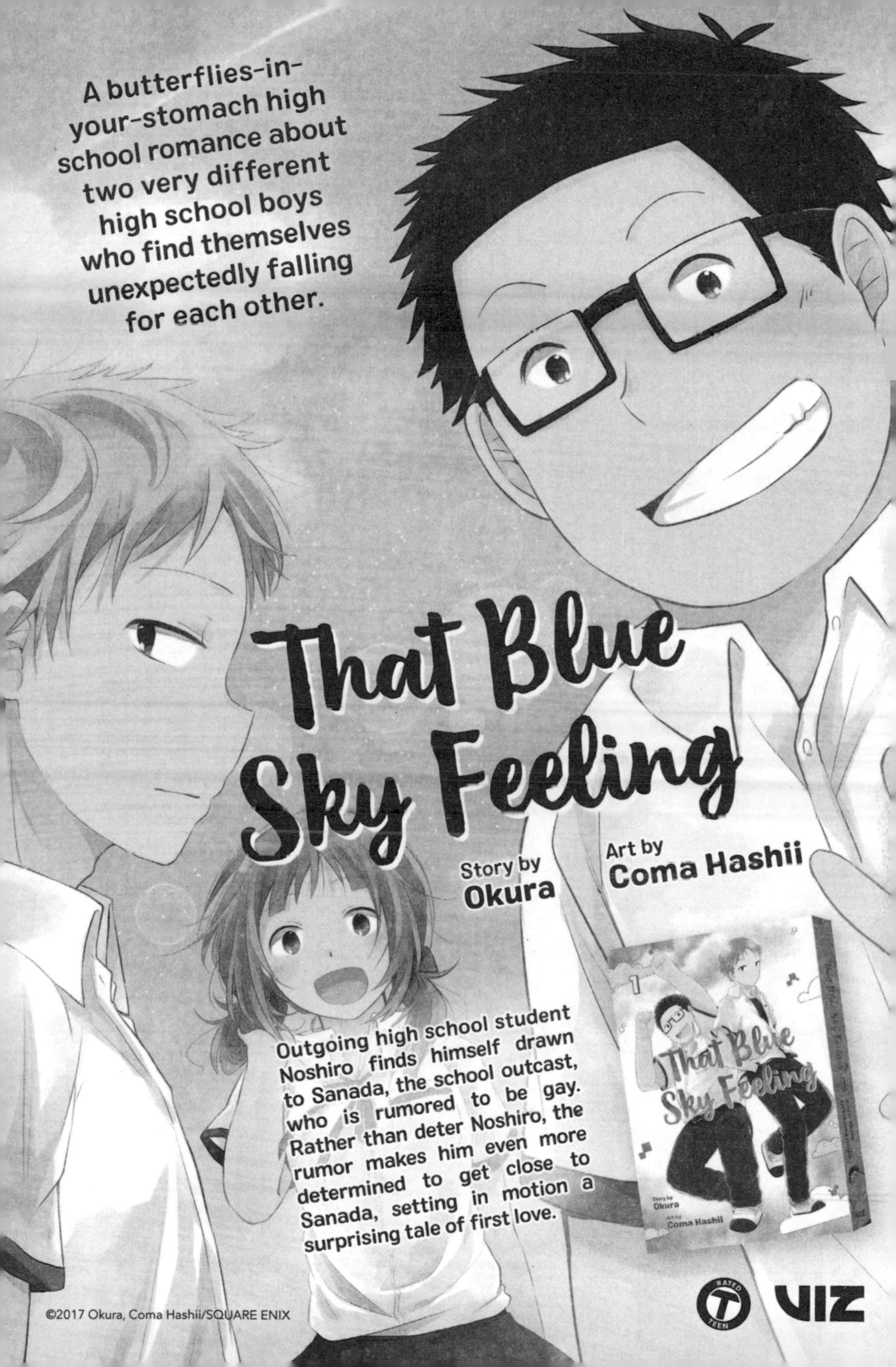

A butterflies-in-your-stomach high school romance about two very different high school boys who find themselves unexpectedly falling for each other.
That Blue Sky Feeling
Story by Okura
Art by Coma Hashii
Outgoing high school student Noshiro finds himself drawn to Sanada, the school outcast, who is rumored to be gay. Rather than deter Noshiro, the rumor makes him even more determined to get close to Sanada, setting in motion a surprising tale of first love.
RATED T TEEN
VIZ
©2017 Okura, Coma Hashii/SQUARE ENIX

Ao Haru Ride

STORY AND ART BY
IO SAKISAKA

Futaba Yoshioka thought all boys were loud and obnoxious until she met Kou Tanaka in junior high. But as soon as she realized she really liked him, he had already moved away because of family issues. Now, in high school, Kou has reappeared, but is he still the same boy she fell in love with?

Honey
So Sweet

Story and Art by Amu Meguro

Little did Nao Kogure realize back in middle school that when she left an umbrella and a box of bandages in the rain for injured delinquent Taiga Onise that she would meet him again in high school. Nao wants nothing to do with the gruff and frightening Taiga, but he suddenly presents her with a huge bouquet of flowers and asks her to date him—with marriage in mind! Is Taiga really so scary, or is he a sweetheart in disguise?

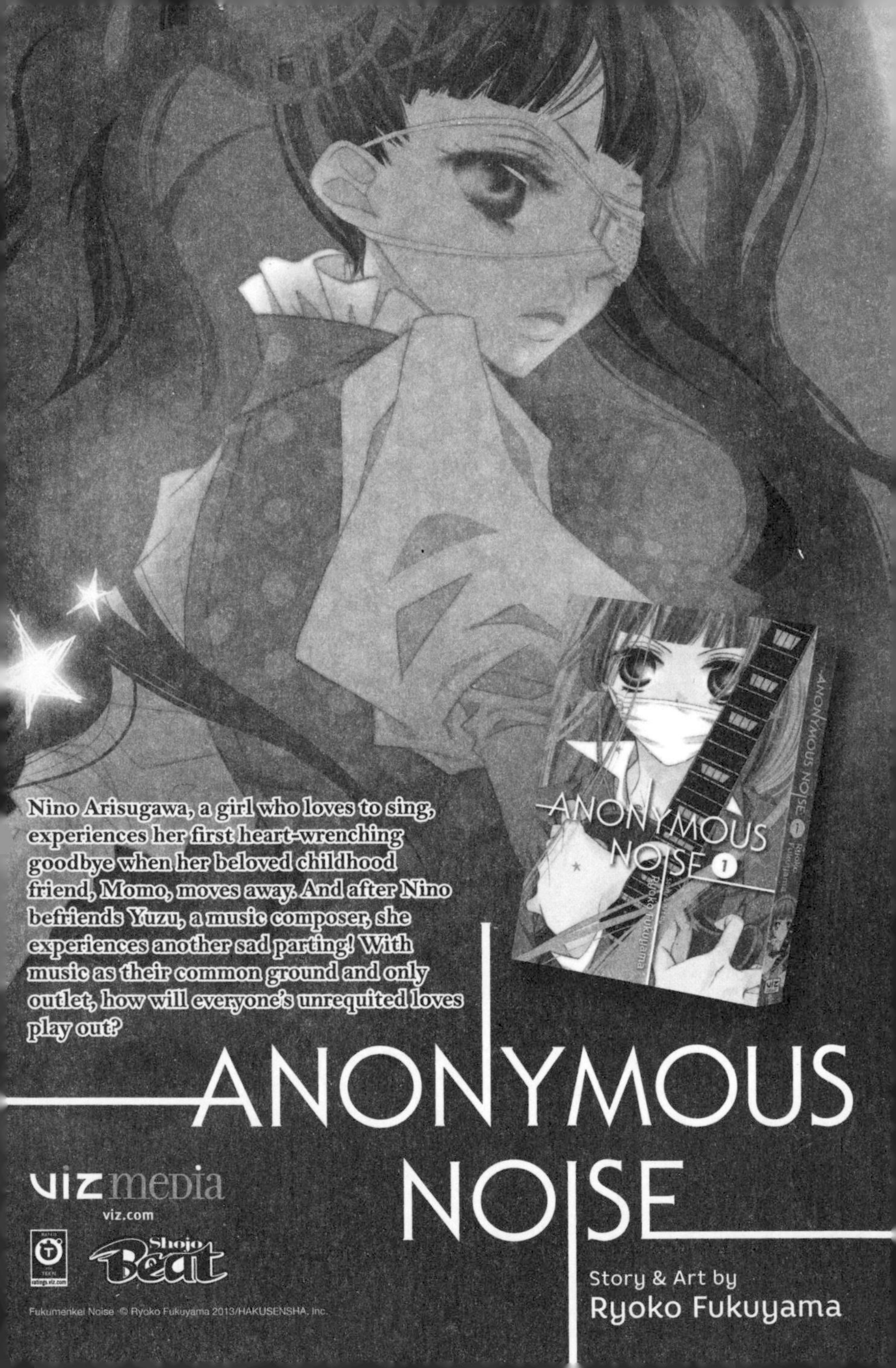
Nino Arisugawa, a girl who loves to sing, experiences her first heart-wrenching goodbye when her beloved childhood friend, Momo, moves away. And after Nino befriends Yuzu, a music composer, she experiences another sad parting! With music as their common ground and only outlet, how will everyone's unrequited loves play out?
ANONYMOUS NOISE 1
Ryoko Fukuyama
ANONYMOUS NOISE
viz media
viz.com
RATED T FOR TEEN
ratings.viz.com
Shojo Beat
Story & Art by
Ryoko Fukuyama
Fukumenkei Noise © Ryoko Fukuyama 2013/HAKUSENSHA, Inc.

Behind the Scenes!!

STORY AND ART BY **BISCO HATORI**

From the creator of Ouran High School Host Club

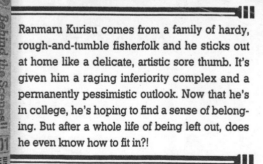

Ranmaru Kurisu comes from a family of hardy, rough-and-tumble fisherfolk and he sticks out at home like a delicate, artistic sore thumb. It's given him a raging inferiority complex and a permanently pessimistic outlook. Now that he's in college, he's hoping to find a sense of belonging. But after a whole life of being left out, does he even know how to fit in?!

IDOL dreams

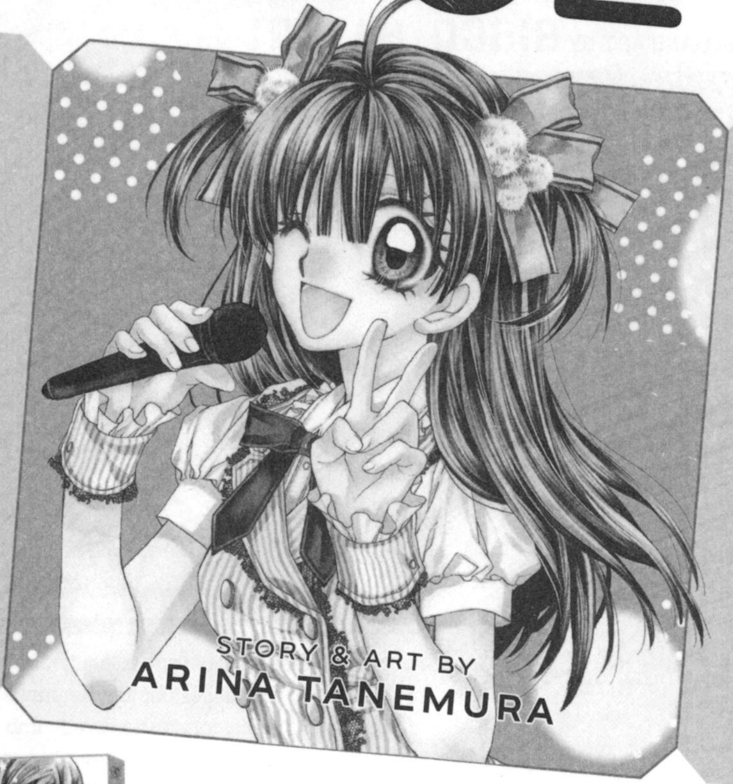
STORY & ART BY
ARINA TANEMURA

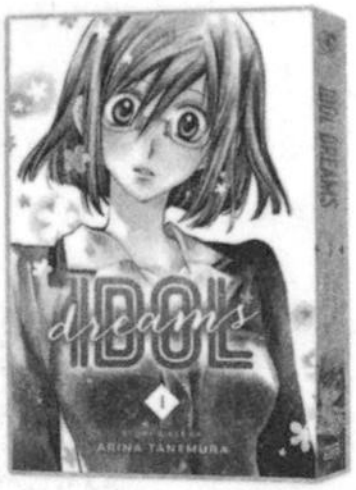
IDOL dreams
1
ARINA TANEMURA

At age 31, office worker Chikage Deguchi feels she missed her chances at love and success. When word gets out that she's a virgin, Chikage is humiliated and wishes she could turn back time to when she was still young and popular. She takes an experimental drug that changes her appearance back to when she was 15. Now Chikage is determined to pursue everything she missed out on all those years ago—including becoming a star!

Shojo Beat VIZ T RATED TEEN